Holocaust Graphic Narratives

Holocaust Graphic Narratives

Generation, Trauma, and Memory

VICTORIA AARONS

Rutgers University Press
New Brunswick, New Jersey, and London

Library of Congress Cataloging-in-Publication Data

Names: Aarons, Victoria, author.
Title: Holocaust graphic narratives : generation, trauma, and memory / Victoria Aarons.
Description: New Brunswick, New Jersey : Rutgers University Press, [2019] | Includes bibliographical references and index.
Identifiers: LCCN 2019008414 | ISBN 9781978802568 (cloth) | ISBN 9781978802551 (paperback)
Subjects: LCSH: Holocaust, Jewish (1939–1945), in literature. | Graphic novels—History and criticism. | Autobiography. | Holocaust, Jewish (1939–1945)—Influence. | Literature, Modern—20th century—History and criticism. | Literature, Modern—21st century—History and criticism.
Classification: LCC PN56.H55 A238 2019 | DDC 741.5/358405318—dc23

LC record available at https://lccn.loc.gov/2019008414

A British Cataloging-in-Publication record for this book is available from the British Library.

∞ The paper used in this publication meets the requirements of the American National Standard for Information Sciences—Permanence of Paper for Printed Library Materials, ANSI Z39.48-1992.

www.rutgersuniversitypress.org

Manufactured in the United States of America

For my sons,
Aaron and Gabriel Salomon,
and in memory of my father,
Zelig Aarons
(1912–1996)

Contents

Holocaust
Graphic Narratives

Introduction

Visual Testimonies of Memory

> Pictures that lock the story in our minds.
> —Susan Sontag, *Regarding the Pain of Others*

> When the historians close their books, when the statisticians stop counting, the memorialists and witnesses can no longer remember, then the poet, the novelist, the artist comes and surveys the devastated landscape left by the fire—the ashes. He rummages through the debris in search of a design. For if the essence, the meaning, or the meaninglessness of the Holocaust will survive our sordid history, it will be in works of art.
> —Raymond Federman, "The Necessity and Impossibility of Being a Jewish Writer"

Art Spiegelman's *Maus*, the first graphic narrative to receive a Pulitzer Prize (1992), established the genre of the graphic novel as a legitimate form of Holocaust representation. Spiegelman's groundbreaking work created an opening for Holocaust graphic storytelling, legitimizing further experimentation with the graphic form as a meaningful, even provocative genre of literary expression of the Shoah. The success of *Maus* provided graphic novelists and illustrators a kind of literary license, as graphic artist Miriam Katin put it, "permission"[1] to enter the space of Holocaust history and memory in order to tell their own and their families' stories of survival and devastating loss in this unconventional, experimental, and potentially problematical genre. As Leonard Rifas has suggested, Spiegelman's *Maus* "did more than any other single work to establish comics as a legitimate medium for communicating serious stories."[2] In doing so, Spiegelman stretched the limits, the range of possibilities, and the definition of the genre, opening the comics medium to a layered, complex expression of both individual and historical trauma. *Maus*, "arguably the world's most famous work of comics," as Hillary L. Chute proposes, not only introduced a new and richly figured genre of Holocaust testimony but also expanded the reach and possibilities for the medium, "forever altering the terrain of comics in America and worldwide."[3] Spiegelman implicitly stages his extended, visually and verbally narrated story of a Holocaust survivor's harrowing experiences and the imprint of the deeply engrained past on the psychic life of the inheritor of that history against generic expectations and incongruities of form and content. In drawing upon both discursive modes of storytelling and visual elements of comics, Spiegelman reconceived the ways in which we envision and narrate the broader strokes of history as they inform and are informed by personal histories. Spiegelman's work envisions the intimacies of history, providing midrashic—interpretive, expansive, elastic, and performative—moments of exploration and adjudication, extending the narrative of the past into the present and thus reading history responsively. *Maus*, in many ways, then, created not only an innovative outlet for comics but a new genre for Holocaust expression, new ways of "seeing" and bearing witness to the Holocaust and its haunting aftermath for generations extending beyond that history.

The genre of the graphic narrative, in the past two decades in particular, has moved from underground to mainstream. Graphic narratives have emerged from the experimental, avant-garde underground to the forefront of literary production and consumption. Once considered an icon of the emergence of pop culture, an extension of the generic mixing implied by the neologism "commix," the graphic novel has taken on the dual representational seriousness of the authentically personal and the complexly political. As Ariela Freedman proposes in the introduction to a special issue of *Partial Answers* devoted to "Comics and the Canon," "The new respectability of comics has been especially evident over the last three decades, as comics, graphic memoirs, and graphic novels have continued to emerge as literary, artistic, and cultural artifacts of central importance. Comics are no longer seen as outside what we might broadly call a literary and fine-arts 'canon,' as objects belonging to low culture rather than high culture, as ephemeral items rather than artworks of lasting and iconic significance, as lesser hybrids of word and image rather than as belonging to a specific demanding medium."[4] Thus in the decades since the initial publication of *Maus*, from its original serial distribution in *Raw* magazine as a countercultural artifact to its two-volume book form (as well as its subsequent iterations in *MetaMaus*, *In the Shadow of No Towers*, and *Breakdowns*), the graphic novel has become a recognized genre of Holocaust literary representation. Since the publication of *Maus* (volume 1 in book form in 1986, volume 2 in 1991), an array of graphic novelists and illustrators in the United States and abroad have attempted, to varying degrees of success, to give voice to the extended trauma of the Holocaust.

With memory as the controlling trope, these graphic writers and cartoonists, through the juxtaposition of text and image, extend the narrative of the Holocaust into the present, creating a midrashic imperative to reconstruct and reanimate the experience of the Shoah, giving voice to unrecoverable loss. By midrash, in this context, I am referring loosely to an interpretive process of storytelling, a response to those moments of interruption, pauses, and gaps in a narrative that open themselves up to further analysis and commentary. Here we might consider Scott McCloud's definition of closure in comics as a process of midrashic interpretation. Closure, as McCloud defines it, actively engages the reader/viewer in "the phenomenon of observing the parts but perceiving the whole."[5] As we navigate our way among the interstices between panels, the empty spaces on the page abut and leave room for interpretive intervention. We thus perform a midrashic perceptual leap in response to the perceived incompletion of the text. Midrashic practice begins with a primary text open to interpretive possibilities. In the Holocaust graphic narrative, individual eyewitness accounts and experiences form the primary narrative as it extends generationally in this dialectic of part and whole, itself representing the fragments of memory and offering potential responses to rupture.

The popular and critical reception of *Maus*, then, changed many of our assumptions about the capacity of comics to cross over into a domain of conceptual structures and approaches, taking up, in longer narrative form, those subjects, patterns of narration, literary conceits, and rhetorical tropes conventionally associated with more traditional, discursive literary forms such as the novel, autobiography, memoir, and creative nonfiction. While, to be sure, the comics medium has a long tradition of political cartooning (i.e., political critiques, satires, caricatures) and, more specifically, World War II cartoons circulated for the purposes of both propaganda and censure, the Holocaust as the subject of extended "sequential art" narratives, as pioneering cartoonist Will Eisner defined the genre, has a more limited and restricted history.[6] The publication of *Maus* was largely responsible for the development, over the past twenty years or so, of the art of graphic comics storytelling as a medium for the representation of war and of natural and human-made catastrophe.[7] These extended graphic narratives engage history in complex representational and perceptual modes of interpretive discovery. These are complicated visual and verbal narratives that, as Martha J. Cutter and Cathy J. Schlund-Vials propose, "enable not only recitation of past trauma but also a reevaluation of what is at stake in the envisioning of history itself."[8] The interplay of distinct moments in history and the reach of the imagination unrestricted by temporal, spatial, and geographical boundaries create urgency and immediacy. Here the reader/viewer and the author/graphic artist are cocollaborators in the movement across time and topography as they enter the muddied borderlands of memory. An intersection of personal and collective histories characterizes these graphic narratives. This intersection produces a sense of historical rupture and disequilibrium, joining potentially an individual's connection to the past with the cumulative, wide-scale effect of moments in history. In this way, Holocaust graphic narratives create a visual testimony to the past, to devastating loss as well as to survival.

The juxtaposition of image and text fundamental to the graphic narrative emerges through the structural unit of the individual panel and the white spaces (the "gutters") between and among the panels. As McCloud suggests, the work of the imagination takes place in "the limbo of the gutter," breaks in the unfolding narrative that "transport us across significant distances of time and space."[9] The play of presence and absence that arises with a focus on the individual panels in sequence freezes the frame of history and experience for moments of moral and ethical reckoning. This tension between the spoken and the unspoken, emerging in the spaces among the panels, mediates the representation of trauma. These material, visual spaces, in which time is frozen, not unlike the framed photographic pose that freezes a particular moment temporally and spatially, juxtapose the seen with the unseen. As Chute suggests in *Disaster Drawn*, an eloquent study of documentary comics, the nonfictional graphic narrative that reimagines historical moments of traumatic rupture is "a form of witnessing," an architecture for the expression of individual and collective trauma.[10] Not surprisingly, the idea of a Holocaust graphic novel, at least in its nascent stage, raised the question of appropriateness. Is "a comic book" an appropriate medium to represent atrocity? Might the very cartoon form unavoidably trivialize the subject or fictionalize the historical reality of the Shoah? Does the form itself distract from the seriousness of the subject? Is the comics structure by necessity reductive, thus threatening to minimize the subjects it illustrates? The design and popular history of the genre as well as common assumptions about the audience for both comics (e.g., infantile, "kiddie fare,"[11] the "funnies") and commix (an underground venue for the portrayal of prurient and sexually explicit content, drugs, gratuitous violence, etc.) would seem to suggest that the subject of the Holocaust was "untouchable" in this art form. Simply put, the argument might look something like this: the reality of the Holocaust is far too complex for comics artists to convey given the formal structures of the genre (i.e., the minimalism and economy required by the cartoon's balloon of speech, the containment of the panels, spatial representation, caricatured drawings, and so forth). In a medium that, by its very nature, is predisposed, as Joshua Lambert suggests, to "stylize and simplify and exaggerate," a comics aesthetic would seem antithetical to the enormity and complexity of a subject such as the Holocaust.[12]

Thus the art of graphic storytelling and graphic narratives in general have, in the past couple of decades, expanded not only their thematic and narratological scope but also their claim to generic seriousness. In this expansion of scope and seriousness, extended "novelistic" graphic narratives have incorporated diverse modes of graphic storytelling: graphic memoirs, autobiographical graphic narratives (both what Gillian Whitlock refers to "autographics" or the "aesthetics of life narratives"[13]), graphic novels, graphic histories, graphic documentaries and journalism, graphic adaptations of traditional literary works, and so forth. This is not to say, however, that issues of the appropriateness of the comics graphic form and the aesthetics of Holocaust representation, in general, are not still debated both in and out of the academy. The "cartoon strip" still carries with it the residue of previous conceptions regarding the seriousness of the form, a structure more suitable to comic exaggeration and distortion and thus *mis*representation. Indeed, "Holocaust humor," and thus its implicit relation to the cartoon strip, continues to be the source of fraught and "not so funny" dispute.[14] Of course, such a volatile and divided response to the question of whether the Holocaust can ever be the subject of comedy, or parody, or caricature, or lampoon (or any style of "entertainment") is more than a matter of "taste." The issue of form and function in this regard raises long-standing concerns related to an aesthetic of Holocaust representation as well as a caution against "fictionalizing" the Holocaust, providing yet another opening for Holocaust denial and antisemitism.

Whether Holocaust "comics" and graphic novels are, as Philip Roth might have said, "good-for-the-Jews or no-good-for-the-Jews"[15] or whether even such discussions are productive is not something I intend to take up here. Instead, simply put, no longer the "poor stepchild" of literary production, graphic novels and nonfictional graphic narratives currently hold their place among traditional literary forms and genres; they are, as Ariela Freedman proposes, "in conversation with an established literary and artistic canon and . . . make a claim to cultural centrality and significance."[16] In many ways, graphic narratives speak to the age in which we live. Regardless of one's reaction to the form and its possible generic limitations, the graphic novel, with its juxtaposition of both the comics structure (panels, gutters, icons, cartoonish figures, speech balloons, etc.) and text, has become increasingly a medium for a serious and complex expression of individual and collective histories.

The genre of the graphic narrative has become a platform for evoking defining and rupturing traumatic moments of history—both individual and collective—and thus for an emerging aesthetics of memory. Especially in the years following the turn of the twenty-first century, the graphic novel has shown itself to be an innovative stage upon which to enact the participatory engagement of storyteller and reader in bringing to life the increasingly remote and inaccessible events of the Holocaust at an important time in history, a time that will witness the end of direct survivor testimony. Through the interplay of visual and textual design, graphic authors and illustrators, ever since Spiegelman, have created, as Baetens and Pylyser have suggested, "real and open inquiries that pay great attention to the possible resistance of what it means to be a historical witness and the material resistance of what it means to present the successful or failed encounter between victim, eye or hearsay witness, inquirer, and artist with the help of words and images."[17] The graphic narrative creates the dynamic, elastic conditions for a collaborative effort in bearing witness and sustaining memory. Rather than a static or flat representation of history, the genre generates a graphic performance of individual stories set against the backdrop of the historical period of the Shoah.

In large part because of its juxtaposed elements—the tension between form and subject and the destabilization thus achieved through such antitheses—the comics structure can have a jarring, disturbingly arresting, and engaging effect. Thus the genre can provide a powerful antidote, as Lambert argues, to "Holocaust fatigue," to the suspicion that our culture has become saturated with Holocaust "paraphernalia"—with all "things" Holocaust—the Holocaust as a current "favorite" referent in discussions of persecution in contemporary culture. As a result, as in the way of all such terms in the popular lexicon, *the Holocaust* runs the risk of becoming diluted, diminished by overuse, misuse, and appropriation by rote. That is, Holocaust memorial discourse can play out in unthinking idioms, the great accomplice of indifference and historical amnesia and, as George Orwell famously wrote, of political quietism.[18] Thus as Lambert has proposed, "How important, and how powerful, it is for a topic that demands reverence to be treated in a medium that is allergic to it": "Whether it's humans drawn as animals [*Maus*] or a young boy's survival of Auschwitz as a cartoon mutant's origin story [*X-Men: Magneto Testament*], there's something off about these works. And that's true even of graphic works of simple, straightforward testimony, because rendering speech and historical experience into strips of cartoons involves so much distortion that a reader cannot forget . . . that this is a highly unnatural, profoundly deliberate way of communicating . . . which gives them the power to stop us from feeling like we've already seen it all."[19] Whether or not "Holocaust fatigue" is an accurate assessment of the media-saturated, catastrophe-driven predicament of our age or whether the term itself has simply become "fashionable"—yet one more "trending," commercialized, media-hyped slogan—the telling point here is that the discourses surrounding the Shoah need to be revitalized. Such discussions suggest the need for new forms of Holocaust expression, a reawakening of attention and conscience in the continuing attempt to articulate, to reckon with, and to calculate the defining events of the Shoah and its implications for the future. The graphic narrative defamiliarizes the discourse of Holocaust testimony by transplanting it into this new medium.

Graphic storytelling, especially narratives that return to specific moments in history—both recent and distant—can provide a visual and textual shape to "voiced" memory. The antithetical, incongruous, and largely experimental nature of the graphic narrative (though no longer as unconventional as it once was) opens up possibilities for further expression, history "unfrozen," as the novelist David Grossman puts it.[20] The ongoing extension and expression of Holocaust memory is thus in defiance of historical amnesia, of indifference, of silence, of an eliding of the past—of those who, like the narrator of Saul Bellow's *The Bellarosa Connection*, "would like to forget about remembering."[21] The genre of the Holocaust graphic narrative, then, provides a means of writing against adversity, "a resistance to the sapping of memory," as Edmund de Waal writes in *The Hare with Amber Eyes*, the story of the inheritance bequeathed intergenerationally to him of the valuable collection of netsukes, the legacy of his extended family hidden during the Nazi appropriation of their home and property.[22] Graphic storytelling, then, creates an architecture of memory, a grammar and structure for vivifying and materializing memory in the figurative and literal landscape of the past as it orchestrates the fluid perception of space and time. We thus come into history by way of individual histories, stories that demystify the actualities and the expressibility of that history.

These are very personal stories, "counter-narratives of witnessing and testimony," as Jeffrey Clapp puts it,[23] polyphonically voiced in a way that situates individual lives against the backdrop of historical catastrophe. Such graphic narratives that, as Chute suggests, "bear witness to authors' own traumas or to those of others materially retrace inscriptional effacement; they repeat and reconstruct in order to counteract."[24] In doing so, the graphic artists I am looking at here reimagine and retrace specific moments and individuals rather than attempt to reproduce or represent a panorama of Holocaust history. The narrating voices in these works are not distanced, omniscient tellers of history. Rather, the guiding voices we hear are deeply invested in the stories they tell, memoirists of the frame. They are immediate, urgent speaking voices. If not direct witnesses to those moments in history, they are, nonetheless, active participants in the stories they tell. These stories thus are narratives of self-identity set against the backdrop of the Holocaust, identities that significantly have been formed by the histories of others, by those whose lives—if belatedly—come to inform the author's own.

By and large, the stories visually told combine individual and family histories with the larger and extended scope and generational range of Holocaust history. These are participatory works in which the writer/illustrator, whose authorial ethos is complicated at moments when the narrative voice splinters, creates multiple telling voices and reanimates the defining events of the past, defining that past in terms of individual identity and also the shape of history. Thus these graphic narratives attempt to create presence where there is absence. They create a whole out of fragments. The structure of the graphic narrative, as Chute suggests, "through the work of marks on the page creates it as a space and substance, gives it a corporeality, a physical shape," the material shape of history but also of traumatic rupture, fragmentation, and loss.[25] After all, the image, as Didi-Huberman remarked, is the "very attestation" of absence.[26] That is, the manifestation of the image, the material presence of the image, evokes its absence all the while constructing a material because of its visual connection to the past. As Chute elsewhere proposes, "Against a valorization of absence and aporia, graphic narrative asserts the value of presence, however complex and contingent."[27] In these graphic narratives of entire communities elided by war, presence is set against a landscape of loss, of absent lives and topographies made present for the moment of discovery and recovery.

The absence that surrounds the Holocaust—that is, the tentacles of loss and those stories that have gone unheard because of a protective or defensive silence, because of belated pursuit or awareness, or simply because there is no one left to tell—is the place of midrashic invention. The graphic artists who write and draw amid the rubble of Holocaust history do so in order to reconstruct, reckon with, and reanimate the past not only to make claims to memory but to visualize and memorialize the lost. Especially for generations increasingly removed from the events of the time, the Holocaust, as Andrea Simon writes in her memoir *Bashert: A Granddaughter's Holocaust Quest*, "is one big empty hole."[28] Thus we find here, as elsewhere in Holocaust narratives, a performative response to the gaps in individual and collective stories of the Holocaust, a process that both shows and tells—that is, a metanarrative that self-consciously comments on the rupture even as it enacts it. Midrashic extension, then, creates a bridge between past and present and extends the memory of the Shoah. Moreover, as we find in the graphic narratives that we will examine here, both visual and textual elements participate in the process of midrashic interpretation; it is at the intersection of text and image (and the spaces in between) that the story is enacted. As with the aperture in the lens of the photographer's camera, the space through which light passes, here the aperture of narration—the seeing light of narration—clarifies and reframes the experience. The aperture fractures the narration into separate focuses, distinct moments, voices, panels, and images in order to bring them into focus, to reunify the parts—past, present, and future—in an arc of discovery.

The graphic narrative is simultaneously a condensed, elliptical, minimalist form and a dilating one. Literal gaps between panels open themselves to the readerly creation of time, distance, and space. Limitations in language and visual form (limitations on what can actually be represented) distill to compelling materiality the abstractions of loss and its traumatic consequences. The stark economy of the graphic narrative lends itself to the midrashic imperative of Holocaust testimony. Testimony is, as Lawrence Langer suggests, "a form of remembering."[29] Testimonies are living expressions of both individual and collective history, "human documents rather than merely historical ones."[30] Through the graphic form, the writer/illustrator gives a human "face" (indeed, the panel might be considered a kind of "face") to the ongoing, participatory act of remembrance. In re-creating moments of traumatic rupture, dislocation, and disequilibrium—primary tropes of Holocaust representation—such graphic narratives contribute to the evolving field of Holocaust literary studies by establishing a visual testimony to memory.

The range of Holocaust graphic narratives (fiction and nonfiction) is considerable. Some of the works that compose the overarching genre include, but are by no means limited to, the following: Joe Kubert's *Yossel: April 19, 1943* (2003); Pascal Croci's *Auschwitz* (2004); Bernice Eisenstein's *I Was a Child of Holocaust Survivors* (2006); Martin Lemelman's *Mendel's Daughter* (2006); Miriam Katin's *We Are on Our Own* (2006) and its sequel, *Letting It Go* (2013); David Sim's *Judenhauss* (2008); Jason Lutes's *Berlin* saga (2008); Greg Pak and Carmine Di Giandomenico's *X-Men: Magneto Testament* (2008); Polish writer Michael Galek and illustrator Marcin Nowakowski's *Episodes from Auschwitz* (2009); Carla Jablonski and Leland Purvis's *Resistance* trilogy (2010, 2011, 2012); Trina Robbins's *Lily Renée, Escape Artist* (2011); Belgium-born Israeli cartoonist Michel Kichka's *Second Generation: The Things I Didn't Tell My Father* (2012); French novelist Jérémie Dres's *We Won't See Auschwitz* (2013); Israeli commix novelist Rutu Modan's *The Property* (2013); Reinhard Kleist's *The Boxer: The True Story of Holocaust Survivor Harry Haft* (2014); German graphic novelist Barbara Yelin's *Irmina* (2014); Amy Kurzweil's *Flying Couch* (2016); and Emil Farris's *My Favorite Thing Is Monsters* (2017). Other graphic narratives tangentially refer to the events of the Holocaust, such as Marion Baraitser and Anna Evans's *Home Number One* (2006). So too there is an established genre of illustrated children's books about the Holocaust—including such well-known works as *The Search* (2009) and *A Family Secret* (2009) by Eric Heuvel; *Good-Bye Marianne* by Irene Watts and Marianne E. Shoemaker (2008); and *Hidden* by Loic Dauvillier, Greg Salsedo, and Marc Lizano (2012)—as well as a number of graphic renditions of the *Diary of Anne Frank* produced primarily for a young audience. Notably all these publications appeared in the early decades of the twenty-first century, with the exception perhaps of a most curious Japanese series that came out in the late 1990s:

Osamu Tezuka's *Adolf: A Tale of the Twentieth Century* (1995–1996), which begins in Berlin during the Olympics and follows the lives of four characters, the Japanese Sohei Toge, the German Japanese Adolf Kaufman, the Jewish German Adolf Kamil, and Adolf Hitler. Although, because of its length, not formally a graphic novel per se—that is, an extended work of sequential art—we might include in this list Bernard Krigstein and Al Feldstein's utterly remarkable eight-page comics strip "Master Race," written only a decade after the end of the war (and to which I will return in the final chapter). This list of titles is, by no means, exhaustive, and I include only those graphic works that were either originally written in or translated into English. There are others that I have not included because they refer only briefly or in passing to the events of the Shoah. My focus here is on those graphic narratives that have at their center the events of the Holocaust and that were published primarily in the first two decades of the twenty-first century, a period that has seen an appreciable return to the subject of the Shoah across genres (including a considerable number of novels, memoirs, and films), over half a century since the end of the war and the liberation of the concentration camps, a time defined, in large part, by the end of direct survivor testimony.

Let me return briefly to the related issues of definition and genre as they emerge from any study of graphic sequential storytelling. Both generic definition and generic convention assume the centrality of narrative voice(s) to narration. *Graphic novel* is the customary catchall generic term for the range of texts that I'm discussing here. That is, *graphic novel* has become the designation, no doubt in large part for marketing purposes, of a novel-length work in graphic form, its definitional usefulness in distinguishing it from, say, the formal shape of traditional prose fiction but also from comics. The designation *graphic novel* summons a kind of literary weight that the comics strip lacks. I don't want to go into the history of the term *graphic novel*, a subject that has been well covered in the literature.[31] Part of the categorical problem of what we commonly call the graphic novel stems from its relative growth in production as well as its relative newness in the field of literary studies and its inclusion as part of a developing literary canon. The graphic novel is a hybrid form by its very structure: the intersection and interplay of text and image. Thus it defies categorical simplicity and singularity and draws from both. More to the point, for our purposes, graphic "novel" does not really get at the complexity, the intricacy, and the relation of modes of narration to the subject of the works I examine here. That is, if "novel" suggests, descriptively, a work of fiction—crudely put as something that is not true, the stuff of the imagination—then the categorical marker does not adequately reflect the texts that we are looking at. These hybrid works not only merge text and image in complicated ways but bring together and blur a variety of perspectives and positions from which the narrator and the implied author/graphic artist view the subject: fiction, to be sure, but also memoir, autobiography, biography, historical fiction, journalism, and creative nonfiction.

Therefore, while some graphic novels are works of fiction, many are not. And some, of course, are semifictional. Thus while I will refer to the term *graphic novel*, in particular, when I am referencing specifically the novelist's craft, I prefer the term *graphic narrative*, since that seems to me to describe more accurately the kinds of works that define the richly constructed stories of the Holocaust that compose the genre. As Chute rightly explains:

> Graphic novel is often a misnomer. Many fascinating works grouped under this umbrella . . . aren't novels at all: they are rich works of nonfiction; hence my emphasis here on the broader term *narrative*. (Indeed, the form confronts the default assumption that drawing as a system is inherently more fictional than prose and gives a new cast to what we consider fiction and nonfiction.) In *graphic narrative*, the substantial length implied by *novel* remains intact but the term shifts to accommodate modes other than fiction. A graphic narrative is a book-length work in the medium of comics.[32]

Significantly, as Chute points out, "Graphic narrative suggests that historical accuracy is not the opposite of creative invention."[33] Graphic narrative, thus, is a more apt description of the hybridity of the genre in several interrelated ways: the merging of otherwise distinct genres, the collaboration of and conversation between visual and written text, the characteristics of creative nonfiction, the doubling of narrating voices, and the activity of the reader in simultaneously viewing and reading the pages as they unfold.

This twofold complexity of definition and genre is complicated by the subject of the Holocaust. It is so because the subject itself, in a variety of discursive forms, draws upon a hybridity of literary structures and conceits. Holocaust literature, in general—novels, short stories, memoirs, graphic narratives—engages a variety of modes, patterns, and tropes to reenact what I have referred to elsewhere as a genre of rupture. In "The Genre of Rupture: The Literary Language of the Holocaust," I propose that Holocaust literature constitutes its own genre and that it is situated in the two long-standing Jewish literary traditions of midrash and lamentation.[34] Such a framework for interpretation and traumatic expression creates the conditions for the performance of "a language and a landscape of rupture, of discursive disequilibrium, and of narrative disjunction in an attempt to enact the very conditions they evoke," thus "inviting the reader to participate in an ethical act of reading and bearing witness."[35] I argue that, in doing so, Holocaust narratives (primarily prose narratives, but not exclusively so) perform the midrashic interpretive hybridity that defines the form. That is, in order to make emphatic and to respond to the experiential and conceptual gaps in making sense of the enormity of Holocaust history, such works call upon a deviation from and a defamiliarizing of conventional boundaries and structures. If convention suggests an organizing, guiding principle with which to structure experience (the experience of reading, of negotiating ethical norms of civility and humanity, of—very simply—living in the world among others), then the historical fact of the Holocaust erodes all such structures.

Thus in attempting to represent or extend such an elision, such a shattering of ethical and moral touchstones, Holocaust literature becomes a measure of disintegration and severance. In achieving such a disarming effect of mimesis, Holocaust literature, as Berel Lang has proposed, is shaped by a "blurring of traditional genres."[36] This "blurring effect," Lang argues, "reflects two principal sources—the character of the Holocaust as a subject for literary representation and the role of historical and ethical causality in shaping the genres, and thus the forms, of literary discourse."[37] This blurring or blending of otherwise distinct genres and modes of expression and representation responds to the perceived failure of traditional forms and structures as well as the failure of ordinary language to represent adequately the historical and ethical complexities of the Holocaust. Therefore, as I suggest, "The convergence of historiography and literary invention in Holocaust writing lends itself to wide-ranging texts that call upon diverse discursive strategies. Such works attempt to shape Jewish collective memory, linking personal and collective identities with traumatic history. Throughout the varied corpus of Holocaust literature, we find works that, through the imaginative re-configurations that engage the Holocaust as a subject of testimony and moral reckoning, attempt to create a particularity of expression to represent the trauma of dispossession."[38] Thus we find a characteristic merging of the more formal categories of autobiography, biography, and history but also the intertextual troping of language, those figures that shape and texture language and, thus, experience and, in the case of the graphic narrative, the mosaic of images juxtaposed to words.

I am primarily interested here in those Holocaust graphic novels that, in reconstructing the events of the Nazi genocide, focus on individual familial experiences as a metonymic or synecdochic expression of collective suffering and that blur both genre and temporality in an attempt to re-create and reimagine the events that have shaped the landscape of a post-Holocaust world, thus bridging the gap, as third-generation memoirist Daniel Mendelsohn has suggested, between distance and proximity.[39] As such, I focus primarily on Miriam Katin's memoir, *We Are on Our Own*; Martin Lemelman's account of his mother's survival in hiding, *Mendel's Daughter*; Canadian graphic artist Bernice Eisenstein's second-generation narrative, *I Was a Child of Holocaust Survivors*; Amy Kurzweil's third-generation narrative, *Flying Couch*; and Joe Kubert's imaginative rendering of the Warsaw Ghetto Uprising, *Yossel: April 19, 1943*. These central works will frame the individual chapters, opening themselves up to discussions of other related graphic narratives. I have selected these texts in particular because, looked at together, they represent a multigenerational illocutionary braiding, a multivoiced response to the Holocaust as it extends in both recollected and imagined memory over time. These narratives go back in time as a conceit for the enactment of memory and also as a means of laying the groundwork for self-assessment, historical reckoning, and a measure of the continuing legacy of the Holocaust and our mediated and mediating responses to it. Through temporal and locational shifts and the dialogic arrangement and intersection of text and image, these graphic narratives create the uneasy condition that exists, as Amy Kurzweil's autobiographical narrator puts it, "between all we've lost . . . and what we can't get rid of."[40]

I have selected these texts because they demonstrate, in concert, through the collaborative arrangement and interplay of words and icons, diverse perspectives on inherited and mediated memory and on the role of the narrator in the transmission of memory. Read together, they participate in a midrashic, interpretive response to the Shoah. These works—directly or indirectly—are self-consciously preoccupied with possible configurations of narrative perspective. That is, the shifting narrative perspective that defines these graphic narratives reflects the intersection of personae, of speaking voices, and of histories, both individual and collective, that are given shape through the multihued articulation of trauma and its extended aftermath. We find in these narratives a kind of chiastic crossing, overlapping and intersecting narrating voices whose stories are conveyed through the fractured and indistinct lens of time and through conscious self-construction and the largely unconscious defenses of the ego. As always, point of view governs the unfolding of the story. But in Holocaust graphic narratives, through illustrated narrative perspectives—the varyingly distanced positions from which the narrators view the events of reconstructed and imagined memory—point of view becomes reified, made visual, and thus concretized. What happens to narrative voice in graphic storytelling is important in this regard: voice is shaped, materialized, and thus made palpably emphatic by the "ectoplastic cartoon's balloon of speech,"[41] the bracketed felt experience and manifestation of voice. Here the speech bubbles create the shaped expression of voice as it coexists alongside images, iconic representations, together creating a narrative immediacy that gives voice—competing and consanguineous voices—to the visual contiguity of the past as it coincides uncomfortably with the present. Voice is thus contained within the frame of the image, bracketed by its restricting borders or existing just outside of the panels, a distinct, arbitrating "voice," both figured and embodied. The effect is often jarring, an economy of sound that exposes its antithetical adversary—silence—a metonym for loss, for words unspoken. Here the chorus of voices, in a simulacrum of speech and image, create the uneasy conditions among that which is seen and unseen, visible and invisible, present and absent.

Before opening up this study to the individual chapters, I would like to mention what I have omitted from this work. I have left out comic books. There are a number of comic strips that effectively engage the Holocaust in their story lines, including some of the early Superman and Captain America comics. To this end, I would like to draw the reader's attention to an excellent collection of comics that portray superheroes and other figures set against the forces of Nazism, *We Spoke Out: Comic Books and the Holocaust*, edited by Neal Adams, Rafael Medoff, and Craig Yoe.[42] This book gathers together some of the more iconic comics artists and crusaders and provides an animated historical portrait of the response to the Holocaust from the decade following the war to much more recent Holocaust-related comics storytelling. Additionally, while I refer to Art Spiegelman's *Maus* and, to a lesser extent, some of his other works, I have not devoted an entire chapter to this pioneering graphic artist and his deeply influential Holocaust work. I have not done so primarily because there is already a large and significant body of scholarship that engages Spiegelman's oeuvre, especially *Maus*.[43] What I'm primarily concerned about here is, simply put, what happens after *Maus*. If Spiegelman's foundational work is the standard against which other Holocaust graphic narratives are measured and the point of origin for further explorations of modes of graphic representation through the structure of comics, then what has *Maus* set in motion? That is, if *Maus* is, as Samantha Baskind suggests, "the touchstone of the genre," in what ways has this foundational work of comics—war comics, trauma comics, memory comics, testimonial comics—shaped what we now think of as the genre of Holocaust graphic narratives?[44] Where has the Holocaust graphic narrative "gone" since *Maus*? What directions in the genre have a new generation of graphic artists taken and to what end?

What I'm not suggesting is that Holocaust graphic artists borrow from or follow any fixed guidelines established by Spiegelman. On the contrary, *Maus* opened up the possibilities for a wide range of complex structures, intersections, and modes of memory making and the visual-textual shape and performance of trauma, creating the space, as Wendy Stallard Flory puts it, "for an imaginatively engaged and strongly affective response to some details of the enormity of the Holocaust."[45] Spiegelman, through the production of *Maus*, created a new hybrid language for witnessing the events of the past, an intimate form of testimony that has moved Holocaust representation into the twenty-first century. What I imagined for my book, then, was a single work devoted to a representative selection of Holocaust graphic narratives that have been published almost exclusively since the turn of the twenty-first century. (My discussion of "Master Race," in the concluding chapter is the exception.)

Thus I have limited my focus to what I consider some of the primary, exemplary works of Holocaust graphic narratives. By doing so, I hope to suggest the richly figured and deeply complex narrative designs that have gone into these works. In limiting my scope, I pay close attention to reading some of the complex issues in the field of Holocaust literary representation raised by these works. As I hope to show, the medium of comics as it elasticizes itself to shape around and maneuver text performs the tensions, the gaps, and the mediating intercessions that reflect the complicated ways in which memory travels through time and space. As it does so, the medium metanarratively calls attention to its own craft, to its artifice, the story itself an act of storytelling, performing its own narration. The largely generational approach that I take reflects the myriad and labyrinthine ways in which the traumatic memory of the Shoah is transferred through time. We discover in these narratives the unveiling and swelling of Holocaust history through various stages of unconcealment and layers of mediated memory and reception. They evoke the passage of time and memories both personal and collective and thus produce a material extension of trauma. These graphic works capture a sense of memory through fading or disintegrating imagery in the construction of figurative and literal landscapes. As the stories open up to history and to generations, we find a widening of the lens of perspective, a multidirectional, polyphonic chorus of voices and positions from which the past is unfastened, retrieved, and negotiated.

The graphic narratives that follow, then, pose contrasting yet overlapping generational perspectives through which memory is shaped and re-evoked: *We Are on Our Own*, a graphic memoir written by a child survivor, whose memory is indistinct and unformed and thus whose story is filled in by her mother's memory (Katin); a second-generation memoir, *Mendel's Daughter*, which depicts through the visual focus on hands and eyes the ways in which memory is "handed down" to and absorbed by the children of survivors, interpreted and mediated through the individual lens of both narrator and witness (Lemelman); a contrastive second-generation memoir, *I Was a Child of Holocaust Survivors*, that foregrounds the intersection of past and present in the graphic artist's coming-of-age (Eisenstein); *Flying Couch*, a contemporary third-generation narrative that interweaves the lives and stories of three women as they are influenced by the mutating shape and transference of trauma (Kurzweil); and finally a counterfactual "what-if" narrative, *Yossel: April 19, 1943*, in which the graphic novelist creates a double of his imagined self, a member of the resistance in the Warsaw Ghetto Uprising who, at the narrative's end, dies, but only after showing the kind of heroism that the artist can only draw into fantasized memory (Kubert).

These five framing narratives—in many ways very distinct in terms of artistic invention and the extent and fashioning of corresponding text—all nonetheless approach the subject of the Holocaust with a self-conscious attention to the angle from which the past is viewed, a critical matter of perspective: one from the limited perspective of a child survivor; one from an adult child of a survivor, who only after his mother's death can draw her story onto the page; one from the child of survivors as she negotiates her own place in her parents' history; one from the grandchild of a survivor who must navigate her grandmother's past through the competing lens of her mother's equally invested perspective; and finally one from the perspective of an invented, fantasized double, a "second self," drawn into a narrative already set by history. The visual field of the graphic novel makes possible this perspectival reach. That is, the field of vision creates an occasion for the stretching and lengthening of both genre and perspective, points of entry and departure that extend the legacy of the Holocaust. As the second-generation memoirist is cautioned by his mother in Lemelman's *Mendel's Daughter*, "Sometimes your memories are not your own."[46] They become part of the accumulation of another person's sorrow, of collective mourning.

1

The Performance of Memory

Miriam Katin's *We Are on Our Own*, a Child Survivor's (Auto)Biographical Memoir

A thick and densely populated silence.
—David Grossman, "Confronting the Beast"

There is no easy story in legacy. What is remembered and what is forgotten?
—Edmund de Waal, *The Hare with Amber Eyes: A Hidden Inheritance*

So, where does a story begin?
—Miriam Katin, *Letting It Go*

Miriam Katin's graphic memoir *We Are on Our Own* (2006), the story of her experience as a child in Hungary during the Nazi invasion, is told from two competing and often conflicting perspectives: the limited vantage point of a young child survivor—Katin is two years old at the time of the German invasion of Budapest—and that of her mother, whose memories of their experience in hiding are mediated through her daughter's illustrated articulation of them. *We Are on Our Own*, through the dialogic interplay of text and image, mediates these differing perspectives. It is only through the hindsight born of age and experience that Katin, as an adult with a child of her own, can belatedly recover and attempt to articulate the events she was subjected to as a child as well as the approximate emotions and sensations of an experience that she only now obliquely—guided by her mother's stories—"remembers." Katin, animator and graphic artist, came to this project late in life, drawing her first memoir when she was in her sixties. Commenting on the belated origins of her attempts to draw the narrative of the past, Katin explains, "The stories my mother told me about our life and survival during WW2 and the fate of our family . . . were always with me. A daily uninvited and unwanted presence. They begged to be told. But . . . I thought who needs another Holocaust book anyway. However, when I discovered for myself the world of comics, I realized that I can draw these stories."[1] *We Are on Our Own* is Katin's attempt to perform the memory of her childhood encounter with the Nazi assault on Hungary's Jews, with the aggressive incursion of the Russian troops, and with her and her mother's perilous and uncertain escape. In doing so, Katin draws herself into the trauma of her past, creating an aesthetic of affect, the textures and collisions of memory. Drawing largely upon expressionistic and impressionistic images of affect,[2] Katin is able to "visualize . . . to herself"[3] that which she can only "remember" through her mother's fragmented stories as well as those artifacts of the past, those personal letters and postcards her mother had written to her father and the more impersonal, public accounts and documents of the period. Katin is thus both the subject and object of her memoir. In drawing herself as a child pursued by forces over which she had no control, she creates the conditions in which she both appraises and observes as *other* and at the same time is a spectator of the outside world from inside the position of her younger, imagined incarnation.[4] Subject and object, observer and observed are conflated in her attempts to reenact the complexity of the experience and the articulation of memory.

Beginning in Budapest in 1944, "a city of lights, culture, and elegance,"[5] her story narrates a life ruptured and inverted, the very precepts and patterns of belief and the shape of the world she and her parents inhabited eroded by the Nazi occupation of Hungary. In graphic form, Katin draws the abrupt and devastating reversal of her family's condition: the Nazi onslaught, the legislated rise of overt antisemitism, her father's enlistment in the Hungarian army, and their displacement from home and community. Disguised as Hungarian peasants—"a village girl with an illegitimate child"—mother and daughter alone will navigate on foot through the Hungarian countryside, taking precarious and itinerant refuge where they can.[6] Moving from one temporary shelter to another, motivated by the predatory pursuit of those who hunt them down, theirs becomes a life circumscribed by flight, by disguise and concealment, and by the imminent danger of exposure. Katin charts the condensed experience of their lives together in hiding from 1944 to 1945 as they navigate the tentative generosity of strangers, the constant fear of discovery, the passage through unknown and hostile terrain, and the confusions of an uncertain future. In doing so, Katin disrupts the temporal, spatial, and narrative linearity in her graphic manipulation of panels and page layouts in an attempt to materialize the visualization of trauma in order to evoke both the complexity of the extended moment and the complexity of giving voice to the memory of the experience.

The title of Katin's memoir suggests the lesson learned well by the child who survived only because of the fortunes of circumstance and her mother's ingenuity and fortitude. One thing is very clear: as the narrator's father, reunited with his family at the end of the war, unequivocally pronounces, "We are on our own. . . . That's all there is."[7] Theirs is a condition without intercession or arbitration, as even the young child perceives, "Not anybody at all."[8] Indeed, throughout most of the narrative, mother and daughter together are "on their own," cast precariously about, abandoned by the civilizing interventions of human decency and restraint but also by exhausted notions of god. The first page of the graphic memoir consists of a large, slightly off-centered square darkened by scribbled black lines and swirls that extend haphazardly beyond the borders of the panel. Inside the large black block is a smaller square, left uncolored save for the inside edges marred by the uncontrolled scribbles of lines. The opening image thus evokes a child's attempts to draw the square within the square, a child's drawing that is, as yet, unformed—lines that cannot be contained within the experience of the frame within the frame. Right from the start, then, Katin emphasizes that the story we are about to be told is from a child's perspective. In fact, the construction of the book itself reminds us of a young child's illustrated book, its cover made of hard cardboard, its small, square size designed for small hands, the pages a thicker, more resistant weight, the images on the cover as well as the internal pages, as Tal Bruttmann suggests, "drawn in the graphic style of a children's book."[9] Yet the juxtaposition between form and content suggests a disturbing antithesis in which the appearance of the book and the subject matter of the drawings that proceed are at odds; right from the start, something is off. Such an ironic juxtaposition produces a jarring effect and establishes the uneasy anticipation that will be played out on the pages of the memoir.

Indeed, the background of the book's cover is black, as is the large square that confronts us on the first page. The book thus promises to begin in a state of chaos as is made emphatic in the writing within the white square in the small center of the large black square askew on the first page: "In the beginning darkness was upon the face of the deep."[10] The "face" of the black square consists of the diminishing light that takes us back to a mythic time before the formation of life itself, an appropriate beginning that anticipates the formation of a coherent universe out of the chaos of the deep dark. The opening page is followed by a close-up of a black splash that, in the next two panels that zoom out, is shown to be a Hebrew letter that begins the text of the making of the world in Genesis, God's creation of the light that is only the beginning of the covenantal promise of a future. Yet as the young Katin's mother explains to her daughter in the following panel, "God divided the light from the darkness," only on the following page to take back that first act of creation, the dark rapidly eclipsing the light.[11] In many ways, Katin's memoir is a meditation on the death of god, or the death of an idea, a civilizing structure, and an ethical frame for living among others. God as the architect, evaluator, and judge of all things and created, in the young child's hierarchical order of importance, "the dark, then the light, then mother and me and then the others" and pronounced the light "good," only to abandon—arbitrarily and in something of an afterthought—the covenant.[12]

Here not only is the credibility of a benevolent, meaningfully designed universe forsaken, but such a framework for belief is irreversibly capsized: the opening pages of the narrative show the Hebrew words of Genesis eclipsed by the regressive impulses of malevolence, the Hebraic letters replaced by the symbol of the swastika and captioned with the unnerving liturgical cadence of the line "God replaced the light with the darkness."[13] We view this rapid exchange on a two-page spread; thus we are asked to see this abrupt reversal as one—that is, as a reimagining of beginnings, of the origin story. Such a re-envisioning of the point of departure disturbingly recalls Melvin Jules Bukiet's received knowledge that, for the children of survivors, "in the beginning was Auschwitz."[14] Indeed, Katin opens her memoir with varying temporalities, geographies, and narratives in what would seem to suggest her attempts to locate an introductory framing, organizing principle for the narrative: in rapid succession, the opening pages shift from the child and mother in seeming ease poring over the scriptural text of the Hebrew Bible, only to shift in the next page to the Nazi flag overtaking the view from what we imagine to be their window, to shift again as we turn the page to the year 1968, to an adult Katin with her new child, surrounded by family and warmth, only to transfer again on the facing page to 1944 and Budapest before the Nazi occupation, followed once again by the threat of impending disaster. Such jarring, erratic, juxtaposed movement from scene to scene, from one time to another reflects the instability of memory and also traumatic recall. Thus Katin conflates in these opening pages time and comportment, inviting the reader to see the predicament of individual lives within the sweep and arc of the wider historical moment and its aftermath for the author and her mother.

Katin's narrative perspective is complicated by her age at the time of the events she relates, events that she can only now, with the guide of maturity and experience as an adult with a child of her own, begin to understand. Thus Katin writes from a dual perspective: she is both a survivor, a witness to events she experienced directly yet whose implications she did not at the time appreciate, and a second-generation chronicler of events filtered through her mother's memory and her own imaginative, projected reinvention of both the events and their meaning at the time of their occurrence. Complicating further this mix of perspectives and an amalgam of all these is her perspective as an authorial presence in writing the memoir. Putting herself in her mother's place, Katin displaces her deferred anxiety onto her mother, but she also displaces her mother's past terror and dread onto her own more proximate and residual fears and her belated awareness of the danger she was in. Thus the remnants of memory as they exist on the periphery of her consciousness as well as the unconscious return of past trauma control the unfolding of the narrative.

Katin is part of what Susan Suleiman refers to as the "1.5 generation": "child survivors of the Holocaust, too young to have had an adult understanding of what was happening to them, but old enough to have *been there* during the Nazi persecution of Jews."[15] As Suleiman suggests, these were survivors for whom "the trauma occurred . . . before the formation of stable identity . . . and in some cases before any conscious sense of self."[16] As a very young child at the time of her ordeal, Katin does not have distinct memories of the events that her mother has related to her, and thus she must reach into her mother's memory of the past in an act of imaginative creation. Her position is characteristic of other young children for whom the memory of their displacement and imminent peril exists only on the periphery of their consciousness. As such, the child's limited consciousness of events and surroundings complicates the process and articulation of memory. As Katin said in an interview with Samantha Baskind, "As I was very young, my real memories of that year are very scant. I am grateful for that. What I most remember is connected to food and the lack thereof; the little dog that I befriended and then had to leave behind when my mother and I were on the run, which I describe over the course of several pages, culminating in the dog being killed and my mother and I later finding him bloody in the snow; and the bombing that I witnessed."[17] Such limitations and "flawed," imperfect memories, however, do not detract from the literary expression and production of repressed memories, according to Suleiman, "powerful accounts of what it felt like to be a child . . . during the Holocaust, encountering loss, terror, chaos [in which] we see both the child's helplessness and the adult's attempt to render that helplessness, retrospectively, in language."[18] Similarly, child survivor Irena Klepfisz, whose wartime experiences in hiding in the Polish countryside were not unlike Katin's, describes in the prose poem "Bashert" her lack of awareness during the time in which she and her mother—both terribly alone, ill, and desperate—were imperiled and in disguise: "I am over three years old. I have no consciousness of our danger, our separateness from the others. I have no awareness that we are playing a part."[19] While child survivors who were too young to remember the events or even to have perceived their peril at the time in which the events were taking place look back into an empty space where memory conditionally might have been, such vacuity is in part compensated for through a creative reenactment of their experiences.

It is thus through the narrated repetition of events that the child survivor is able to wrest some control over the uncontrollable past and perhaps conquer the belated fear of what might have happened. Cathy Caruth, in *Literature in the Ashes of History*, a very interesting study of psychoanalysis and the disappearance of history, argues that the failure of memory symptomatically results in repetitive return narratives, "a return to the site of catastrophe to grasp an origin that marks the beginnings of [the] urgent desire to remember."[20] Such a "return" might be figured in an actual return to the physical site of the catastrophe or an imaginative return through, as Caruth suggests, "the creative act of language."[21] Caruth's discussion of Freud's example of the child who engages in the repetitive game of departure and return, of "fort" and "da," "gone" and "here," as a means of negotiating the fear of the loss of the mother is pertinent to our discussion of child-survivor return narratives. The graphic reconstruction of the catastrophic time before memory might be likened to the repetitive game played as a means of gaining control of one's unconscious impulses and fears. The "repetitive game," then, played out indirectly by way of the narrative, constitutes a return to, or repetition of, the "lost" experience, the origin of the anxiety not only about absent memory but also about the contingency of a life that might have been lost. The "return of the traumatic experience," as Caruth suggests, "is not the *direct* witness of a threat to life but rather the attempt to overcome the fact that it was *not direct*, to master what was never fully grasped in the first place. . . . The life of the survivor becomes the repetition of the reality that consciousness cannot grasp."[22] Thus returning to the traumatic moments or occasion of the past, in the instance of Katin's child-survivor narrative, might be thought of as a way of performing or reenacting the trauma in order to control it.

Thus Katin's mother's stories evoke in her a kind of imaginative recall, a symptomatic response to experiences that she absorbed unconsciously as she witnessed and *felt* her mother's fear in the way that children are deeply in some primal way attuned to changes in their mothers' affect. After all, the extent to which Katin's young life was so dramatically ruptured and reconfigured cannot be overestimated: a once present but suddenly absent parent, the result of her father's conscription in the Hungarian army; the loss of her beloved dog Rexy, turned over by order to the Nazis in the legislated appropriation of all "Jewish dogs";[23] watching her mother burn the family documents and photographs, anything that could link them to their past; leaving the only home and community she had ever known; assuming a new name and identity; the abrupt substitution of one life for another, one of transit; the unexplained experience of hunger, cold, and discomfort; the necessity of silence and restraint. Such disruptions and reversals—a new vista of sensory experiences—would have created a shift in Katin's developing consciousness about the contours of her environment and the stability of her relation to that changing psychic and physical landscape. The stable markers and structures of identity and place were eroded at an impressionable age for the young child, who now, decades later, advances upon that once unknown territory in an attempt to shape and give meaning to the structures of memory.[24] Katin, speaking at the New York Comics & Picture-Story Symposium, explained that drawing her first graphic memoir involved "translating a handful of childhood photographs" and gathering "flashes of memory," amending that "she did not want to depend on memory alone, no matter how strong it resonated."[25] Such resonances of memory, then, contribute to the complexities and paradoxes in adjudicating such knowledge, especially when memory fails or when memory becomes memory transferred. When, in other words, are Katin's memories of the events she experienced as a young child her own and when are they her mother's memories that Katin has absorbed through the process of telling and retelling and thinking them through?

Paul Valent, psychiatrist and child survivor, born in Bratislava in 1938, and who spent the war years in hiding with his family in Hungary, discusses his own vague memories of his early life under Nazi occupation:

> There was a general but unformed sense which I had at the time of people disappearing. I have photographs of three cousins with whom I had stayed on the farm when my parents were deported by the Nazis who disappeared. But even while I was with my parents the dread of disappearances remained unformed. Why dread? Because as a four year old, I had already experienced the disappearance of our live-in housemaid. And other frightening things had already happened. I remember clearly even now the fear when we crossed the border at night and how the next day I was given a new identity, a new history of my short life. My body became a source of fear.[26]

While Valent's early childhood memories may be imprecise, the fear he experienced is not. The "unformed dread" was embedded in the fabric of his young life, *there* in anticipation of the increasingly unexplained absence of people he knew and with whom he identified.

The assumption and acquisition of fear, a transference of that to which the young Valent was exposed and with which he must have identified, *felt*, in others was subsumed in the embodied self. His fear, the reigning emotion of those years in hiding, became, to borrow a phrase from Katya Bloom, the language of the body.[27] Here the embodied self is the locus of affect and feeling. The very "language" of fear becomes embodied *in* the developing sense of self and thus is indistinguishable from one's sense of identity. As Bloom argues, "Consciously or unconsciously, our identity is firmly linked to our felt experience of being 'bodied.'"[28] That is, the way in which one comes to perceive himself or herself is articulated in the body's affect, the language of emotion imprinted on the body. Bloom puts it this way: the "body is an important site of knowledge about self and relationship."[29] The language of the body is thus defining of self and, especially in the case of child survivors of the Holocaust, the self as seen in relation to others, to the antagonistic other as a source of danger. And thus, as Valent suggests in his self-analysis, he does not remember feeling fear, but rather and significantly, his "body became a source of fear"—that is, he embodied the shape of fear; his body contained or was the "source of" fear, the cause and fount of fear.

In response to interviews conducted with child survivors of the Holocaust, Valent analyzes the childhood memories of those who lived through the Shoah and the effects of these early traumatic memories on the survivors as well as on future generations. Valent came to his memory project with the following questions, ones that seem particularly pertinent to our discussion here: "Do children remember what happened? How important are memories, and is it better to have them or to forget? What makes one remember or forget? What difference does the age of the child make to the outcome in survivors?"[30]

It is revealing in this regard to consider the perspective of another child survivor of the Holocaust. Psychoanalyst Dori Laub, five years old in 1942 when his family was deported from their home in Romania, says this of the imprint of that traumatic rupture of his young life: "I have distinct memories of my deportation, arrival in the camp, and the subsequent life my family and I led there. I remember both these events and the feelings and thoughts they provoked, in minute detail. They are not facts that were gleaned from somebody else's telling me about them. The explicit details . . . which I so vividly remember, are a constant source of amazement to my mother in their accuracy and general comprehension of all that was happening."[31] Laub qualifies the interpretation of his memory by recognizing in it the retrospective lens through which he now mediates and arranges such memories: "But these are the memories of an adult. Curiously enough, the events are remembered and seem to have been experienced in a way that was far beyond the normal capacity for recall in a young child of my age . . . and feel almost like the remembrances of another child, removed, yet connected to me in a complex way."[32]

Such a displacement of ownership or possession onto another, the *other*, is a not uncommon response to the early traumatic experiences of child survivors. In part echoing Laub's qualifications, one of Valent's interviewees, five years old at the time of the Nazi invasion of France, refers to the same kind of displaced and distanced position from which she regards the fragmented memories she maintains of her past and her past self: "Even the memories I have are difficult to associate with myself. I could not feel emotion for that little girl, because it felt as though these things happened to someone else altogether."[33] Imagining the self in another would seem to create a kind of safe distance from the past, from the self as the subject of the traumatic rupture, and thus create the condition for a critical assessment of the self as object. That is, stepping outside the experience creates a kind of escape from the closed interiority of the emotional response to the events that, at least from Laub's perspective, reemerge in uncanny clarity.

In Valent's study of child survivors, however, the memories of past experiences appear far more fragmented and indistinct and, in this way, reflect a recurring trope not only in child-survivor narratives but also in second- and third-generation attempts to reanimate and reimagine the events of the Shoah. In contrast to such indirection is the kind of vivid recall that would seem to define the memories of adult survivors, such as Katin's mother, who eventually narrates the past and thus awakens in her daughter a conscious awareness of the perilous times they encountered and the risks associated with their eventual escape. But the narrative of their wartime existence was withheld from Katin during her childhood. As she explains at the end of her memoir, "My parents took care not to burden me with history at a young age. The war was mentioned only in gently shrouded ways."[34] Arguably, there may be more vulnerability in not knowing the narrative of one's family history than there is in knowing. As Valent suggests, interestingly, "second-generation children were in some ways more vulnerable than child survivors because they carried scars and emotions with no possibility of remembering their origin. While they had the advantage of being born in an objectively better world, they were subject to the memories, anguish and struggles of their parents, who often kept them in the dark about them."[35] Child survivor testimonies, in many ways, parallel second- and third-generation accounts of their parents' or grandparents' pasts. Katin, for example, shares many characteristics of the children and grandchildren of survivors, especially since she does not have easy access to the memories she attempts to articulate. Her recollections of her own "embodied" experiences are muted and limited by her age and lack of acute awareness at the time.

In such instances, memories of the past reappear as fragments, as one of Valent's child-survivor interviewees describes them, "just some images, like some stills in a movie."[36] We find in these discussions, here and elsewhere, a variety of metaphors in an attempt to get at the experience of "remembering." Another child survivor, in response to the question "What does a child of three and a half remember?" replies, "I have no doubts about what I remember. . . . I have seen it in front of my eyes, in my pictures, slides, if you like, and I can see myself in them."[37] Such recurring references to "images," "movie stills," "slides," and "pictures" are all metaphorical attempts to reify, concretize, and visualize memory in an attempt to stay memory and thus construct meaning from such fragments. However, as one child survivor amends, "The real story is probably between the images."[38] Despite the fragmentation, disjointedness, and uncertainty of memory for those whose early childhood lives were interrupted and to a large extent suspended by the events of the Holocaust—those in hiding, dislocated, separated from family, and otherwise disrupted—Valent emphasizes that "in a core part of themselves children *did* know what was happening."[39]

There is a moment in Katin's memoir that seems to speak to Valent's point regarding a child survivor's unconscious awareness of her vulnerability. In a disturbing scene that brings the memoir to its conclusion, Katin draws a sequence of panels in which the young child acts out her confusion, anger, and trauma as she plays with her toys. This episode occurs at the conclusion of the war, only when Katin and her mother are safely reunited with her father. This closing sequence parallels the opening reference to the beginning as depicted in Genesis—the invention of the light amid the darkness, "upon the face of the deep"—and thus frames the memoir.[40] Here we find Genesis reconceived in the child's amended interpretation acted out in play: "First," the young Katin narrates, "there was snow, then . . . some bad soldiers came. It was cold . . . so very cold."[41] As the child narrates the events of her recent past, she reenacts with her toys and dolls the destruction—the sounds and confusions to which she was exposed: her father's forced abandonment of the family, her mother's helplessness, the death of her dog. Reiteratively playing out the shattering events of the past year, Katin concludes the episode by stabbing a fork into a doll, signifying by implication what only the older narrator recognizes as the death of a civilizing, moral agency. The final scene in this sequence shows the child poised in an internal frame surrounded by a larger black square as if we are looking into a chamber: God's death in the crematoria. The image is accompanied by the child's ballooned question, "What if mommy burned that God after all?"[42] In drawing her younger self aggressively stabbing the doll, Katin suggests the way in which the child, through play, attempts to work through her unresolved response to the violence and trauma she experienced by assuming some—if belated—control over her life.

Psychoanalytically, such repetitive play (e.g., stabbing the doll over and over again with the fork, acting out the advent of catastrophe with sound effects—"Wooooowooo . . . zooooom! Booom! Booom! Crash!") is performed in an unconscious attempt to work through her anxieties, fears, and anger.[43] The doll that bears the brunt of the fork in the final panel serves as a stand-in for the enemy, the antagonist, for a god who, after all, betrayed them. This episode is prefaced by the child overhearing her father's ominous words issued in response to her mother's prayers: "How can you give thanks to a deadly sky. . . . We are on our own, Esther. That's all there is."[44] In response to overwhelming emotions over which she has no control, the young child thus plays out her unconscious feelings as a means of alleviating and resolving her deeply felt anxiety. Previously helpless, defenseless in the face of forces she barely understands, the child will act out in play what was not possible in life. Thus the internal conflict is performed outwardly in an attempt at relief. She retaliates against that over which she had no control.[45] So too we might consider Katin's memoir a playing out of her deferred anger and fear and her recognition of her helplessness and defenselessness as a child during a time of war as well as her anger at what she now knows from her mother's stories of trauma (her mother's fear that they will be exposed, her repeated rapes by the Nazi commandant and the Russian soldier, her desperation).

To the problem of how child survivors "adjust[ed] subjectively to their threatening worlds," Valent concludes that "they accepted it."[46] But he amends that such acceptance was, as he implies, both a submission to that over which one had no control and a defense against it: "Just as there was knowing and not knowing, there was feeling and not feeling."[47] Katin, it would seem, through her graphic self-portrait, might have been spared the trauma of knowing but not the trauma of feeling. This paradox, however, is complicated, since belatedly, of course, she experiences the trauma of "not knowing," of absent memories. Valent, perhaps speaking for himself as well as his child-survivor subjects, argues finally that such memories are crucial, especially at our present moment, a time in which, as he concludes, "The Holocaust is now only memories. Child survivors are living representatives of the Holocaust, and only their memories give it flesh and blood. One is one's memories. One cannot exist without memories. Memories connect the past, present and future, they connect oneself with the world. Without memories there is a nothingness, an irrational deadness. . . . Thus one may be more at the mercy of memories one cannot remember than those one can."[48]

Such experiential, diachronic, and structural gaps in the narratives go a long way in explaining the emphasis on artifacts as tangible objects of memory. Artifacts—photographs, diaries, letters, postcards, and the like—become openings for stories, an invitation to envision the past through the object relation. British writer Edmund de Waal, author of *The Hare with Amber Eyes*, charts the story of his quest to uncover the history of the inherited collection of the netsukes that were originally owned by distant members of his extended family, that were appropriated by the Nazis, and that fortuitously, five generations later, came into de Waal's possession. After the family's displacement and rupture, all that remained was the valuable, exquisite collection of delicate objects, metonymic representations of a world unaccountably lost. These diasporic artifacts embody, for the distanced bearer of the legacy of the past, a found presence in the lacunae of his family's history. As de Waal explains, "I want to know what the relationship has been between this wooden object that I am rolling between my fingers . . . and where it has been. . . . I want to know whose hands it has been in. . . . I want to know what it has witnessed."[49] The object here is a substitution for that which was destroyed and the narrative that was lost. Thus de Waal animates the artifact as a way of giving voice to history: "I need to find a way of unravelling its story. Owning this netsuke—inheriting them all—means I have been handed a responsibility to them and to the people who have owned them."[50] The object, in many cases, is all that remains. Artifacts thus become telling, living histories, openings for the transmission of memory. As Katin suggests, old photographs of her family became the "inspiration" for her graphic memoir, an invitation to enter the space of memory.[51] Thus as de Wall acknowledges, "It is *how* you tell their stories that matters."[52]

The problem of memory remains the catalyzing and controlling narrative arc of Katin's graphic memoir. As Jean-Philippe Marcoux, in "'To Night the Ensilenced Word': Intervocality and Postmemorial Representation in the Graphic Novel about the Holocaust," suggests, "*We Are On Our Own* takes the reader into uncharted postmemorial territory by presenting the author, not as the mediator of her parents' experience, not as translator of the witnesses' testimonial voices but as a passive and innocent firsthand witness of the trauma of experience."[53] Memory is both antagonist and a sought after, uncanny presence. Memory is thus performed on the page of the graphic narrative: the shape of memory (what is remembered, what is forgotten) creates a shadow image in the background of the events that Katin discloses even as she demonstrates metadiscursive attempts to fathom and to visualize the events of the past as she narrates them. To make emphatic this dissociation and the limits in knowing and remembering, Katin breaks the narrative progression, interrupting the story of their dangerous passage through the Hungarian countryside with temporal and geographical shifts to future moments in the memoirist's life. Such moments occur at important junctures in the unfolding narrative. Early in the memoir, for example, the Nazi flag overtakes the page (and is to overtake the lives of mother and child), and on the following page, the story jumps two decades after the end of the war, far from the Nazi terror. No longer in Hungary, we find ourselves in 1968 New York, as the narrator, looking into a pastoral distance with her own child cushioned on her lap, considers, in a cartoon bubble designed with wavy edges meant to represent internal thought, "So peaceful here . . . so calm and secure."[54] In this six-panel layout, mother and child, drawn in the soft pastels of warmth and peaceful repose, are joined in the final panel by the extended family gazing affectionately at Katin's baby safe in his bassinet. Here, the horror of the previous page momentarily recedes. And instead we are introduced to the future, to the promise of a happy ending.

The mother and child in the initial pages of the memoir are a silhouette to the afterimage of another generation of mother and child; the child in the early pages is now a mother herself, granted a future that threatened to have been eclipsed by the onset of "darkness" that introduced the graphic narrative, establishing the anticipation of events to come.

In doing so, Katin constructs an alternate reality to the one foreshadowed by the opening scene. As Charles Hatfield suggests of the comics structure in general, "Much of the action depends on waiting for things to happen."[55] Here the anticipatory nature of the narrative's design heightens the developing tension. Her equanimity is a momentary reprieve. The final panel of the page undercuts the narrator's composure, the young mother's final thought heralding the past, which will now be the future outcome of the Nazi invasion. The conditionality of the narrator's contemplative musing of the security of their reinvented lives, that "one can almost believe that it can last," is but an apprehensive prelude to the adjacent scene in which we abruptly return to Budapest in 1944 and the narrator once again as a young child with her mother is unprepared for the upheaval that will define their lives in the foreseeable future. The reiterative return to the site of traumatic origin—*once again* in peril—suggests the ongoing nature of traumatic recall, the way in which the trauma is not contained in the past. Hillary Chute, in *Disaster Drawn*, the study of graphic narratives and the expression of trauma, argues that "graphic narratives that bear witness to authors' own traumas or to those of others . . . repeat and reconstruct in order to counteract."[56] Such temporal and spatial ambiguities are thus destabilizing, since past, present, and future are not distinct; instead, they collide on the page, "this contortionist's backbend of time."[57] Conventional chronology and linearity give way to the artful reconceptualization of time and space.

Chute, in this regard, speaks to the internal "logic of arrangement that turns time into space on the page. Through its spatial syntax, comics offer opportunities to place pressure on traditional notions of chronology, linearity, and causality—as well as on the idea that 'history' can ever be a closed discourse, or a simply progressive one."[58] We see this turning from traditional modes of telling in Katin's graphic memoir in which shifts in time and place suggest the fluidity and instability of time's passage through memory. The present comments on the past, just as the past comments on the present and the future, allowing for, as Hatfield proposes, an "ongoing intertextual or metatextual commentary."[59] Harriet Earle suggests that writers who engage the traumatic past "introduce atypical narrative techniques, especially in relation to time and disrupted narrative linearity; not only is this disrupted sense of personal chronology an important trope in the representation of a traumatic rupture . . . but it is also something that the author can manipulate to great dramatic effect."[60] To this end, Katin, in *We Are on Our Own*, complicates both the textual and visual narration, moving from the graphic expression of her mother's memories—the transposition of her mother's stories to the pages of the memoir—to the interpreted mediation of what are now the appropriated memories of their shared past. Their memories are entwined in the narration and transmission of them. While this account is the story of Katin's attempts to reconstruct and piece together her early, tenuous life, the memoir is, centrally, a tribute to her mother—her fortitude, ingenuity, and self-sacrifice—a model of character against which she, as the older narrator and memoirist, measures herself and finds herself inadequate.

Katin's memory is one that is and is not her own, a memory filled in by her mother's recollection of their shared past, although the figure of her mother appears in the narrative almost exclusively in the distant past, drawn into the story by the hand of the graphic artist. There is, however, a notable exception to the way Katin "places" her mother in relation to the past: alone on the final page of the book is a reproduction of a photograph of Katin with her mother Esther taken in 1946, the year after their rescue. This closing photograph appears on the page adjacent to the last drawing of the young Katin, a retrospective self-portrait of the child who is, at the time of the production of the memoir, no longer a child. These contrastive images set adjacent to one another signify the blurring and tangling of temporality and location that contribute to the intertwining of perspectives. This final drawing, a black-and-white sketch of the young Katin poring over a map that is half her size, depicts a retrospective cartography of their movements during the war, as she explains, "The very same map my father carried around while tracing our steps trying to find us."[61] Just as the borders of their experience are difficult to measure in cartographic representation, the boundaries of time are indistinct. The cartographical code, as Katin discovers in the years following the war, is rendered inaccessible, "a tattered old map with mysterious pencil marks." And the map, as Katin laments, "like so many other things," has "vanished."[62] On this page, Katin draws herself in the center of a panel—a parody of a photograph—framed by a broad, uneven black border whose scribbled lines extend beyond its edges, as if to suggest that memory cannot be contained, nor is it of a piece. The drawing of the young child shows her in profile, while on the facing page, the reproduction of the photograph shows both Katin and her mother head-on, facing out of the page. While the photograph lends itself to a realistic depiction of their shared history and the authenticity of their survival, the past, as depicted in the memory of the graphic artist, is partially concealed, existing behind the frame of the captured photographic image. In both images, however, the frame separates us from its subject, a reminder that we are distanced spectators to and observers of the events of the past, as is to a significant extent the narrator.

Susan Sontag's discussion in *On Photography* of the image as visual memory seems particularly appropriate in thinking about the way in which the image is narrated in Holocaust graphic novels. Although Sontag makes the distinction elsewhere between the photograph and the image—the photograph's capacity "to show" and the power of the image "to evoke"[63]—to capture an image, photographed or drawn, as Sontag suggests, "means putting oneself into a certain relation to the world that feels like knowledge."[64] The image, as Sontag puts it, creates "the look of the past and the reach of the present," images that "do not seem to be statements about the world so much as pieces of it, miniatures of reality."[65] The image, then, as Sontag says, "makes us feel that the world is more available than it really is."[66] In drawing and narrating the image, either with accompanying text or in the textual silence of the panel, Katin makes the past seem more accessible than it really is. Here Katin makes a space to enter the past in an ethical engagement with that history, creating, like the photograph, "a thin slice of space as well as time."[67]

The concluding two-page spread in *We Are on Our Own*, from which we view the two panels concurrently—the drawn image of the child holding the map of her history in her hands contrasted on the adjacent page with the reproduction of the photograph of Katin and her mother after liberation—offers the reader/viewer two interpretive views of the aftermath of their dire experience in hiding. These final few pages function as something of an epilogue to the narrative, an addendum that includes an abbreviated account of the aftermath of mother's and daughter's survival. While the additional information about their lives after the war takes us into the future—their return to Budapest in the direct aftermath of the war, the 1956 Hungarian uprising, their move to Israel where Katin served in the army, their eventual move to the United States, Katin's marriage, the birth of her sons, her professional life—all of this more proximate history is postscript. The extended period of time following the war that brings Katin to the completion of her memoir (more than half a century) exists on a condensed two-page spread. By contrast, the single year in which they were in flight and in hiding composes essentially the entirety of the narrative. The memoir embodies "the story" to which Katin, only at narrative's end, gives belated "stage directions." This has been, as she only now explains, the story "of our escape and life in hiding during the year of 1944–1945. I could somehow imagine the places and the people my mother told me about, but a real sense of myself as a small child and the reality of the fear and confusion of those times I could understand only by reading the last few letters and postcards my mother had written to my father. They survived the war with him."[68] Instead of introducing the book with the context for the events that will be performed on the pages of the graphic narrative, Katin includes such background information as an afterward, an afterthought, a gesture toward her own belated understanding of that period of her life. Just as *We Are on Our Own* is and is not a memoir—for it is Katin's experience as well as her mother's story, both set against a larger historical narrative of Hungary at war—such a generic hybridity, characteristic of Holocaust narratives, creates the conditions for a blurring of voices, of perspectives, of temporality, and of spatial conditions that represent and enact the fractured, chaotic condition of their time. Katin's memoir thus enacts at the level of its form a temporality of belated disclosures as it graphically destabilizes time.

The literary representation of the Shoah—memoirs, fiction, and poetry—is distinguished by an overlapping of traditionally defined genres. Such an amalgam of structures and intersecting forms create narrative "confusions" and collisions but also connections, a transgenerational expression of the ongoing discursive and imaginative response to the events of the Holocaust. The "blurring of traditional genres"—the merging of biography, autobiography, historical fictions, coming-of-age narratives, fables, semiautobiographical vignettes, testimony, and so forth—as Berel Lang suggests, is a response to "the character of the Holocaust as a subject for literary representation and the role of historical and ethical causality in shaping the genres, and thus the forms, of literary discourse."[69] In drawing upon different levels of representationality in Holocaust representation, such generic hybridity attempts to capture the complexity of the unraveling of events both as they occurred and in the extended aftermath of the Nazi assault on humanity, a moral and ethical reckoning that continues well into the present age, so much so that, as Lang argues, "the pressures exerted by [the subject of the Holocaust] are such that the associations of the traditional forms . . . are quite inadequate for the images of a subject with the moral dimensions and impersonal will of the Holocaust."[70] Thus we find attempts to refashion new genres, redesigned forms of literary and representational expression. We see this too in the ongoing constructions of and arguments surrounding Holocaust memorials, art, and architecture, a matter of reconceptualizing expression. In literary narratives, as Lang suggests, the blurring of otherwise distinct genres and modes "pushes certain features of writing to their limits."[71] We find in the rapid growth of the graphic narrative, since the publication of Spiegelman's *Maus* and increasing in the early decades of the twenty-first century, the sense that conventional forms of expression fail to evoke the traumatic rupture both for the survivor but also for subsequent generations of Holocaust writers. Such a generic blurring, then, or destabilizing of conventional genres, creates the conditions for a multiplicity of narrating voices and "memories." Is Spiegelman's *Maus*, for instance, a survivor's account of his harrowing experience in Auschwitz, or is it the story of a son's deferred attempts to come to grips with his life lived in the shadow of the Holocaust? In other words, is Spiegelman's deeply complex, layered, and interwoven two-volume masterpiece a biography? Autobiography? Novel? Historiography? If genres are meant to give formal shape to the expression their structures contain, then such restrictive categorical distinctions are, in many ways and especially in the graphic narrative, beside the point and fail to give meaning to and enact the layered complexities, density, intricacies, and dissonances of Holocaust memory and imagination. The fluidity and hybridity of generic intersections in large part create the scaffolding for the fusions and juxtapositions of spatial and temporal shifts.

In *We Are on Our Own*, past, present, and future coalesce (a recurring trope in Holocaust narratives); temporal distinctions give way to a blurring and to the chiastic crossings of time and space. Writer, artist, and child survivor Ava Kadishson Schieber describes this phenomenon as a layered mosaic of the "present past," past events grafted on the present that indelibly shape the future.[72] Time here is a trope for the impermeability of the past, for the ways in which time is pulled back and arrested, the effects of trauma creating the cessation of ordinary rhythms of temporal and spatial movement. Time and space are conflated in the graphic narrative, and they are so in the interest of traumatic replay. To this end, Chute explains that "the grammar of comics . . . shapes time and space . . . and it presents a non-linear experience of time." The past thus intrudes on the present, "the imbrication of the past with the present," an overlapping of temporal edges.[73] The effects of such intrusions and interruptions have a disruptive influence on the narrative progression. Such destabilizing of time and place is emphasized graphically at moments in the narrative in which past and present are shown on a two-page spread; we see both concurrently, in concomitant, coexistent relation.

In Katin's layered account, past and present muddy, suspending time even as the narrative advances us into the future. Katin's narrative moves between past and present, between a reconstruction of her mother's terror and her attempts to contextualize her younger self within it. The past—its shape and scope—is the defining trope of the graphic narrative. Basically, Katin's memoir has three narrative threads, all of which attempt to enjoin—to order and to direct—the past: (1) her distant past in the advancing moments of the occupation and in hiding, (2) her more proximate past as a young mother, and (3) a more immediate past witnessed by those panels in which she and her mother discuss the frightening moments of their shared history and those in which we see her reflecting on those moments with her own child and the challenges she faces, given that history, in raising him as a Jew. While the first of these conceits constitutes the majority of the unfolding narrative, the other temporal moments comment on and show the lingering effects of the past on the present and the encroaching future. These convolutions of time enact the memoirist's attempts to sort through the past, to seize and arrange the bombardment of memories, impressions, and anxieties that inform and complicate her efforts to concatenate these disparate moments. Katin attempts throughout her graphic narrative to negotiate varying ranges of distance through the creation of narrative intervals. The more recent "pasts" visually become interruptions in her autobiographical thread. Interestingly, these narrative moves in time take up her autobiography when she is the mother of a young child herself, omitting all the years that stand in between her childhood experience in hiding and the birth of her first child. The focus on this particular event, the birth of her child, is, I suspect, a transferential moment for Katin. She will "replace" her mother; that is, she will become the parent her own mother might have been save the events of history, of time and place. In this way, by drawing herself in parallel moments, Katin gives her mother an alternate history: not a young, Hungarian Jewish woman with a child during the Nazi invasion of Budapest, forced to summon the means for their survival alone, but rather reinvented as a young mother in New York, raising her child in relative safety, in "the summer sunlight of upward mobility," as the postwar writer Grace Paley once put it—though ironically so—unencumbered by external constraints, by the fear of capture, arrest, deportation, erasure.[74]

In these transferential moments, Katin reflects what she imagines must have been her mother's anxiety and apprehension; she thus identifies with and outwardly projects her mother's deep unease, foreboding, and confusion. She internalizes and transforms the chaos of their times into the disarray of her own sense of obligations and possibilities. Her identification with her mother is most transparent in the intermittent sequences that interrupt the developing narrative of the distant past. At an important juncture in the memoir, as Katin draws her mother and herself running from the anticipated retaliation of drunken Soviet soldiers, the episode is suddenly aborted in midflight, and we turn to an intervening scene in which Katin, now a mother herself, is playing with her young son. This is a brief, one-page sequence that begins with mother and child sitting together on the floor of the child's room building a structure out of blocks of various shapes and sizes. After completing the structure, the child happily knocks the blocks down, taking childlike, innocent, and uncomplicated pleasure in erecting and destroying—an implied contrast to the near destruction of Katin's family's circumstances and their attempts to rebuild their lives. Here, Katin's child can take control of his actions; he can make things happen, a sharp contrast to the younger Katin and her own mother, whose lives are out of their control. The episode concludes with mother and child outside in the yard, where the child, standing amid piles of leaves, head tucked down, calls out, "I am hiding Mom! Find me Mom! Find me!" The final panel shows a delighted child gazing up at his mother as she reassures him, "Oh! There you are!"[75] His playful hiding is shown in sharp and direct juxtaposition to the images of Katin and her mother on the adjacent page, together in hiding as they are pursued by the menacing face of danger and fear.

The book is open to both pages, the one facing the other in dissonance but also in implied conversation with one another. The reader/viewer sees both moments in time simultaneously; constrained and contained in dialogue on the facing, connecting pages of the graphic narrative, these scenes—arrested in narrative time—stand still, reflecting the memoirist's suspension between these moments. Katin thus projects the one image onto the other, and the former memory refracts the latter. The two sets of mother and child function here as doubles but also as foils. Significantly, Katin is the constant in both episodes: the child in the first episode and replacing her mother in the subsequent set of panels. Katin displays two abutting "versions" of hiding: the one a desperate necessity in dire circumstances, the other a pleasurable game of hide-and-seek. In the latter instance, of course, much of the child's delight is in the unconscious surety that he will be "found," that his mother, ever constant, will be there when he uncovers his eyes. The one sense of being "found" is measured here against its implied contrast: in the first set of panels, sketched in shades of menacing shadows of black and white, mother and child can't afford to be "found"; they must remain hidden. In showing the one sequence in close proximity to the other, Katin evokes such a pleasant moment at playful hiding with her own child—drawn in the warm tones of color—set against its contrastive, antagonistic other. Thus moments of pleasure are arrested, tempered by, and encased in *the other*, in a scenario in which, in this case, hiding signifies a marker of the Holocaust, a flight response to a set of specifically defined historical conditions. As Katin makes very clear, the seeming lack of external threat is not a panacea for the kind of internal debilitating impulses that extend well beyond the defining moments of her history. Both these contrastive episodes reflect shared experiences between mother and child, and though binding them in radically disparate ways, both moments, we are meant to understand, will be given permanence in memory.

The past, almost entirely, is depicted in sketchy black-and-white drawings. The exception to this is an early introduction of the ominous appearance through a window frame of billowing Nazi flags set against a blue sky. The reader finds herself on the inside of the building looking out; we view the advancing Nazi flag as do Katin and her mother. The various images of the flag, colored in red contrasted with the imprint of the menacing black image of the swastika, subsume the frame, panning in until the black of the image fills the window through which the child views her shrinking world. In the last panel of this sequence, the black of the swastika eclipses the sky above, blocking out everything, concealing "the light with the darkness" (fig. 1.1).

Significantly, as I have suggested earlier, the narrative opens with the young child's point of view. It is from her limited perspective through which we see the events unfold. But this limited perspective is mediated throughout the narrative by other mitigating perspectives, rounding out our understanding of the story she tells. In this particular instance, the image of the swastika as it comes into view through the window of their apartment in Budapest, gradually showing itself from the corner of the window frame until it takes over the

FIGURE 1.1. God replaced the light. Miriam Katin, *We Are on Our Own: A Memoir* (Montreal, Quebec: Drawn & Quarterly, 2006), 5.

view completely, illustrates the calculated advancement and systematic closing in on the lives of Europe's Jews. The sequential movement of the flag as it overtakes the window suggests the systematic, successive, and uninterrupted steps of the Nazi machinery. At the same time, the dramatic shift to color suggests the shocking suddenness of the upheaval and eradication of the known world. Thus Katin creates the historical reality of the time and, simultaneously, her innocence and lack of awareness as she is caught up in it.

The various shades of black-and-white pencil drawings that represent the distant past are in part drawn from old family photographs that inspired Katin's work and that later appear replicated on some of the pages of the memoir.[76] As Katin has said of her stylistic design, "The past comes to me as black and white and gray," the colors of memory.[77] The sparsely interspersed images of the more proximate past and the present—those that reflect the adult Katin with her own husband and child—are drawn in color, bright hues of oranges and reds that create a startling contrast to the shadowy pattern of black and white that constitutes most of the images and that defines the position from which Katin views the events of the past. Of course, Katin both did and did not experience these events, if by experience we mean a conscious awareness of the reality of the danger to which she was exposed. The gradations of shadowy, sketched lines of black and gray represent the obscurities and shades of memory, fading in and out on the edges of awareness. The representation of the distant past constitutes memories that she takes as her own. She places herself in the frame of her mother's memories. To this end, Katin draws what she imagines to have been her own misinterpretation of events as they unfolded, an innocence that contributes to the authenticity of the telling. Such a layering of perspectives suggests the generational differences in the way in which we observe, access, and adjudicate both the events that we experience and their implications, inferences beyond the reach of a child's limited vision.

In Katin's graphic memoir, this pleating of textual and visual points of view creates a kind of double-voicing in which the young child's perspective is tempered by and mediated through her mother's more mature cognizance of the dangers they faced as they experienced them. Such a doubling of voices creates a doubling of vision, the experience of witnessing simultaneously different levels of awareness. If narrative voice draws upon the accumulation of tones (attitudes or emotions) that creates a whole—that is, an identifiable character and the position that character takes toward an event, an idea, and so on[78]—then the doubling of voices, such as we "hear" in Katin's graphic memoir, produces, as Wayne Booth once described it, "a chorus of voices, each speaking with its own authority."[79] Such a doubling of voices can take the form of a literary "voice over," akin to film, in which the narrating voice creates a kind of overlay to the action that is taking place on the "screen" of the text. That is, while we see, for example, the young child Katin oblivious to the threatening conditions that encompass her as she and her mother take provisional shelter in the home of Hungarian strangers or when they run from the Russian soldiers or barely navigate their way through the blinding storm, we experience the silent yet guiding "voice" of the implied authorial presence, who arranges the panels and draws the events to guide the reader/viewer's response. In this way, that older, retrospective narrative voice acts as escort and companion to our experience of reading and viewing the events as they unfold before us as well as directing our emotional, affective response to these events.

We thus "hear" two voices here: the younger Katin in the past who is unaware of the danger she is in and the distanced author/illustrator, who even in the distant future can see more clearly than she could at the time. We see this separation and merging of perspectives in, for example, an episode in which Katin and her mother, disguised as a servant girl and her illegitimate daughter, have taken provisional shelter in the home of Hungarian villagers.

Katin's mother, because of her beauty, has become the object of a German commandant, who, bored by his command in the small town, travels throughout the wine region and beholds Katin's mother in his sights. Recognizing that "this Nazi Bastard has his eyes on" her, Katin's mother has no choice but to yield to his sexual advances.[80] In this extended sequence, the German repeatedly arrives bearing gifts—stockings for Katin's mother and chocolates for the child—in an attempt to distract the young child as he leads her mother into the bedroom. While we do not witness the assault taking place, we understand that Katin's mother has been raped repeatedly: we see the aftermath of the rape as she cowers in bed while the German dresses. The young child, of course, is unaware of what is taking place in the nearby room. In fact, when she finds her mother in tears after the commandant has departed, she attempts to comfort her mother by reassuring her, "He will come back Mommy. Don't cry."[81] In this very disturbing scene, not in the least because the German suspects that they are Jews—her mother's "dark eyes and olive skin"—Katin skillfully presents two voices, two positions from which her narrators experience the events as they transpire.[82] Such an ironic coupling of voices reflects different conditions of awareness. While the young child is unaware of the implications of the "nice man" who brings her candy and leaves her mother devastated, her mother's anguished position—her fear and helplessness—is juxtaposed with her daughter's innocence. We are invited into both perspectives simultaneously; such dissonance creates the condition of uneasy anticipation and complicates the world cast before us. As Chute argues, the comics structure lends itself to a double-voicing in which the "grammar" of comics "exhibits the legibility of double narration—and stages disjunctions between presence and absence and between word and image—in order to pressure linearity, causality, and sequence: to express the simultaneity of traumatic temporality, and the doubled view of the witness as inhabiting the present and the past."[83] Such double-voicing in the tensions between text and image thus gives depth to the experience of witnessing.

In this complex web of voicing, Katin creates simultaneous conditions of unawareness and awareness, a layering of different perspectives—at moments conflicting and at others harmonizing—different positions, temporalities, and histories viewed by us *as a piece*, and this wholeness contrived of fragments is crucial for the enactment and expression of the complexity and the chaos of the time in which they lived. As Booth makes emphatic, such a multiplicity of telling voices is not simply a rhetorical or, in his terms, a "technical innovation" but rather an "ethical invention," calling attention to "the ethics *of* readers—their responsibilities *to* stories."[84] Such a double-voicing or "double-telling," as Cathy Caruth suggests in *Unclaimed Experience: Trauma, Narrative, and History*, makes emphatic "the story of the unbearable nature of an event and the story of the unbearable nature of its survival."[85] The obligatory call to participate in the narrative of the Shoah—a reckoning of its disposition and its aftermath—requires responsible telling but also responsible "listening," as the distanced reader, the handler of the text of extreme suffering and labored survival, enters the space of memory aware of the limitations of such knowledge. Katin complicates this doubling of voices further by creating a trifold of voices or positions from which the events of her narrative are told: her younger self at the time of the Nazi occupation and those moments of upheaval, flight, and hiding; her older self, the more knowledgeable and experienced narrator, who retrospectively reconstructs and comments on the past (both with text and graphics); and her mother's perspective of the same events as Katin imagines them to have been.

The images that Katin draws make emphatic the blurring of perspectives but also the limitations of memory. The black-and-white drawings of the past reflect the distance from which the older writer/artist views her childhood. The images of the past lack the clarity and immediacy of the drawings that reflect the intensity of the narrative present. Color is more distinct, creating more contrasts, subtleties, and visual proximity. The images that represent the past are increasingly indistinct as they are when they represent a danger that Katin can only "remember" in her projected hold on such remote memory. Katin's illustrations are characteristically softly drawn sketches. As the narrative progresses and the danger increases, however, the drawings become increasingly blurred and jarring. Thus the images here reflect both the indistinctness of memory and those moments of trauma replayed. The illustrations are sketchily drawn, as if the artist is hesitant to commit to a memory that she can't quite distill but also one that evokes the shape of fear and the difficulty in articulating the peril that exists just beyond language or understanding.

We see such blurring of both vision and memory in the graphic depiction of mother and child fleeing both a human assault and the torrents of the physical world—the one inhumane, the other indifferent—as they attempt to outrun the advancing incursion of the Russian military and the severe storm that obstructs their movements. At the mercy of both human malice and the malign indifference of the natural world, the young child and her mother exist on the muddied and indistinct borders of shelter, emphasized by the shadowy and blurred images of mother and child traversing their way through a hostile landscape. This stark series of panels, with minimal accompanying text, shows Katin and her mother navigating the fragmentary nature of episodic memory. The individual panels represent distinct moments in time. In the first of the panels at the top left of the page, mother and child set off, initially followed by a stray dog that captures the interest of the young child, chasing them as if in play. Contrasting their two radically different perspectives, the child looks back over her mother's shoulder at the playful dog while Katin's mother trudges through the storm, the wind pushing against her as she holds her daughter against her shoulder with one arm and drags her suitcase in her other hand. In the second panel, on the top right of the page, Katin's mother falls to her knees as she makes a sled of their suitcase in order to pull her child—too heavy to carry—against the dragging blizzard of the storm, the dog, tail wagging, sniffing the child's hand as she reaches for him. The third panel in the center of the page shows that the child's attention is riveted behind them on the dog that is receding into the background; she is shown either waving her hand as if in departure or beseeching him. Like the first, this panel abandons all text, a representation of the silence that encases them, words, we are meant to understand, that require too much energy to speak. The final image and the largest panel at the bottom of the page depicts mother and child almost obscured by the gales of wind against which Katin's mother is bent in the direction of their uncertain, arduous journey. Her mother's gaze is directed ahead as she forges through the storm. These four panels that depict their perilous passage through the storm are sketched obliquely, lines erratically scrawled across the frames and across the more "concrete" figures of mother and child to represent the confusions and blurring of memory but also the distortions of time and place (fig. 1.2).

As this sequence progresses, the scene becomes increasingly erratic; each of the four sequential panels depicts the escalating turmoil of the wintry elements until the chaos of the storm itself imperils their movement. But this is also a deeply expressionistic moment in the narrative, if not in a formal sense, then in the close-ups of the faces of mother and child. It is Katin's mother's face that draws our attention, emphasizing that her perspective is the central guiding lens through which we witness the events. While the child's eyes suggest the traces of worried concentration—is it because she is cold? Confused? Disappointed that they have left the dog behind?—her mother's expression is unambiguously sketched, but curiously so, since her face is shadowed by textured strokes and contrastive shades of light and dark pencil lines creating emotional depth. The intensity of the moment is expressed by the somber tones and layering of gray and black strokes.

Katin draws her mother headed into unknown territory; her uncertainty and obstructed vision as she forges their way through the tempest of the storm are a measure of her disorientation and fear at attempting to locate safe harbor for herself and her child. Katin thus creates, through the sequential movement of the panels, both fragmentation and wholeness. Both time and space are compressed. Each panel is viewed separately, a distinct moment in their laborious forward motion. The fragmented movement represented by the distinct panels separated by frames enacts the traumatic moment. As Jane Chapman, Dan Ellin, and Adam Sherif suggest in their study of the representational strategies of comics, "When representing traumatic events, it is perhaps a strength of sequential illustrated narratives that the form of the panels itself

FIGURE 1.2. Mother and child in the tempest. Miriam Katin, *We Are on Our Own: A Memoir* (Montreal, Quebec: Drawn & Quarterly, 2006), 62.

is a fragmented narrative."[86] In re-creating the traumatic moment, the graphic artist slows the motion of the experience; we see each moment as a singular instant arrested, thus extending the traumatic rupture. Yet we also fill in the gaps between the panels, thus completing the passage of time; here the white spaces create room for the implied connections and movements among the panels as they extend over narrative time. Scott McCloud, in his classic text *Understanding Comics*, describes in this way the impulse to complete the experience of time and motion: "Each panel of a comic shows a single moment in time. And between those frozen moments—between the panels—our minds fill in the intervening moments, creating the illusion of time and motion."[87] Just so, "when the content of a silent panel offers no clues as to its duration, it can also produce a sense of timelessness" and thus the ongoing "unresolved nature" of the traumatic event.[88] We view the scene as simultaneously moving forward and arrested, dragged back in time, an effect created by panels that "fracture both time and space, offering a jagged, staccato rhythm of unconnected moments" that create a totality of suffering.[89] As McCloud suggests, much of the work of the imagination happens in the gutters, a largely unconscious process by which we create "a single idea" from separate images.[90] As Chute suggests, "The gutter is both a space of stillness—a stoppage in the action, a gap and a space of movement."[91] By conceptually filling in the gaps, the reader thus participates in the interpretive midrashic project of extending memory, actively, to borrow a phrase from one of Bernard Malamud's characters, "to make happen what happens."[92] Post-Holocaust literature in general creates such midrashic moments of filling in the gaps in understanding that past history and its imprint on the future. In a graphic narrative like Katin's *We Are on Our Own*, the graphic form, with its panels, its gutters, its sequential iteration of action in minimalist form, compels the reader to fill in the gaps of the narrative and thus of its ethical implications in a way suggestive of the interpretive practices of midrash.

Thus in enacting the prolonged traumatic moment, Katin conveys emotion and action through the combination of simple, restrained text and image, thus creating a "perception of 'reality' [as] an act of faith, based on mere fragments."[93] In filling in the gaps between the panels, we provide "closure," in McCloud's terms, completing the movement that is only implied through the separate images, a process of "observing the parts but perceiving the whole . . . mentally completing that which is incomplete."[94] The juxtaposition of completion and incompletion here, as elsewhere in Holocaust graphic narratives, mimics the imperfect and fragmented condition of memory and its traumatic iterations. In this particular sequence of mother and child lost in the storm, the images themselves are tremulous, tangled, swirling lines, suggesting the movement of the wind but also Katin's mother's panic. As Harriet Earle suggests in a brief piece on the representation of trauma in comics, the "aim of a traumatic text [is] to create in us some part of the psychological disturbance that undoubtedly plagues the traumatized within the text. . . . In comics of trauma, the symptoms of traumatic experience are mimicked in the formal techniques of the comic."[95] In re-creating the traumatic moment, Katin's characters appear blown about, barely able to stay on course. The swirling effect creates the confusion and disarray of their immediate condition but also their uncertain future. Both the child's face and her mother's visage are drawn in miniature, the middle panel distanced, projecting the remoteness of memory and its inaccessibility. Their destination is unknown both to them and to us as they are projected out of the frame. The bottom panel shows the child being pulled in the now open suitcase, emptied, we imagine, of most of their belongings, reflecting her mother's ingenuity but also her desperation and exhaustion: the final image of her mother's face is shadowy, blurred, murky, and indistinct, but her fear is not. We see these panels as separate moments arrested by the white spaces of the gutters, but we also view them as continuous, a continuous movement that extends off the page onto the as-yet-unknown.

In these minimalist, relatively simple drawings—a mother, a child, a suitcase, and a dog—the confusions of memory as well as the confusions of the moment are exposed. Thus we have multiple, concomitant perspectives interacting to represent the uncertainty of their condition: the child in narrative time, oblivious to the threat of capture and death; the mother's anguished perspective the central lens through which we see their vulnerability; and the older narrator's distanced perspective as she acknowledges her own scattered and hazy memories of the event. The figures have a kind of ghostly, wraithlike shape as if to suggest the fleeting, transitory moments of their journey but also the timelessness and seeming endlessness of their protracted efforts. Indeed, the final panel becomes increasingly blurred, lines scribbled over one another, the image darker, the mother, bent against the wind, facing the final border of the frame, suggesting both the possibility of escape (she is exiting the frame) and also the very real possibility of capture, detained by and held in the frame. Her passage is blocked by the border of the frame. In this moment, time is frozen. We are reminded here of Walter Benjamin's point that "to articulate the past historically does not mean to recognize it 'the way it really was.' It means to seize hold of a memory as it flashes up at a moment of danger."[96] This stark moment frozen in time and space is less a representation of fear and more the performance of fear. Katin enacts, *draws* fear, materializes fear on the page, thus inviting the reader to witness, to look in on that protracted moment of abject terror as it is both contained in the frame of the panel and uncontained in its sight beyond the artificial constructs of the panel as it exists as a distinct moment in time. Here, incongruously, Katin creates both motion and stasis. She slows time to reflect the traumatic moment in which they are held, "the representation of . . . episodic truth."[97] This episode is protracted, four panels with minimal mediating text that essentially tell the same story. But the repetitiveness of the panels and the absence of any text at all in two of the panels freeze mother and child in time, thus re-creating in graphic form the traumatic moment, moving, as Earle suggests, "with agonising slowness," causing the reader to "linger on the page longer than we would perhaps usually do," caught up in "the chaos of the subject matter and action within the panel[s]."[98] There is a kind of severe minimalism of expression established here as elsewhere in the narrative. Only two of the panels include brief text, and the duration of the storm is depicted in only four, sparsely populated images. Yet we are meant to imagine that their rough passage through the storm is protracted, taking place over hours rather than moments. As McCloud points out, "In a medium where time and space merge so completely, the distinction often vanishes."[99] Here time is depicted in the isolated space of the storm; there is no time outside of the arrested motion. The image seized in a moment of danger exceeds spatial constraints and extends beyond the borders of chronological and narrative time. In other words, the image outdistances time and space.

Time, thus, shows no constraints, but rather temporal borders are shown to be elastic, fluid, influenced by the subjectivity of memory, by the interiority of agency, and by the ongoing historical rupture of the Shoah. We thus find, here and elsewhere in the genre of Holocaust narratives, differing yet interconnecting temporal structures: *historical* time—what happened when, where, under what specific circumstances, to whom, by whom; *imaginative* time—moments that both go back in historical time and extend, through the imagination, into the future through the reconceptualization and reanimation of those events and their protracted aftermath; *narrative* time—the interpretive telling of the story of what happened, time's movement over the space of the page; and *psychological* time—the imprint of the past on the narrator's and the reader's psychic "space."[100] These are temporal moments that collide, time that is in dialogue with historical and personal memory. Such temporal layering serves in the interests of a spatial representation and spatial interpretation of memory that expand moments in time. As Chute suggests, the graphic form "fundamentally relies on space—the space of the page—to represent the movement of time; it presents a temporal map, juxtaposing frames on the page."[101] The collage of images and panels that structure the genre of Holocaust graphic narratives speaks to the experience of being inside and outside the borders of time and space—the space, that is, of memory. Such narratives thus self-reflexively ask how one orders—arranges, controls, chronicles, narrativizes—both time and space.

Characteristic of Holocaust writing, time and space are distorted in part to "explore the space between reality and representation" but also to create the conditions of rupture, confusion, and fear.[102] It is in large part through such minimalist, economical representation that Katin, in *We Are on Our Own*, creates the conditions of rupture that the narrative enacts. Here, minimalist understatement heightens the traumatic moment. Litotes, a figure of understatement, pushes to the foreground the enormity of the situation mother and child face. Understatement, in the form of a reduced number of panels and minimal, "sketchy" line and figure rendering, thus functions metonymically. The characters' solitary experiences in the stark representation of extreme distress reflect the whole of their experience, just as the individual fragmented panels are brought together in our understanding of the extreme weight and significance of that experience. In Holocaust narratives, understatement and magnification are interchangeable; the former creates the latter through what is left unspoken. The genre of comics—of graphic, sequential art—lends itself to this effect, creating "amplification through simplification . . . stripping down an image to its essential meaning."[103] These elliptical moments, figures that create understatement in order to magnify that which they depict, represent the dismantling and shattering of a world at odds with itself and fragmenting under the combined weight of hatred and aggression. Such minimalism contributes to the way we are: as Rocco Versaci suggests, "assaulted by the image"—assaulted, that is, by history and memory.[104] Katin thus creates a kind of scattershot of memory in her frenzied images in part to reflect the way in which one is seized by memory and the fragmentary character of the fleeting past. As Benjamin put it, "The true picture of the past flits by. The past can be seized only as an image which flashes up at the instant when it can be recognized and is never seen again."[105] The past is exposed in pieces, fragments, and images made possible in the formal arrangement of the graphic narrative in which separate panels are suggestive of distinct moments of time.

A similarly drawn series of panels appears later in the narrative, where, again, mother and child are in flight. Again, flight itself is re-created in the panels and in the spaces between panels, ironically as a way of making emphatic arrested motion. Mother and daughter's reiterative patterns of flight expose the fraught conditions of their tenuous, provisional survival. Katin returns to this scene in an effort to replay, play out, and thus control the memory of the traumatic moment. Such repetition calls attention to the insistence of memory. The repeated scene functions as a pattern of emphasis. The reiteration stops the narrative in its tracks but also moves the narrative inside the experience—that is, inside memory. The reiterative need to return to the scene of near exposure and capture, for Katin, is a symptom of the attempt to master the fear of how limited her ability is to know the events that became a measure of her life. Returning the narrative *once again* to the moment of confusion and dim recollection is both a reaction to and a working through of the extended trauma of this particular history. In motion, they are motionless, caught in the traumatic moment. In these scenes in which they are lost in the snow, there is no defined space; instead place gives way to memory imagined. Here, Katin draws her mother once again carrying her child through the snow as she approaches a village. Positioned in the central panel of the page to which our eyes are immediately drawn, mother and child appear lost amid the swirls of falling snow and gales of blowing wind. Standing hand-in-hand against the onslaught of the tempest, mother and daughter are minimized, reduced, and obscured by the storm that threatens to eclipse them (fig. 1.3).

The effect of zooming out, fixing the now remote characters in the distance, makes emphatic the way in which the older narrator is lost in the vortex of memory but also how mother and child were almost lost to, obliterated by, the circumstances of history. As Chute suggests, "'Materializing' history through the work of marks on the page creates it as a space and substance, gives it a corporeality, a physical shape," and thus makes that which is "absent appear."[106] Katin does not take us back in time so much as she materializes a particular moment in time. In these panels, Katin replicates both motion and sound; the force of the gales, the currents of the storm, and the howling winds create a

FIGURE 1.3. The confusions of the storm. Miriam Katin, *We Are on Our Own: A Memoir* (Montreal, Quebec: Drawn & Quarterly, 2006), 71.

simulacrum of motion and sound in ironic contrast to the absence of any text. The two conjoined panels on the bottom left of the page show her mother trapped in the interiority of the frames. This doubled image palpably re-creates her mother's reimagined distress: she is depicted looking first in one direction and then in the other, the panels connected by her tangled knots of hair mixed with the aggressive snarls of wind. Katin thus moves on this page from zooming out a panoramic shot, emphasizing the scope of their fear, isolation, and confusion, to zooming in on an image of her mother in extremis. In this silent close-up, Katin's mother seems to call out to the reader—although her gaze is averted and she has no accompanying text (fig. 1.4).

Such silent panels interrupt the narrative in an implied aside or indirect address to the reader. As Hatfield suggests, such "silent panels revealing lone characters in unguarded moments of reaction . . . serve as dramatic punctuation, offering revealing snapshots of individual character."[107] In this diptych, Katin draws a double image of her mother, a reversed mirror image that enacts at the level of form her entrapment. Here Katin enacts a doubling of vision and also a double vision; she is trapped in the interiority of her emotional response to her situation. While the direction in which she is looking may be different, the expression on her face is not. The inverted composition, not unlike a negative's contrastive image, uncannily superimposes what is seen upon what is not seen. In this oppositional doubling of images, Katin's mother both is prevented from seeing her way through the whirling obscurity of the storm but also sees the predicament she faces. She may be looking in opposite directions, but she sees the same thing. Thus the separate frames give way, dissolve, a representation of her blindness in the storm and also the reality that she does not know where to turn, nor does she have anywhere *to* turn. Everything is blurred by the snowstorm; the shades of white, gray, and black shadowing create a verisimilitude of their terrifying aloneness, a solitary journey. Their isolation as they navigate their way through the countryside is heightened as they pass through an abandoned village, Katin's mother wondering aloud to her cold and hungry child, "So quiet here. No smoke. Not a sound. Everybody left."[108] Their aloneness is a measure of the threat of other

FIGURE 1.4. The shape of fear materialized in the moment. Miriam Katin, *We Are on Our Own: A Memoir* (Montreal, Quebec: Drawn & Quarterly, 2006), 71.

human beings who hunt them down, those from whom they flee. Here again, in the chaos of the storm, they are made vulnerable, exposed, and disoriented. In the scene's final panel, the diminished figures of mother and child, decentered and telescoped to such an extent that they all but disappear, are overtaken in the frame by a stranger driving a horse and cart. The mother's arms are raised in entreaty or in surrender, either a fitting response to their plight, as Katin's mother—imploring, "Please take us with you! We will freeze! I have a ring. It is gold!"—casts their lot to chance once again.[109]

Katin's re-creation of their defenseless passage through the storm, significantly, is juxtaposed to an immediately preceding scene that takes place in the narrative present. The adult memoirist is looking out of the window at the softly falling snow while speaking to her aged mother on the phone. Here, contrastively, Katin is on the inside looking out. The vantage point from which she views the snowy landscape through the window while being safely ensconced in the warmth of her home brings back pleasant and more immediate memories of her father's love for skiing. For her mother on the other end of the phone, however, images of the snow signify memories far less temporally proximate but just as immediate in her haunted recollection of them: her child suffering from the freezing cold in a hostile countryside, her inability to find shelter, and their immediate danger. In the final panels of this episode, the mother's memory and her accompanying sorrow take over the narrative and adjusts her daughter's perspective, and Katin's facial expression changes from pleasure to regret as she acknowledges her deficient ability to remember the events her mother can't forget. When asked by her mother in the final frame, "Do you remember . . . ?" her daughter can only admit, with the uncertainty born of uncanny recognition, "I don't think so."[110] In the juxtaposition between past and present, Katin makes emphatic the tension between what we know and what we can only infer. In doing so, she raises the problem of what it means to know and what it means to be a survivor. Here I take Arlene Stein's definition of survivor that she poses in her second-generation account, *Reluctant Witnesses: Survivors, Their Children, and the Rise of Holocaust Consciousness*: "The 'Holocaust survivor' . . . is any Jew who lived under Nazi occupation during World War II and who was thus threatened by Nazi policies but survived. This includes those who were confined to ghettos, forced labor camps, concentration camps, those who were in hiding of living under false identities, refugees who left their families behind, those who fought with the partisans, those who were sent away in the *kindertransport*, and others." I like this inclusive definition because it leaves room for a number of different responses, experiences, and memories, as well as narrative possibilities.[111]

In Katin's posture, we see the tension between the desire and felt obligation to remember, on the one hand, and her deep ambivalence in evoking the trauma of that experience, on the other. In *Letting It Go*, the sequel to *We Are on Our Own* and the story of Katin's fraught response to her grown son's decision to reside in Berlin, the graphic artist, in attempting to collect and circumscribe her fears, self-reflexively asks, "So, where does a story begin? And if you are inside that story right now, in that situation and it hurts and say you can draw, then you must try and draw yourself out of it."[112] While here Katin wishes to "draw [herself] out of" the narrative of anxious dread, in *We Are on Our Own*, Katin draws herself into the story of the terrifyingly fraught past. She draws herself into the trauma. She does so in part because she knows the outcome of this earlier narrative, whereas the future for her son in Germany and her own participation in his life in the long-vilified locus of antisemitic execution is still undefined; it is not yet in the past. In the artful Holocaust memoir of the year she and her mother spent in hiding, Katin recognizes the benefits of having been too young to retain a conscious memory of the events she experienced, and her relief is qualified by the psychic chasm such obliviousness has created and also by the uncanny shadow of unease and apprehension imposed by the unconscious.

Thus in *We Are on Our Own*, Katin's memories are and are not her own, a fraught condition foreshadowed by the image on the cover of the memoir: it is a split panel; on the left is a drawing of a defeated Nazi banner in a heap on the ground, the image of the swastika partially obscured by the flag's folds; on the right is a picture of mother and daughter, over whose heads flies a Soviet banner (fig. 1.5). The narrative that promises to follow is both mother's and daughter's memoir braided together, the barest fragments

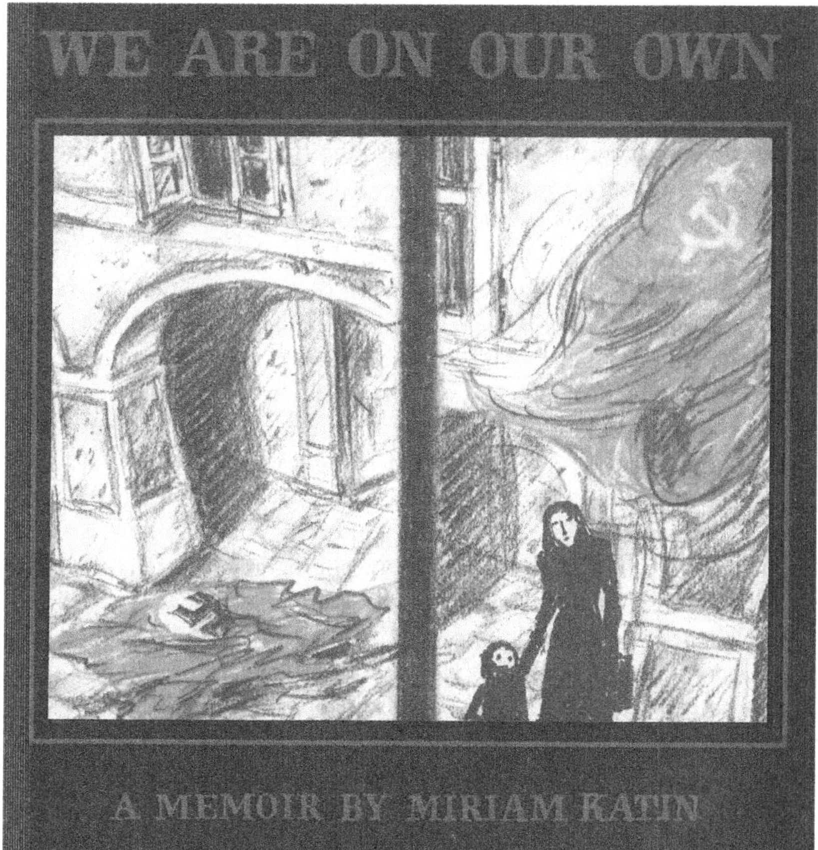

FIGURE 1.5. Mother and child against the backdrop of history. Miriam Katin, *We Are on Our Own: A Memoir* (Montreal, Quebec: Drawn & Quarterly, 2006), cover image.

of childhood memory produced by and "remembered" by way of a direct witnessing mediated by trauma. Thus the memoir ends with a final parallel image to that on the cover. The last image we see is a reproduction of the photograph of mother and daughter in 1946, after the war. Here, as on the cover, mother and child stand hand in hand, Esther on the right of the composition. Her daughter standing to her mother's right, they both look directly out of the frame as, together, they meet the viewer's gaze. This final image mirrors that on the right panel of the book's cover, where mother and child are drawn in black and white, standing against the billowing red Soviet flag that has overcome and replaced the torn, crumbled Nazi flag shown on the ground in the panel to their immediate right (on the viewer's left). While on the cover, the expressions on the faces of mother and child are yet to be distinctly formed, as is their future, the final image at the close of the memoir shows them smiling in open embrace of a new and hopeful life. Their postures create a window into affect. On the cover image, mother and child stand in the lower left-hand corner of the panel, diminished by the red Soviet flag to which our eyes are immediately drawn. The bottom half of the child's body is reduced by the closing frame, and her mother too is cut off right before the hemline of her dress. The child's eyes are two circular black dots against the blank whiteness of her face that is encased in black. Her mother's angular face is also white, upon which is drawn the bare outlines of eyes, nose, and mouth. Contrastively, in the final photograph, we see mother and daughter fully figured. And while the old photograph is in black, white, and faded sepia tones, the textures and implied colors of their clothes are distinct and multihued. No longer shrouded in black, the child wears a white dress with white ankle socks and a white bow in her parted hair. Her mother too is adorned in the clothes of her time: a plaid skirt, white ankle socks, Mary Jane shoes, and a necklace hanging from her neck. Her hair has been curled, and in a relaxed pose, one hand loosely in her pocket, the other encasing that of her child, Esther looks, simply put, very happy.

The inclusion of the reproduction of the photograph functions as memorial text. As Elisabeth El Refaie suggests, "Coming as it does at the end of a harrowing tale of narrowly escaping the Nazis and living in hiding, the photo acts as material evidence of the author's survival and as a kind of monument to her mother's bravery."[113] In this final image, Katin achieves a kind of intimacy between the subjects inside the frame of the photograph and the viewer on the outside who holds their direct gaze. Mother and child, as they have all along, stand against the backdrop of history. Characteristic of the genres of life writing as well as Holocaust graphic narratives, historical and personal stories coexist and simultaneously intersect; the borders of the one cross over into the other. Here, Katin's story of their individual histories is contextualized within the wider landscape of the collective history of the Shoah, illustrating here and elsewhere Earle's contention that in the graphic novel, "history gets humanized."[114] The deeply personalized nature of the genre—in the dialogue achieved through the fluid relation of text and image—both emphasizes and, for the moment of the narrative, contains the menacing scope of history at large. Thus we have been "let in" to the deeply personal, intimate story of the most threatening and vulnerable moments of their lives as well as a witness to their survival. Representations of the Shoah, because of the massive scope and the enormity of that history, run the risk of eclipsing the individual, eliding or obscuring individual *histories* for the larger reach of *history*. After all, as Susan Sontag reminds us in *Regarding the Pain of Others*, "All memory is individual, unreproducible—it dies with each person. What is called collective memory is not a remembering but a stipulating: that *this* is important, and this is the story about how it happened, with the pictures that lock the story in our minds."[115] The two images that bookend their shared history then—the first and final images of the memoir—frame the story that is graphically narrated through a layering of perspectives, screens through screens, a perspectival mosaic through which the past is navigated and mediated. The final image is, fittingly, a frame through which we see into the past by way of the jointly constructed story that has just been told but also a window from which both mother and daughter are looking outward toward the future.[116]

2

Memory Frames

Mendel's Daughter, a Second-Generation Perspective

> As if you could speak the unspeakable.
> —Eduardo Halfon, "The Polish Boxer"

> Consider that this has been.
> —Primo Levi, "Shema"

> To search for traces in the ash: this is the story of an impossible quest, not for what lies buried beneath the ashes, but for what may be impossibly, evanescently, inscribed upon them.
> —Cathy Caruth, *Literature in the Ashes of History*

In Holocaust graphic narratives, such as Miriam Katin's *We Are on Our Own*, the blurring of perspectives and narrative points of view is emphasized by the overlapping and crossing of genres. Both genre and point of view are illustrative vehicles in these narratives of intersecting generations and generational lives in response to the continuing legacy of the Shoah. Katin's child-survivor account of her experience fleeing the Nazi occupation of Hungary from 1944 to 1945 is a memoir—a brief period in her life that shows itself in the traumatic extension of memory. But her graphic narrative is also a biographical depiction of her mother's endurance, self-sacrifice, and resourcefulness in rescuing herself and her daughter. This biographical/autobiographical chronicle is further complicated by the filters of imagined and reconstructed memory as recounted through the transmission of a mother's stories passed on to her daughter years after the conclusion of their safe passage. Katin's understanding of the events is aided by archival documents and extant artifacts, such as letters, postcards, and photographs that survived the war. Thus the layering of memories and stories, inevitable with time's passage, get tangled in the imagination and thus are "fictionalized," filtered through Katin's graphic and narrative rendition of them. Memory is, after all, not entirely reliable, susceptible as it is to unconscious defenses, repression, fantasies, and intervening experiences, all of which penetrate and mediate past events.

In graphic narratives that return to the catastrophic rupture of the Shoah, as with the multifaceted, hybridized genre of Holocaust literature in general, the self-reflexive awareness of the inconsistencies and limitations of memory calls attention to the possibilities for an ethical engagement with the past. Here the relation of the narrator to the stories told is complicated by the passage of time and by gradations of distance and proximity—logistical, temporal, emotional, affective, and experiential. As we move from survivor accounts to post-Holocaust narratives, the intergenerational and transgenerational extension of individual and collective memories and stories engage in complex forms of visual and discursive expression. This chapter introduces a second-generation account of the events of the Shoah as narrated by a son of survivors, one to whom, as the second-generation writer Eva Hoffman suggests, "the guardianship of the Holocaust" has been bequeathed.[1] "The legacy of the Shoah," Hoffman writes, "is being passed on to us. . . . The inheritance . . . is being placed in our hands, perhaps in our trust."[2] What follows is the perspective of one adult child of survivors—one of several second-generation perspectives that I examine in this book—as he attempts to navigate, through the dialogic intersection of image and text, the reality of his mother's history, a legacy now "placed in his hands." With panels as memory frames, the graphic form materializes the ethical face of the image in making visible the past.

As with Katin's child-survivor account, Martin Lemelman's graphic depiction of his mother's experiences in hiding during the Nazi occupation of Poland, *Mendel's Daughter*, is subtitled *A Memoir*.[3] In this second-generation graphic narrative, Lemelman attempts to re-create his mother's past, a past from which he has been excluded: her prewar life in Poland, the murder of her parents by the Nazis, her escape and concealment in a hole dug in the forest—a "grave" she inhabited with her sister and two brothers—and the deportation and death of members of her extended family.[4] The narrative Lemelman reconstructs through image and text is the story told to him by his mother, a story initially recorded on videotape in 1989. It is not until 1996, however, following his mother's death, that Lemelman "managed to find a video of [his] mother talking about her life," the testimony of a dead woman, words from a more recent grave. Her found voice, once buried, becomes the impetus for Lemelman's narrative encounter with the past.

An early sequence of images in the memoir shows Lemelman retrieving the videotape from a storage box and, subsequently, inserting the tape into a television monitor. On the screen, the opening text mimics a documentary's expository intertitle or title card, Lemelman's "voice" thus providing the frame for the opening "credits" and backstory superimposed on a blank screen. The prefatory remarks are, ironically, shown to be something of an afterthought, as is his belated interest in his mother's past: "Come to think of it, I haven't watched the tape since I recorded it in 1989."[5] Lemelman thus identifies himself as director and producer of the video we are about to see reproduced in the book's images. Such self-reflexive, authenticating conceits—such as videotape, tape recorder, pen, and notebook—are characteristic tropes in second-generation writing, establishing the second-generation narrator as documentarian. Art Spiegelman, for instance, shows his autobiographical narrator at moments in *Maus* in the act of writing down his father's words on a tablet (see, for example, the image of father and son at the kitchen table, top two panels, page 29; panels 3 and 4, page 30; bottom page 37; and so forth, volume 1) and, at other instances, holding a tape recorder in his hand as he records his father's story, explaining, as he does so, that "writing things down is just too hard."[6] When Spiegelman interrupts the narrative at one point to put down his pen and, stretching his arms, says, "My hand is sore from writing all this down," the graphic artist returns to the narrative's backstory, reminding us of the artifice of his project and his guiding role in it.[7] We find such self-conscious conceits throughout both volumes of *Maus*. Such an artifice in *Maus* functions, as Charles Hatfield suggests, as a "prop," a "documentarian's tool . . . to underline the activity of Spiegelman as artificer. . . . The tape recorder thus performs a kind of ironic authentication, destabilizing *Maus*'s claims to literal truth."[8] A similar artificial prop frames the narrative of Lemelman's *Mendel's Daughter*. In foregrounding his hand inserting the long-forgotten-but-now-reclaimed videotape of his mother "talking about her life," Lemelman will thus construct this conceit as a way of turning the story over to his mother all the while keeping his own "hand" in it as he draws the images that accompany the text of his mother's words, signaling his own subjectivity in and contribution to his mother's narrative.[9]

Lemelman is fast to lay claim to the authorizing source of the story in crediting his mother for the narrative that will follow: "This is her story. It's all true."[10] While Lemelman may begin the graphic memoir with direct authorial intervention and mediation, he turns the telling over to his mother. Such attempts at establishing verisimilitude in the framing of the narrative suggest Lemelman's self-reflexive efforts to create historiographical authenticity in the face of storied and long-stored memory. Lemelman's pledge of historical accuracy stands alongside a panel in which he draws a doubled image of his head. Lemelman positions himself with his back to a mirror; he is facing outward, gazing somewhere to the side and beyond the reader. We see both the front of his face and the back of his head simultaneously as this split image of him is reflected in the mirror. He is thus looking in two directions: the one facing forward as he looks to the future, the other backward as he looks to the past; in the mirror we see his eyes cast into the distance beyond the reflection. This is a complicated and rich image, signifying, in the juxtaposition of text and image, that he is seeking the right direction from which to witness the events of his mother's story, suggesting that it is the survivor's story that will guide the unfolding of the narrative. The image of the author/illustrator's face, as Jessica Lang suggests, reveals "the fractured nature of postmemory, the province of the second generation."[11] Thus Lemelman visually re-creates the condition of postmemory, graphically depicting what Marianne Hirsch defined as the position from which a post-Holocaust generation views the past, "distinguished from memory by generational distance and from history by deep personal connection . . . a powerful and very particular form of memory precisely because its connection to its object or source is mediated not through recollection but through an imaginative investment and creation."[12] Such a postmemorial reenactment of the very fractured position from which one views memories that are not one's own but that form a significant part of one's legacy and identity sets the stage for the fusion of arbitrating voices and perspectives that control the unfolding of the narrative.

"Memoir," then, is in many ways a curious categorical marker and subtitle for the book. On the title page, Lemelman lists his mother's name alongside his own as coauthors of the narrative that will follow: "Gusta Lemelman • Martin Lemelman." Thus the narration from the very beginning promises to be complicated. Whose story is it? What is the relation of the narrator to the story that he and she together will tell? Lemelman follows the title page with a dedication to his mother, "In loving memory of my mother Gusta," as well as to the memory of those in his extended family who perished in the Holocaust and others of his more immediate family. Once again we find a narrative complicated by the doubling of perspectives, a double-voicing in which the survivor's story is mediated through the filter of the son, who did not witness the events he imaginatively recalls, events, nonetheless, in which he is deeply invested. Moreover, in Lemelman's palpable anxiety about authenticating his mother's story, and of thus authenticating his own relation to it, there is a corresponding anxiety about appropriation, with the felt need to tell rubbing up against the worry about the ownership of the narrative and the imaginative projection of the contemporary narrator's desire. So here, the survivor's experience is not solely imagined but authenticated generically. It is a story heard and recorded, the words transcribed onto the page accompanied by fabricated images of what the graphic artist/son of survivors imagined his mother's world to have looked like.

Indeed, following the insertion of the tape into the VCR, Lemelman steps aside, and following these prefatory remarks, part 1 begins his mother's narrative in his mother's transcribed voice. As Lang points out, with this move, "the narrator here suddenly shifts . . . and for the rest of the memoir his voice is sublimated by his mother's voice."[13] We have, in fact, anticipated this shift from the opening pages of the book. Early on, Lemelman introduces the reemergence of his mother's "voice" by likening his own experience in conjuring his mother's presence to her previous insistence that her own father, Menachem Mendel, "spoke to her in dreams."[14] Although Lemelman is quick to declare his skepticism to this and to other magical interventions, the image he draws of himself shrugging, with hands raised, palms up, to either side (raised, that is, to the heavens), is one of surrender, conceding to his mother's narrative authority. However, despite the disclaimers of his own intervention, the text of his mother's Holocaust experience is mediated through images, Lemelman's drawings that accompany and steer his mother's words. Both mother and son together are narrators of the survivor's story. Lemelman seems committed to notions of authenticity, but he is also concerned about their function and motive. Instead of the construction of text bubbles, Lemelman places text—his mother's and his own words—next to the images, thereby establishing two voices, two perspectives, a structural choreography of narrating voices; the text of the survivor's narrative exists alongside the images that Lemelman draws. Lemelman as graphic novelist but also as one of the narrators (since he draws himself into the narrative at the opening of the book) is thus detached yet invested, a perspective suspended on the axis of distance and proximity, and both survivor and the subsequent generation are responsible for the transmission of the story; both participate in bearing witness to history on an individual and collective scale.

In attempting to evoke the complexities inherent in the ways in which memory is transmitted, received, and extended, Lemelman relies on and draws our attention to images of hands and eyes throughout the narrative. Centered on the title page beneath the book's title and attribution of dual authorship is a drawing of a photograph of Gusta Lemelman as a young woman. Throughout the narrative, Lemelman includes both drawings of photographs and actual reproductions of photographs. The inclusion of photographs is a move toward authenticity and also speaks to the intersection of the real and the imaginary. Actual photographs are scattered throughout the book at moments that serve to remind the reader that those whose lives are made into stories on the pages of Lemelman's mother's account are more than characters in an imagined narrative; rather, they were real people with a pre-Shoah existence, lives terribly ruptured and severed by genocide. We are arrested at these moments in the narrative, and we are asked to see the past with a kind of split vision: the imagined that exists in memory and the photographic face of individual histories. The juxtaposition of the imagined drawings with the photographic real shifts the reader's gaze and creates the conditions for not only a kind of double-voicing but a doubling of vision. That is, the reader is asked to see, to witness, both the extension of memory and specific historical moments in time. For example, at one point in the narrative, Gusta Lemelman describes an *action* in which her mother and other family members are betrayed by their neighbors, captured by the Nazis, and taken away, so that, as she says, "I never see them again."[15] Here, on a single page, exists a double image. On the left-facing side of the page stands a long, vertical rectangular drawing that extends from top to bottom of people huddled together; their penciled faces are drawn, strained, and alarmed. There is no breathing room; they share the same collective fate. Their tightly packed proximity represents the claustrophobic shrinking of their world. Their eyes do not meet the reader's gaze; instead, they are looking on, looking to the side, and looking down as (on the facing page) Lemelman has drawn Gusta's mother as she is dragged off by Nazi soldiers. Our attention is immediately drawn to the figure of Gusta Lemelman as she is assaulted by her captors not only because of the text of the attack and its accompanying image but also by the drawing at the top of the page of the graphic artist's hand, index finger pointed downward, his hand a manicule, directing our attention to the image below and thus making emphatic its importance. The artist's hand here also represents a yad, the instrument with which one reads the text of the Torah, designed as a pointer to indicate the place of the reading but also to prevent the actual hand from touching the sacred text. Interestingly, then, the manicular yad of the artist's hand both calls attention to the image of his mother as she is dragged away by the Nazis but also calls attention to itself—that is, to the self-referential encounter between the second-generation artist and the history he draws.

On the right-facing side of the page is a collage of printed photographs of, we are meant to assume, those same people, the family who were deported and annihilated.[16] The photographs capture the family at a time before the onslaught of genocide; they are posed in the photographs in a pre-Shoah world, at a time before their awareness of the future. But of course, the photographs exist into the future, while their subjects do not. The photographs of the "real" faces of those who take the place of the faces in the imagined drawing to the left are identified by name and relation. Imprinted on each figure is his or her individual identity: "Jenny," "Simon," "Me," "Baba Bashi," "The

Father," and so forth. As Hirsch explains, "Photographic images that survive massive devastation and outlive their subjects and owners function as ghostly revenants from an irretrievably lost past world. They enable us, in the present, not only to see and to touch that past, but also to try to reanimate it by undoing the finality of the photographic 'take.'"[17] Here the photographic images, the "real" faces, take the place of those in the imagined drawing. But both the photograph and the drawing work together to achieve the totality of expression as captured on this single page. Both provide a different type of evidence and of memory.

Memory is complicated in the doubling of image and photograph on this page. The image drawn from the imagination on the left speaks to the process of postmemory, which, as Hirsch explains, "describes the relationship that the 'generation after' bears to the personal, collective, and cultural trauma of those who came before—to experiences they 'remember' only by means of the stories, images, and behaviors among which they grew up. But these experiences were transmitted to them so deeply and affectively as to seem to constitute memories in their own right. Postmemory's connection to the past is thus actually mediated not by recall but by imaginative investment, projection, and creation."[18] The process, then, of imaginative re-creation that is at the heart of the post-Holocaust generation is an approximation of memory, a shaping of memory's imprint on the present. The drawn image on the left, then, suggests memory's malleability; the graphic artist, the son of a Holocaust survivor, will reanimate the dead in a way that reflects his understanding of an experience that he did not witness directly. The photographs that follow alongside the drawn image too reflect memory, a still shot of memory. The family is posed before the photographer's "eye," which suggests a different kind of framing. In the photographs, the subjects are looking outward as their gaze meets the reader/viewer's eye. They are unable to see into the future; they do not look like people who know their impending fate. Here, in the photographs, we are asked to see them not as victims, not as those who are huddled together in misery to the immediate left of the page. But these images exist congruently; past, present, and future coalesce on the page, an "encounter," as Hirsch suggests, "between generations, between cultures, and between mutually imbricated histories occurring in a layered present."[19] Thus the images drawn by the graphic artist and the reproduced photographs together contribute to a living testimony to the past.

While, early on in *Mendel's Daughter*, the inclusion of the drawn photograph on the title page lends a kind of tangible legitimacy to the narrative—we view a realistic image of the woman whose story will follow—the image is visually being handed to us by the artist through whose drawings the survivor's story is mediated. At the top-right corner of the photograph, Lemelman draws a hand, fingers uncurled. Here the artist's hand, rather than grasping the photograph, is portrayed outstretched, both reaching for the image of his mother and also pushing forward the photograph, both an offering and an invitation to attention (pushing the picture forward) to the story that will follow, passed along to the reader, whose participation in the story is essential to its continuing legacy (fig. 2.1). As Lemelman explains in an interview, "My mother never knew I would create a written record of her survival. What she wanted, more importantly, was that I pass on her story to my children"—in other words, to fulfill the Deuteronomic imperative to "teach your children."[20] In this image, the artist's fingers are pointing toward the young woman's eyes, the woman who will become his mother. Such a visual overlay of the present (the hand of the adult son) onto the distant past (the survivor as a young woman) suggests the intersection of temporalities, a mosaic of related histories.

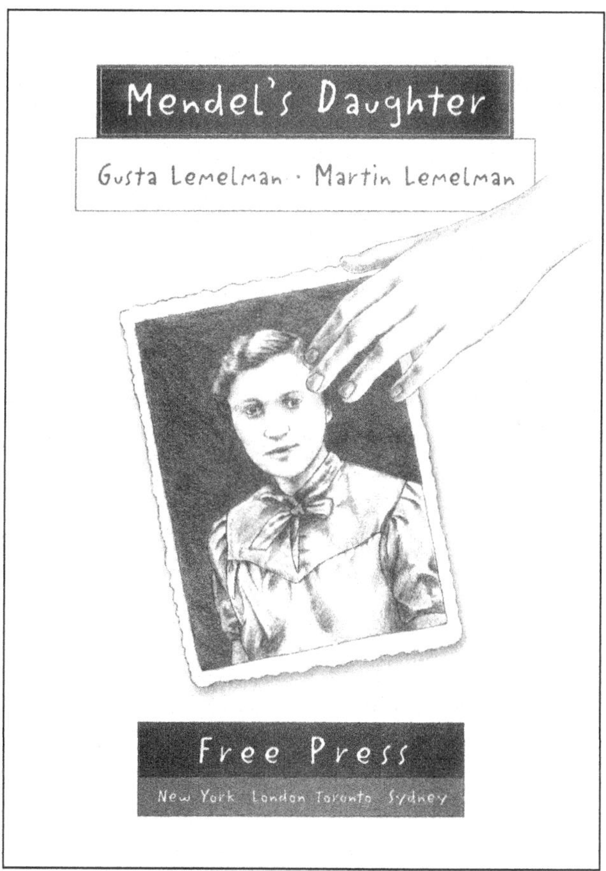

FIGURE 2.1. The artist's mother captured in time. Lemelman, title page. From *Mendel's Daughter* by Martin Lemelman. Copyright © 2006 by Martin Lemelman. Reprinted with the permission of the Free Press, a division of Simon & Schuster Inc. All rights reserved.

The collapsing of generations in Holocaust representation is suggested by this moment: the son points to a picture of his mother in a moment frozen before his birth, before his existence as a bearer of the patronym. What is it, the image seems to ask, that she has witnessed? What does the son see in her image? His fingers touch the photograph as if to reawaken her voice, a material representation of their connection. As Hillary Chute suggests, "In the graphic narrative . . . the presence of the body, through the hand, as a mark in the text—lends a subjective register to the narrative."[21] There is a kind of implied motion in the arrangement of the hand on the image of the photograph, a movement that positions his mother and her story into the foreground. Yet were it not for the hand that brings the voice of the survivor to the page, we would not have her story. Thus Lemelman attempts to bring his mother into a future that is, for her, an absence. He gestures toward *tikkun olam*, repairing the world, from the very personal perspective of family.

This graphic narrative is, Lemelman suggests, from the outset, both their stories. In a lecture titled "The Art of Remembering," Lemelman explains, "It's important to know where you came from. I didn't know."[22] Lemelman seems to suggest that his mother's story locates him in a defining history, one that needs to be reconstructed. On the memoir's concluding page stands a line from the Passover Haggadah: "In every generation, one must look upon himself, as if he personally came out of Egypt."[23] Lemelman thus contextualizes his identity within the frame of these two Jewish narratives: the Holocaust and the story of the Exodus. Through the closing reference to the ancient Hebrew text and the bookending of these related images—the opening reproduction of the photograph and the concluding passage from Exodus—Gusta Lemelman's story is the legacy passed down to her son, establishing generational continuity set against generational disruptions and rupture, generations cut off. What is passed on to future generations is, in a long midrashic tradition of Jewish ritual and belief, the story and, as ritualized in the Passover Seder, its relevance to the present day. Thus Lemelman devotes considerable attention, in setting up in the initial pages of the graphic text, to the framing narrative—that is, to the context within which he receives his mother's story and his place as bearer of that legacy in order to authenticate, substantiate, and give weight to the story he will draw.

Following the title page, dedication, and epigraph is a large drawing centered on the page of a hand extending down toward a face in repose. The caption on the page reads, "My mother died on December 8, 1996. Last night, she spoke to me" (fig. 2.2). The complete caption is severed and separated, made into two moments on the page. The opening clause, "Last night," set against the dark gray of the panel, introduces the temporal moment. The subject of last night's experience that describes, that qualifies and distinguishes "last night"—that, in fact, makes this particular night different from all other nights—is set apart from the image, placed below the image in an isolated rectangular panel at the

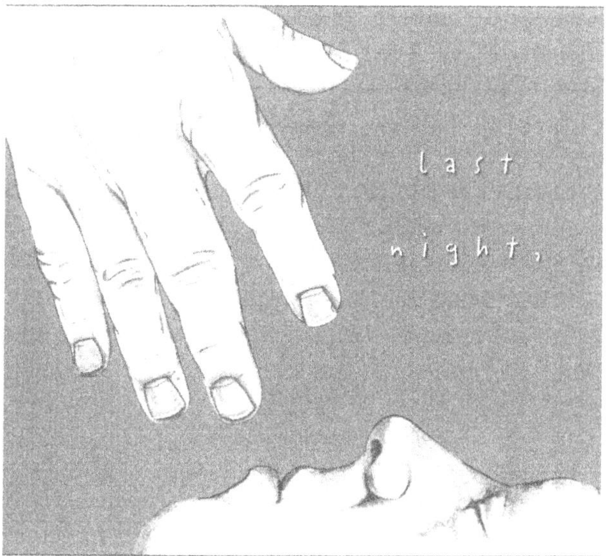

FIGURE 2.2. She spoke to me. Lemelman, 3. From *Mendel's Daughter* by Martin Lemelman. Copyright © 2006 by Martin Lemelman. Reprinted with the permission of the Free Press, a division of Simon & Schuster Inc. All rights reserved.

bottom of the page: "She spoke to me."[24] Singling out this final line, of course, emphasizes its significance for Lemelman. The image is introduced by a correspondingly arranged rectangular text box at the top of the page: "My mother died on December 8, 1996."[25] Both text boxes refer to events in the past, one the more distant past—her death—and the other the more immediate past—her unanticipated "voice." But "last night," positioned with the image of hand and face in a separate panel, is something of an interlude between temporalities. The uncompleted phrase creates a narrative pause; its incompletion and hesitation—"last night"—arrest time and "undoes," destabilizes her death—she may have died, but her voice, as we will see, remains.

The images of both hand and face drawn in profile, eyes closed, are initially ambiguous: does the hand belong to Lemelman, reaching down to his deceased mother's face, fingers almost touching the mouth, as if reaching for her voice? If so, then, as Jean-Philippe Marcoux proposes, in touching his dead mother's face, "Lemelman suggests that the end of her testimony—her narrative death—is the beginning of his intervocalic performance of postmemory."[26] Yet there is ambiguity in this gesture. Whose hand is this? Marcoux proposes that it is Lemelman's, reaching down to raise his mother's story from the dead. This reading constitutes one possible interpretation of this panel. Or to consider another reading, do we interpret this image of the descending hand as that of Gusta Lemelman, the apparition of the mother reaching down to her son's face in sleep? I would argue that we are meant to assume the latter, that the mother's hand, a metonymy for voice, comes to her son in dreams. But the ambiguity in this pose is interesting, and both readings, taken together, suggest Lemelman's complex aim: to interweave the narratives of mother and transferential son in a postmemorial fabric of simultaneous historical recovery and self-construction. Neither face nor hand is gender specific. There's no telling "hair" drawn, although the face might be said to have basic masculine characteristics, even though age tends to diminish those markers. In any event, what is significant here, as elsewhere, is that the lasting connection between Polish immigrant survivor and American-born son is voice, a voiced history bequeathed intergenerationally and functioning as a field of subjectivized memory.

Thus Lemelman's mother "speaks"—in dreams and on videotape—to her fifty-two-year-old son, significantly, as she tells him, "the same age from my father, when he was murdered."[27] Somewhat ominously, these words appear under a drawing of Lemelman, whose face is overlaid by the image of an actual photograph of the murdered grandfather he never knew. Here Lemelman seems to be suggesting that the photograph—that is, the "real" image—is the authentic one, undermining his own hand-drawn self-portrait. His own life is eclipsed by his grandfather's history. Second-generation novelist Melvin Jules Bukiet suggests that the children of survivors are confronted inevitably with an "existential dilemma" that posits itself this way: "How do you cope when the most important events of your life happened before you were born? What does this do to your sense of time? Of authenticity?"[28] Here, Lemelman's image is supplanted by the photograph of his mother's father, suggesting at once their implied consanguinity but also the grandson's insignificance and invisibility in the face of that overwhelming history. How can one compete with—moreover, participate in—that history, that story? Lemelman's face, all but obscured by the photograph of his dead grandfather, nonetheless reveals his distress—brow furrowed, anxious eye looking inward as if to see the image of the man on the photograph whose life overshadows his own. Yet at the same time, the image of the grandfather's photograph faces outward, visible to the reader but not to the son, whose implied likeness to his grandfather is defining. Just as Lemelman is (was) someone's son—*essentially* a survivor's son—his mother is (was) someone's daughter—the child of Menachem Mendel, a victim of genocide. Such interlocking consanguinity speaks to generational continuity and discontinuity.

Below, on the bottom panel of the same page, Lemelman draws an image of his mother on her gravestone, older than her father was at the time in which the photograph was taken and older too than her father was at the time of his murder. She too is facing outward, her hand raised with finger beckoning, pointing toward her own image. Speaking from the grave, she calls to her son: "Listen to me," she insists. "Sometimes your memories are not your own" (fig. 2.3). Are her exclamatory words a warning, cautioning her son against believing himself autonomous, unfettered by the past, by the suffering of others? Are such memories a gift passed down generationally? Blessing or forewarning? They are, I suspect, both. His mother's face, as he draws it on the gravestone, is ever watchful, vigilant, and admonishing, as if questioning his motives, his handling of the story now, literally, in his hands.

FIGURE 2.3. From the grave. Lemelman, 4. From *Mendel's Daughter* by Martin Lemelman.

The gravestone resembles a mirror, yet it is not the viewer whose image is reflected. Gusta Lemelman's beckoning presence on the gravestone is made in rebuke. The way in which Lemelman illustrates his mother's expression here is equally if not more revealing of his own envisioned uneasiness about the project he undertakes. Thus he projects his own anxiety onto her mistrustful gaze, doubtful of his own motives but also his ability to transmit her story accurately, faithful to her history.

In establishing authenticity and in calling attention to the graphic artist's intervening presence in the text, Lemelman creates a scrapbook effect: images accompanied by captions outside of the frames; juxtapositions of imagined drawings of people and places with images of existing photographs; reproductions of actual footage of events; copies of documents issued to family members, such as a "Certificate of Identity in Lieu of Passport," an "Embarkation Card," an "Alien Registration Receipt Card," and other historical artifacts; and multiple mediating voices, all in an attempt to lend authenticity to and to create an accurate picture of his mother's history.[29] As Lemelman explains in the afterword to the book, "I used most of the photographs and artifacts my mother left me. I wanted the book to be as complete a record of her experiences as possible."[30] The juxtaposition of artistic renditions and actual photographs creates a disruptive effect, confusing past and present and capsizing artifice and artifact. This scrapbook of memories comes to represent the complex ways in which the past is contained within the pages of *Mendel's Daughter*, which might be considered a kind of *Yizkor* book of memory and tribute.

At one point in the narrative, Lemelman shows a page, preceded and followed by blank white pages, on which appear a collage of photographs, reproductions of Gusta Lemelman's lost and deceased family members (fig. 2.4). Positioned over the photographs is a drawn image of a hand that both touches and pushes forward the collage of photographs, evidence of the family that once existed. Again, the owner of the drawn hand is ambiguous. Does the hand belong to Gusta Lemelman as she hands these photographic artifacts down to her son to be memorialized in this book of remembrance? Or is this the hand of the graphic artist, who proffers these photographs to the distanced reader/viewer? The ambiguity, I would suggest, is intentional. While I suspect that the hand belongs to Lemelman's mother, the survivor who partially covers the photographs as a protective measure against erasure, the point here seems to be that the photographs, along with the accompanying story, are being handed down to subsequent post-Holocaust witnesses-through-the imagination (to borrow a term from S. Lillian Kremer), both familial and generational.[31] In this patchwork of photographs, the multiplicity of faces, representing voices silenced, lives lost, topple upon one another. The images fall on the page atop one another, a pile of overlapping photographs, a tableau of lives ruptured, their gaze facing outward toward the camera and the future. The figures

FIGURE 2.4. Photographic artifacts of memory. Lemelman, 189. From *Mendel's Daughter* by Martin Lemelman. Copyright © 2006 by Martin Lemelman. Reprinted with the permission of the Free Press, a division of Simon & Schuster Inc.

in the photographs are arrested in a time before the events that would silence them: a wedding photo, a family gathering, women in a garden, and so forth. As Jane Chapman and others have suggested, "By simultaneously bombarding the reader/viewer with a montage of multiple images, ideas and emotions, the sequential pictorial narrative is most successful in its unique ability to represent the power of flashbacks and the victim's incomprehension."[32]

Here we might want to consider what is passed down. What is involved in the transmission of the legacy of the Shoah? How do we measure the appropriate response to such a legacy? And how do such stories inform and shape the lives of subsequent generations? How should they? As the Deuteronomic injunction instructs, "Impress these My words upon your every heart . . . and teach them to your children—reciting them when you stay at home and when you are away."[33] But what, exactly, is transmitted to future generations in "teaching" the legacy of the Shoah? What is the value in the extension of the memory of the past? It is interesting, in this regard, to think about Lemelman's self-conscious reflection of the process of transmission in contrast to a scene in Art Spiegelman's volume of collected underground comic strips, *Breakdowns: Portrait of the Artist as a Young %@&*!* In a brief episode titled "A Father's Guiding Hand," the self-drawn Art Spiegelman, son of Holocaust survivors, presents his young son Dash—the grandson of survivors—with a gift, a treasure chest that, as his father tells him, "has been in the family for years!" and passed along to Art when he was a young boy by his father.[34] Such generational continuity, a rite of passage from father to son—as Art tells Dash, "My dad gave it to me when I was a little boy. . . . And now I'm giving it to **you**! . . . And someday you will be able to pass it on to **your** son!"—now enters its third iteration. "Look at what Papa has for you!" Art eagerly announces to his son, as he hands him his inheritance, a material container of memory. But what is assumed by the excited child to be a treasure chest, once opened, reveals itself to be a casket, a death box of horrors. Holding the key in his hand, the unsuspecting child opens the treasure chest to discover the inheritance he has been bequeathed. In response to his son's horrified question "Whatizzit? A monster?" his father responds, "It's magical! . . . It makes you feel so worthless you don't believe you even have the right to breathe!"

Here the future is seen as irreparably crippled in the face of the past. From the magical chest emerges a monster, a huge, winged, horned dragon, fire billowing from its fanged jaws. Atop its head is perched the striped cap of a concentration camp inmate. From the monster's midsection, a snake-like body with the forked-tongued head of Hitler belches forth, a hideous, inflamed, and enraged monster that expands, increasing in size and ferocity—flames shooting from its mouth—in aggressive pursuit of the young boy who, shrieking in terror, runs for cover. The child runs from the spectacle of horror as the father gleefully and obliviously watches the result of his preservation of "testimony" (fig. 2.5).

FIGURE 2.5. A monstrous legacy. Art Spiegelman, *Breakdowns: Portrait of the Artist as a Young %@&*!* (New York: Pantheon, 2008).

There is, however, no escaping the horrors of the past. Once set loose, freed from its container of history and memory and set in motion, an "object" domesticated and made familiar by a kind of generational piety but now released, the trauma of the past cannot be retracted nor appeased. As Karl A. Plank observes, "An eerie psychological continuity comes out of that treasure box in the form of a survivor's guilt that demands feelings of worthlessness and jeopardizes the confidence of a right to breathe—a death-dealing legacy that seems perpetual as Dash can envision not its end-point, but only the obligation to pass it on, in turn, to his son."[35] The fire-breathing Nazi monster will, in something of a momentary reprieve for the terrified child, be shut back in its box by Art, but the memory of what has been exposed, of what is made known, cannot be undone.

The last panel shows the grandson of survivors crouched in a corner, knees drawn up in a defensive posture. Singed by his all-too-close exposure to a raging legacy that imperils him still, the young boy has been aged and diminished by the experience: hunched over, scorched by the flames, clothes torn. His eyes are closed; his face is partially buried in his blackened arms because he cannot bear to see what is both behind and before him. The future here is now held fast in the grip of the past, a history ominously and palpably still alive. The opening circular panel—signifying the cyclical, unending nature of the trauma—sets the stage for the ominous return of the past. Inside the circle, Spiegelman has drawn a weathered, battered tombstone on which is inscribed the lettering "A Father's Guiding Hand." The grave sits atop a churning, undulating ground from which emerges, as if connected by sinewy roots, a grotesque, gruesome hand, the size of the gravestone. The hand is reaching out, grasping, and punctuating the darkening sky with claw-like, elongated talons. Advancing from the back of the tombstone is a smaller and equally threatening figure drawn in black with what appear to be horns emerging from its head and weapons in its hands. This unknown figure, its motives concealed, materializing from the background, would seem to signify the unconscious fear that past horrors cannot be contained and that the possibility for further danger is yet to occur. Perhaps, as Heidi Schlipphacke suggestively proposes, "Trauma might signal the past, but it might also point to a future threat."[36] Both Spiegelman and Lemelman represent the handing down of memory. But Spiegelman represents that process as ghoulish, even sadistic (the irony of the "father's guiding hand"), while Lemelman gives over to the mother more of the authority of an authentic narrative voice, as Spiegelman does in *Maus*. Thus both Spiegelman's and Lemelman's second-generation graphic accounts explore the ways in which trauma passes intergenerationally but also how subsequent generations differently navigate and internalize the inheritance bequeathed to them, a characteristic conceit of second- and third-generation writing. However, while multiple voiced testimony is something of a palliative for Lemelman, Spiegelman is preoccupied not only with the historical horror but also with its transmission between generations, and he doesn't take himself out of his narrative as Lemelman does—the "father's guiding hand" constitutes an intergenerational imperative to know and feel suffering as part of Jewish identity.

Lemelman thus gives us a complex but less pessimistic version of the ethical motives of handed-down testimony in comparison to Spiegelman's later work. The drawing of Lemelman's hand as it reaches out to touch his mother's grave represents the transfer of memory from survivor to the next generation; her death gives him not only license to continue her story but the imperative to do so. Giving voice to the memory of the Holocaust is a collective, ongoing venture that, we are cautioned, cannot die with the survivor. Living is a voiced experience; so is dying. Thus in telling his mother's story, Lemelman reanimates the dead, giving voice to their memory. He does so both figuratively and in the narrative enactment—by way of text and image—of multiple, intersecting telling voices, all motivated by the son's desire to know. The introductory section of the memoir establishes the transference of story from mother to son and from son to mother, a conceit arbitrated by Lemelman's assurance that the story that will transpire is, indeed, "her story . . . [a]ll true."[37] But interspersed throughout the unfolding narrative of his mother's experiences in the Holocaust are other voices, voices that at least momentarily take over the narration, the voices of other family members, those who survived to tell their stories and those who perished and thus whose stories can only be imagined and drawn into life by the writer/artist. In re-creating a chorus of voices with a voice-over of the writer/artist's arrangement and omissions and inclusions, Lemelman speaks to the nature of testimony, its motivated, constructed character and its hedge against trauma in individual stories set against the backdrop of Holocaust history. *Mendel's Daughter* thus is composed of a chorus of narratives and a compilation of images—drawings, photographs, iconographies, images overlaid with other images—in an attempt to create a multifaceted portrait of the accumulated wreckage of lives, one that reimages the extended historical moment.

Images of hands repeatedly function as a metonymic representation of voice and of the collectivity of memory transferred, the process and project of storytelling a shared enterprise in the transmission of Jewish history and tradition. Indeed, the drawing hand—the drawn hand—appears throughout the narrative. Hands, as we've seen, represent the handing down of memory, and they also function as references of emphasis, a manicular index that calls attention to points of significance. Images of eyes function in much the same way, as a metonymy for bearing witness: what one sees, how one views events, what one cannot bear to see. Eyes here represent visual memory. They suspend movement, creating a stillness of vision that pulls us back in time and all the while projects into the future. The focus on eyes throughout the narrative calls attention to that which is hidden in memory, concealed yet in plain sight. One such image consists of a reproduction of a photograph of Lemelman's mother's eyes, the rest of her face cropped from the picture (fig. 2.6).

Set above the image is the caption, with words spoken by Lemelman's mother, "Sometimes we believe we are going to survive and sometimes we are believing we are going to die."[38] Such a close-up of the "speaker's" eyes creates an urgent intimacy; we are being asked to see what she sees—that is, to see through the lens of her immediate perspective. Yet we are on the outside looking in; we cannot see from her eyes—that is, from the inside of her experience. But we "read" the fear in her eyes and the knowledge with which she sees her world unfold. The precariousness of her condition is expressed in the juxtaposition of text with the close-up of her enlarged eyes, which represent the

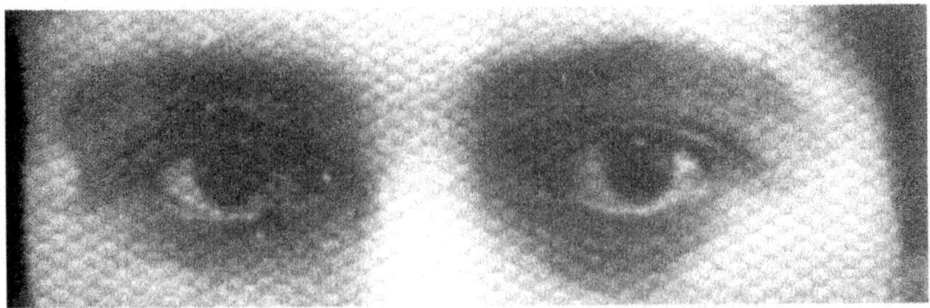

FIGURE 2.6. The eyewitness. Lemelman, 97. From *Mendel's Daughter* by Martin Lemelman. Copyright © 2006 by Martin Lemelman. Reprinted with the permission of the Free Press, a division of Simon & Schuster Inc. All rights reserved.

outward and inward gazes, supported by the tension in the repetitive syntax of "believe" and "are believing." The polyptotonic syntactic structure—the repetition of words derived from the same root in varying grammatical forms in which prefix, suffix, or tense form is altered—tropes time as well as syntax. The repetition and rearrangement of the phrase—"sometimes we believe" and "sometimes we are believing"—makes emphatic the difference between that which is temporary and that which is ongoing, continual. The one is a static moment of hope that is undone by the active awareness of the reality of their condition. The movement from present tense ("we believe") to present continuous ("we are believing") suggests that an important change has taken place for those who now know, those who have seen the reality of their situation (as made emphatic by the close-up of the image of eyes at the top of the page). Their eyes are now open; they "are believing" the worst. The shifting verb tense of the repeated phrase signals and reenacts the traumatic moment of discovery. Such a figure of repetition here, as elsewhere, is not merely stylistic; rather, deviation of the repeated term, its alteration in tense, focuses and directs our attention. It thus moves us inside that experience of what it means to believe that your future is provisional.

While it is the captured voice of Lemelman's mother that moves the memoir to a dramatic close, the interruptions in her narrative create arresting moments of traumatic rupture, visual moments of both the limitations of awareness and the urgency of such representation—as Chute puts it, the "urgent visualizing of historical circumstance that comics aspires to ethical engagement."[39] In a stunning dual image drawn on a single page is a man and a woman separated by frames but linked by the opening words of the Shema: "Hear, O Israel."[40] The left-facing page is blank, emptied of image or "sound." Thus as we turn onto this page, the previous narrative comes to an abrupt halt, signaled by a blank white page. The white page stops us, creating a hiatus in the narrative, a pause before the image that will follow. The empty space marks a traumatic interruption in the narrative and suggests that we are entering the space of a different kind of memory, not the retrospective, chronological unfolding of Gusta Lemelman's story or a return to the opening frame story narrated by Martin Lemelman, the second-generation graphic artist. Rather, both narratives and narrators are interrupted; their stories are suspended for a disturbing moment that takes us back to ancient text, to the biblical command to "hear" (fig. 2.7).

One of the interesting aspects of this interlude is that we have been engaged in doing just that, in "hearing" the story of a survivor's harrowing experience during the time of the Shoah. We have been "aural" and "visual" witnesses to the events as she narrates them and as illustrated by her son, the second generation. Why are we bidden to "hear" at this particular juncture in the narrative? Why, in fact, does this image not preface the story that will follow; why doesn't it come at the beginning of the memoir? For surely, what we are about to "see" and to "hear" as the narrative begins is deeply disturbing, stories that as child-survivor Ruth Kluger insists, "shouldn't even exist to be told."[41] Moreover, the rest of the prayer of the Shema is omitted in this image. Significantly, the basic declaration of Jewish faith—"the Lord is our God, the Lord is one"—that follows the command "to hear" has been elided, suggesting the failure of the covenant. The beginning words of the ancient text are superimposed onto the Holocaust—that is, as witnessed against the atrocities of a more proximate age. "Hear O Israel" are the only remaining words of the Shema here, and they are separated by images that, understood in this particular context, reflect not the affirmation and glory of God but rather the anguish of their time, that to which they bear witness. Indeed, the next image we see is of a Nazi soldier yelling, "Juden Raus!"—Jews out!

In these images, the faces of the figures are covered by their hands, representing the customary disposition for the recitation of the prayer of the Shema but also suggesting that they cannot bring themselves to see outward—that is, to see into an imperiled, conditional future. There are a number of commentaries on the custom of covering one's face while reciting the Shema, among them the explication, attributed to Rabbi Ezekiel Landau (seventeenth-century Prague) and others, that "it would be difficult to express complete faith in God while looking at the pain in the world around us."[42] Here, we are meant to understand, Gusta Lemelman's parents, long since dead, exist on the page in the narrative present with eyes covered; they can't bear to see the future; they can't bear to witness what is happening to them and to those among them in the reconstructed moment of the present. Here the trope of contiguity creates an intersection or fusion of temporality—for what they can't bear to see has, in Lemelman's graphic narrative, already occurred—establishing the conditions for the extension of trauma in the simultaneity of past, present, and the conditional future. It is significant that they are covering their eyes and not their ears, in defiance and fear of the injunction "to hear," for they represent

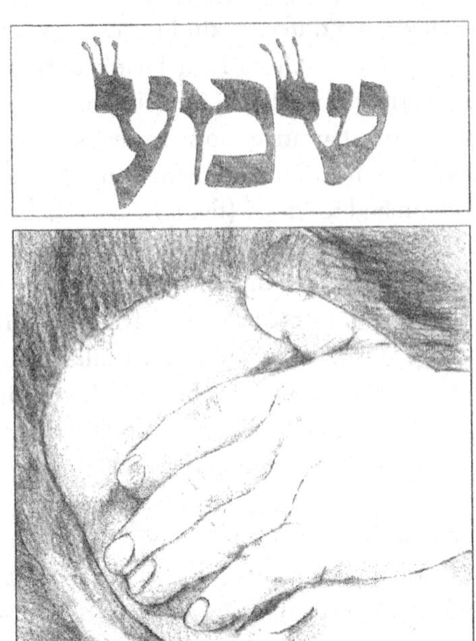

FIGURE 2.7. Hear, O Israel. Lemelman, 117. From *Mendel's Daughter* by Martin Lemelman. Copyright © 2006 by Martin Lemelman. Reprinted with the permission of the Free Press, a division of Simon & Schuster Inc. All rights reserved.

the call to memory, an expression of embodied, inherited, extended memory. This image of hands covering eyes, an image that will be repeated, evokes the meaning of the Hebrew word for "hand," *yad*, which also means "memory" or "memorial."[43] This image stands as a memorial to the dead. The recurring images, then, of hands covering eyes not only refers directly to the Shema but also serves as a caution against the erosion of memory. Significantly, the page on which this image appears is bookended by white space, a blank page on either side, both ushering it in and separating it from the preceding and succeeding narrative. The white pages that encase this image create, as I've suggested, a traumatic rupture and interruption. These moments, similar to the white spaces of the gutters conventionally surrounding panels in comics narratives, create both pauses and the opportunity for closure, the "phenomenon of observing the parts but perceiving the whole," a process that occurs between the panels.[44] As McCloud suggests, in reading the black images up against the white spaces, it is here, "in the limbo of the gutter," those white spaces that separate panels, that the "human imagination takes two separate images and transforms them into a single idea."[45] I would like to propose that it is in the white spaces that the work of midrash is done.

Midrashic moments are those in which we not only fill in the gaps, the spaces in the narrative, but also interpret such lacunae. The white spaces in the formal structure of comics (the gutters) as well as the white pages that separate the pages on which images appear create these moments of interpretive closure. As Jewish legend would have it, the Torah was written in black fire and white fire. The black fire represents the words on the page of the text; the white is the space between the words (as well as between the letters).[46] The white spaces, the silence between the words, are part of and essential to the text. Those white moments might be thought of as pauses in the narrative so as to contemplate and imagine the meaning of the fixed script of the text, moments of meditation but also of meaningful closure—that is, moments that engage in the living narrative. Lemelman's graphic narrative is produced in black-and-white, pencil-and-ink drawings, interspersed with black-and-white reproduced photographs. The black-and-white images represent both the distance of memory and also the authenticity of photography. But the way that Lemelman interrupts and suspends his narrative with the blankness of white pages, pages on which nothing is reimagined, allows the reader/viewer to participate in the transmission of history. The narrative silence of those moments is an invitation for the ethical engagement of the reader/viewer in a reckoning of that history. We only recognize the blank pages because of the black-and-white illustrated pages that surround them. The blank pages, then, create the interval for us to enter the space of memory. Like the conventional gutters that separate comics panels, the white pages constitute "a space of stillness," as Chute suggests, "the figuration of a psychic order outside of the realm of symbolization, a space that refuses to resolve the interplay of elements of absence and presence."[47] The tension between absence and presence creates the conditions for the obligatory alignment between the living and the dead, the engagement with witnessing and the enactment of testimony through silence. Thus the commandment to "hear" prefaced and followed by the whiteness of blank pages suggests that there is nothing left to "hear" but the silence of the dead. The tension exists in the relation of the "heard/not heard," presence/absence, voice/voicelessness, thus creating an ellipsis or hiatus, a narrative suspension or stillness in which what is not heard is ushered in through the rhetorical figure of aposiopesis but a silence that affirms, that articulates, absence as it enacts such loss.

As a means of emphasizing the relation of individual testimony to a history of suffering, a history that risks consuming the stories and lives of those who witnessed the events, Lemelman concludes the memoir with a tribute to the dead. The close of his mother's narrative brings her to 1947, the aftermath of war, the birth of her first child, and, as she pronounces, "for me . . . a new life in America."[48] Following the fortuitous ending to her story, Lemelman introduces the voices of her relatives who did not survive, those whose lives ended in murder: beatings, gassing, and cremation. While they can no longer tell their stories or leave an oral testimony that survives them, Lemelman creates the conditions that allow the grandparents and two great-aunts he never knew to speak for themselves. On this final page, separated on either side by blank white pages, are four panels, each containing two frames (fig. 2.8).

On one side is an image of a member of Lemelman's mother's family—extended family members unknown to him save for his mother's stories. In the corresponding frame, in quotation marks, is a simple declarative statement, told in first-person narration, of each individual fate. Each testimony begins with the opening refrain, "Yes, this happened to me," an affirmation of individual suffering and a validation of self just at the moment of pronounced erasure. The repetition of the affirmative—"Yes, this happened to me . . . yes, this happened to me . . . yes, this happened to me . . . yes, this happened to me"—provides validation in the face of denial, words uttered by the dead. Here the sparse, understated language of trauma articulates a simple truth, and such understatement is a recurring trope in Lemelman's memoir. Litotes, or understatement, creates an arresting point in the narrative unfolding, the suggestion that there is nothing left to say because, paradoxically, there is so much to say that words cannot contain the very images they would hope to convey. Understatement is, I would suggest, a trope of exhaustion, of emotion depleted, words stretched to their limits. As Lemelman's mother says, "So it was."[49] The simplicity of utterance articulates both individual stories and the larger narrative of history: "this happened," a reflection of the greater throes of history; "to me" individuates the experience of suffering. Having no grave

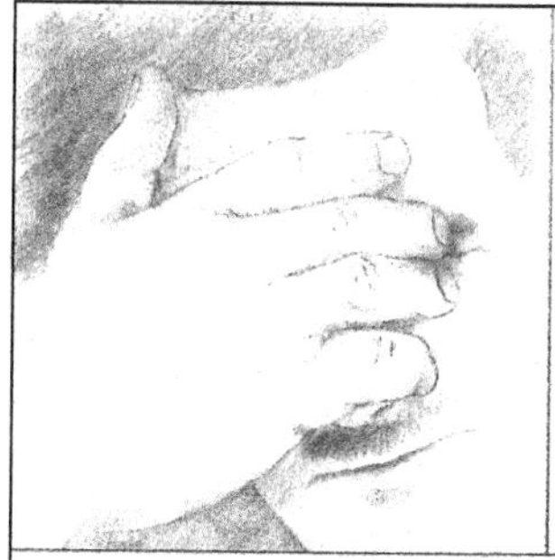

"Yes, this happened to me.
I ran and they shot me.
I was bleeding until I died.
My precious daughter, Yetala,
buried me."
The father

"Yes, this happened to me.
I hid, but they found me, and beat me.
They took me to Belzec,
then Maidanek.
They gassed us, and burnt us."
The Mother

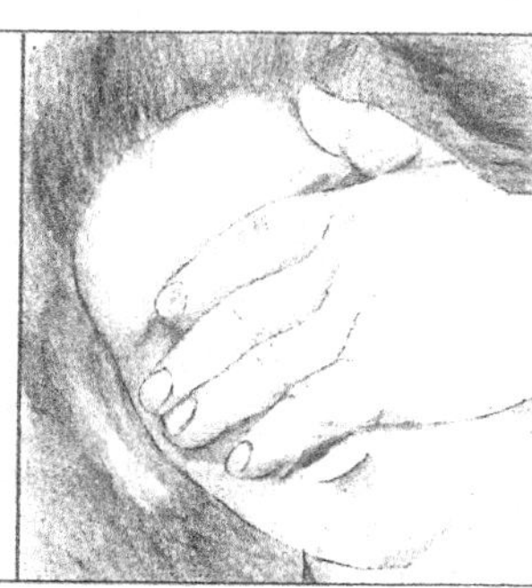

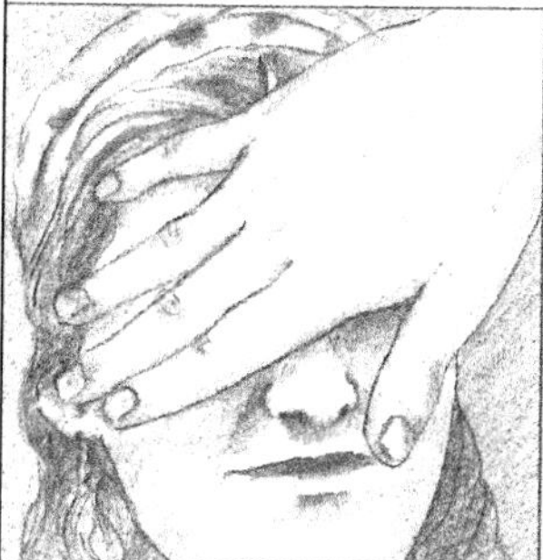

"Yes, this happened to me.
They took me,
and my husband, Feivel,
and my son, Eli.
They gassed us, and burnt us."
Jenny

"Yes, this happened to me.
I was taken with the Mother.
They gassed us,
and burnt us."
Regina

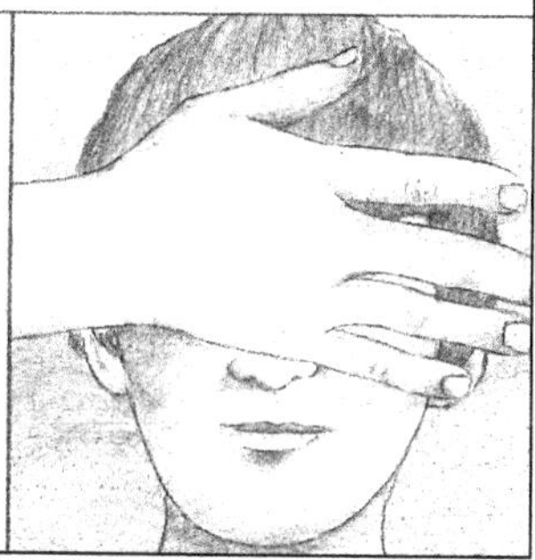

FIGURE 2.8. A tribute to the dead. Lemelman, 217. From *Mendel's Daughter* by Martin Lemelman. Copyright © 2006 by Martin Lemelman. Reprinted with the permission of the Free Press, a division of Simon & Schuster Inc. All rights reserved.

from which to mourn them, Lemelman reanimates his own named dead to give them a place in history and in memory.[50] Allowing them to "speak," creating first-person testimony, words offset in quotation marks, evokes their living just as it exposes their dying. In this way, his memoir is a memorial to the dead, the drawings artifacts of individual tribute and memory. The "I . . . they" refrain suggests their targeted otherness, isolated for extermination: "I ran and they shot me. . . . I hid but they found me."[51] Such first-person accounts make claims to individual lives starkly, unbearably lost. But these testimonies also speak to collective trauma and genocide, made emphatic by the repetitive nature of the horror, the final three testimonies concluding responsively, as if in litany: "They gassed us, and burnt us."[52] In summoning an absent voice, such tropes, as Susan Gubar puts it, "find a language for the staggering horror."[53] In giving voice to absence, rhetorical figures of speech, such as prosopopoeia—a trope that reanimates the dead through the fictional construction of voice—synecdochically creates the "voice" of individual and collective trauma. Such tropes anticipate the very erasure of life that they enact, extending the ongoing narrative of the traumatic impact and aftermath of the Holocaust. Reanimating or reawakening the voices of the dead becomes a way of filling an absence, of defying, in Nadine Fresco's terms, "the void of the unspeakable," and thus metonymically and mnemonically enacting the continuity of memory by evoking the voices of those who were, in fact, silenced.[54]

Evoking Lemelman's earlier illustration of the recitation of the Shema, these figures are drawn with their hands covering their eyes as if in prayer but also because—long since dead—they can't bear to see what awaits them, yet it's a future that already has occurred. Neither can they bear to see the past; that is, the horrors enacted in the past are only now voiced. Thus Lemelman extends his relatives into what might have been a "future," a future that was aborted by the crimes of the past. Here blurring past and present extends the trauma of the Shoah into the future. Set against the context of the Shema, Lemelman creates a midrashic dissonance, a distorted, inverted, and negated invocation, a kaddish of words spoken of the dead by the dead.[55] Thus Lemelman, as others, simultaneously creates the contiguous conditions of absence and presence as a way of identifying the ongoing nature of traumatic rupture and disruption. While the proximate immediacy of absence and presence is a characteristic conceit in Holocaust narratives, the graphic form achieves in its hybridity a traumatic reconstruction created in the intersection of text and image, verbal and visual elements that contribute to ongoing testimony. The graphic narrative combines memorial objects in the form of images with its narrative counterpart. As Laurike in 't Veld argues, "Comics can aptly visualize and incorporate the effects of trauma by using, among other strategies, the tension between the visual and the verbal, the repetition of images and their intrusions into the narrative, and the ways in which past and present can be contrasted and juxtaposed, either in sequence or on the same page."[56] To Laurike in 't Veld's description, I would add self-reflexive and self-referential narrative incursions and intrusions, the placement of flashbacks, the doubling of voices, the shifting generational lens through which we view the events, and the inclusion of the reader in the project of bearing witness.

Loss is evoked in a variety of ways in the graphic form as a metaphorical and literal trope of absence. In Lemelman's graphic memoir, the unrepresentable casts a haunting shadow over the artist's efforts to bring back to life on the page the members of his extended family unknown to him but at the center of his mother's narrative—his mother's loss. While his mother's family dissolves, their traces remain. Here as elsewhere, past, narrative present, and future coalesce; they are not distinct categories. As Thierry Groensteen suggests, when we "go back" in time to the Shoah, "the image . . . at the moment we are looking at it, places before our eyes a scene set *in the here and now*. So that, even if we are not completely in the *present time frame* of the characters and the locations depicted, at least they are offering us their *presence*."[57] In graphically re-creating absence, Lemelman self-referentially calls attention to the process of artistic creation and its appositional, deconstructive counterpart. Forced to separate in their attempt to survive even in the direct aftermath of the war—as his mother laments, "Even with the war over for us, Ukrainian bandits was still killing Jews"[58]—the family is severed, and Lemelman shows them visually deconstructing on the page. In portraying visually the family's erasure, those who were once a vital part of the daily lives of the family, Lemelman draws a portrait of his mother's family at mealtime, where, as Gusta explains, "we eat for one last time in our house" (fig. 2.9).

Here Lemelman shows the family partially erased from the picture by the hand of the artist. Once drawn, those taken from the family can be "undrawn," the erasure marks are in progress, the ghostly remains of the family still partially visible. Although the image is a still, through the partial erasures, Lemelman creates motion; the latticework of blotting out the figures creates movement achieved by the incompletion of the erased figures but also by the jagged, crisscrossing of the smudges made by erasing the pencil drawings. As Hillary Chute, in *Disaster Drawn*, proposes of the graphic narrative, "Comics is about both stillness and movement, capture and narrative motion."[59] As the image bleeds out of the panel and off the page, we thus see the family dissolving; we participate in their leave-taking, in the erosion of the family. Through the partial erasures, we both see the soon-to-depart family members and do not see them. In this way, Lemelman skillfully represents both presence and absence. As Scott McCloud explains in *Understanding Comics: The Invisible Art*, "The art of comics is as subtractive an art as it is additive," a matter of "finding the balance between too much and too little."[60] Thus Lemelman achieves through the smudged erasures the invisibility of the family. This is an image in motion, as it subtracts that

So, we eat for one last time in our house.
I take the father's wine cup, I take some of the Mother's needlework, and I take the photographs from our family.

FIGURE 2.9. A family erased. Lemelman, 186. From *Mendel's Daughter* by Martin Lemelman. Copyright © 2006 by Martin Lemelman. Reprinted with the permission of the Free Press, a division of Simon & Schuster Inc. All rights reserved.

which once was visible. This is a remarkable portrait of a family coming undone as it is drawn. The reader is, as McCloud suggests, "a silent accomplice," a partner and participant in "a silent dance of the seen and the unseen. The visible and the invisible."[61] Lemelman thus creates a visual representation of loss.

In this image, the juxtaposition of the literal and the figurative, or imagined, creates a kind of verisimilitude that shows the erosion of the family and calls attention to the graphic novelist's self-reflexive attempts to re-create on the page the diminishment and loss they experienced. The erasure marks zigzag through the black-and-white drawings of the five family members soon to be out of the picture, mirroring the erosions of life and memory. In doing so, Lemelman creates a kind of realism in the particularity of the loss. It is important that this scene depicts the intimacy of the domestic space in which is framed an intimate view of the simplest of gestures: a family gathered together in the familiarity of their home at mealtime. This simple ritual, however, *as it is being erased*, opens itself up to the larger scope of atrocity, the historical enormity of their times. The reproduced erasure marks also mirror the project of the artist who can bring those lost back into memory just as he or she can obliterate them. The image is both constructed and deconstructed simultaneously in a graphic simulation of the fractured condition and the traumatic rupture of their lives. In doing so, Lemelman blurs the past, present, and possible future. The far left corner of the image extends outside of the panel frame, the room existing in the shadowy image of their lives that existed before the rupture. The drawing on the right side of the panel extends beyond its borders as well; on both sides, the furniture extends beyond the bordering frame suggesting the larger domestic space of the home that lies beyond the kitchen as well as the unknown world that exists outside the frame. What's important here is that the borders constrict so that the family is framed, the family that even as they sit together are being smudged out, cast out of the frame.

On the right-hand facing page, immediately following the scene of erasure, is an image, at the top of the page, of Gusta, as a young woman, in response to the family's dispersal. She is drawn with a cloth clutched in her hand covering her eyes. The reader does the work in this moment: we imagine that she is crying; we visualize the tears behind the cloaked eyes. In other words, we see that which is rendered invisible by the graphic artist. As with the establishment of time and motion, in comics narratives, much of the "action" happens between the panels, in the gaps between panels. In this episode in *Mendel's Daughter*, the one page ends with the family in miderasure, and the facing page begins with an image of the narrator with eyes covered, beneath which is a text box imprinted with four simple, understated words: "And good-bye. We go."[62] At the very bottom of the page is an image, unframed, of a pair of shoes. This is a striking page, less because of what is included as what is deliberately left out, what is omitted from the sequence of images. The three simple gestures—a woman with eyes covered, a brief statement of farewell, and a pair of smudged, worn shoes—function synecdochically as markers of the permanence of loss and the wider scope of the ruptures of war. On the left-facing side of the two-page spread is a parallel image of Gusta Lemelman as the older woman who narrates the story that is drawn in the subsequent panels. In this image of his mother years after her survival, her hand is poised on her face as she cups her right cheek in thoughtful memory, but her eyes are wide open, her vision magnified by the glasses she wears. Thus Lemelman establishes different temporal moments simultaneously: the distant Holocaust past; the time before his mother's death, when she narrates the story into the tape recorder; the present moment after his mother's death in which he listens to her taped eyewitness account and draws it; and finally, the conditional future—that is, the time in which the reader opens the pages of the book.

It is in the simplicity, in the particularity, that the magnitude of their loss is perceived—in the incompletely framed and partially erased image of the fragmenting family around the kitchen table and the three images on the facing page. In the particularity of these images, in their specificity and ordinariness, I am reminded of something that Philip Roth wrote in describing the realist novel. In "The Ruthless Intimacy of Fiction," an address delivered by Roth on the occasion of his eightieth birthday celebration at the Newark Museum in

2013 and published in the recent Library of America collection of his nonfiction *Why Write?* (2017), Roth makes claims for the "passion for specificity" for the realist writer: "Without the crucial representation of what is real, there is nothing. Its concreteness, its unabashed focus on all the mundanities, a fervor for the singular and a profound aversion to generalities. . . . It is from a scrupulous fidelity to the blizzard of specific data . . . from the force of its uncompromising attentiveness, from its *physicalness*, that the realistic novel, the insatiable realistic novel with its multitude of realities, derives its ruthless intimacy. And its mission: to portray humanity in its particularity."[63] While Roth is speaking specifically of the attention to detail as central to the writer's craft in the novel, his insistence on the way in which the physicality of the form shapes the discursive, realist project is relevant to the graphic narratives that attempt to re-create the conditions of the Holocaust. After all, the blurring of historiography and memory lends itself to the kinds of imagined realities that shape the realist novel and create verisimilitude, a simulacrum of reality, especially for a writer such as Roth. It is in the small things—such as a saltshaker on the table; a spoon lifted in midsip; a pair of worn, tired shoes; a gesture of good-bye—that we come to appreciate the larger scope of the circumstances before us.

For Lemelman, these are all visual representations of loss. In another attempt at verisimilitude, Lemelman introduces into the narrative, in something of an aside, reproduced drawings of the holes in the forest in which his mother and her siblings hid. Lemelman draws the images, but here, as elsewhere, his mother's master narrative intrudes; it is she whose specifications set the instructions for the drawings: "Here Yetala and I sleep. Here Simon and Isia sleep. This is how our first grave looks. Here was a pail for the bathroom. Here we was having the stove," and so forth.[64] While Lemelman produces the images, it is his mother whose directions, belatedly uncovered, provide the stage directions. Both survivor and son coauthor the testimony. Thus the images both stand in juxtaposition to the text and imitate what is spoken. When, for example, Lemelman transcribes his mother's words of despair—"I said to myself, 'The world is going under'"—the words are reinforced by an image of his mother as a young woman crouched protectively in the woods, her head bowed into her body, under a sheath of branches and twigs.[65]

Furthermore, the self-reflexive signifiers throughout the narrative link history to the present in foregrounding the relation of witness/survivor to second-generation novelist and to the position of the reader/viewer in relation to the events revealed. We find such self-referential engagement in the evocation of the messenger, characteristic of Holocaust narratives, a figure—often dismissed but more often accurate—who brings news of the catastrophic events. In a kind of parallel structure, Lemelman's mother credits a part of the story she tells to "this man who was there [and] told me this story. . . . He saw what was happening. . . . And he told us what happened."[66] So too Lemelman, secondhand witness, reports the story told to him by his mother, who, at this juncture of her narrative, is in the role of her son: secondhand witness to the story she hears and later conveys. Such self-reflexive narration engages the reader in the process of ethical reading and witnessing. The unknown and unseen "messenger" in his mother's story is a reflection of Lemelman's position as mediator to the story passed along to the distanced reader/viewer of the narrative handed down to us. Thus the repeated images of eyes throughout the narrative suggest what one has witnessed and what one can only see in the imagination. Seeing is thus a metonymy for the perspective through which one visualizes the past. Throughout the graphic narrative, the readers' distanced perspective is contrasted to the firsthand witnessing of the characters. In one close-up of Gusta's sister Yetala's eyes at the center of the panel in the following image, the figure is looking askance, turned inward to the corner of the previous page at something that the reader, whose own eyes are riveted to the image on the page, has just seen on the facing page: an image of her brother falling to the ground.[67] What do we allow ourselves to see? How far into the past does the perspectival reach extend? What are the limits of the imagination? These Holocaust narratives create an ethic of reading that calls attention to what it means to participate in the ongoing burden of testimonial memory, a matter of opening one's eyes to history and to the forms of denial those visions can evoke in us.

Graphic narratives, in representing the Shoah, exhibit a preoccupation with extending the shape of memory and with authentic modes of telling. Lemelman establishes the lens through which he, as graphic artist and narrator, filters the events he describes: the drawings and images are primarily his (with the exception of some reproductions of actual documents and photographs), but the words belong to those who survived as well as those who perished. Although it is Lemelman's mother who would seem to have the last word, her videotaped recording ending with the promise of "a new life," the text of the memoir does not end with such fortunate finality.[68] The final voices are those of the dead, evidence that "this happened," in memorialization narrated by, as Primo Levi once said, the "true witnesses . . . those who saw the Gorgon, have not returned to tell about it or have returned mute, but they are . . . the submerged, the complete witnesses."[69] The unheard victims of genocide, the "real" victims, are those no longer among us to tell their stories. Thus because, as Eli Wiesel has said, "no one may speak for the dead,"[70] Lemelman will caption their own words. The second-generation graphic artist will give the dead the final words: "This happened to me."[71] The final image, significantly, cut off from the lament of the victims, is the passage from the Passover Haggadah, an invocation to "look upon" oneself as part of a community, a community of those who suffered persecution but emerged under the weight of that history: both celebration and lamentation. Thus his graphic memoir calls upon the authenticating histories of Jewish survival.

On the one hand, the memoir lacks a conventional framing device: it begins with the dual authorship and the inspiration for Lemelman's encounter with his mother's past. While Lemelman is quick to introduce himself as the child of a survivor and the recipient of and participant in her story as she narrates it through the medium of the tape recording, he, after the opening pages, draws himself out of the narrative that follows. Early on, Lemelman, as I've already indicated, makes claims for the authenticity of the narrative—"It's all true"—and attributes dual authorship to the memoir.[72] As discussed, one of the early panels shows his hand holding the tape recording of his mother's testimony, visual "proof" of the authenticity of the story but also of the absence of his imposition, intervention, and interference in the plotline of the narrative. In the "Author Interview" that follows the memoir, Lemelman maintains that he views himself "more as the editor than the writer of *Mendel's Daughter*. What was challenging for me was creating a clear and sequential story while retaining the unique flavor of my mother's speech patterns. I would have loved to have illustrated her story solely using the transcript of my interviews with her. . . . I wanted [readers] to understand that what happened in *Mendel's Daughter* happened to real people."[73] Ironically and significantly, however, the images that correlate, expand, and thus interpret the text are their own form of mediated intercession. Lemelman, in doing so, attempts to bridge the gap between proximity and distance by creating an immediacy to the jointly related story and by inserting himself into the narrative, even if only as second-generation recipient and illustrator.

Katin's memoir, *We Are On Own*, narrated in part through the limited perspective of a child survivor, attempts to navigate the space between distance and proximity by twining the child's largely unconscious and fragmented memories with her mother's more reliable and fixed memories of their year in hiding. As a way of acknowledging her distance from the events in which she unknowingly participated and in respecting her mother's wishes "not to use our real names in the book . . . for fear . . . someone will be offended and take revenge," Katin fictionalizes the names of her characters.[74] Creating her own younger persona is a means of establishing both knowing and not knowing but also of establishing her place as both insider and outsider to the experience she relates. The graphic memoirist thus is both inside and outside the text, a witness and spectator to her own remote past. Katin explains in an interview, "As I was very young, my real memories of that year are very scant. I am grateful for that. What I most remember is connected to food . . . and the lack thereof; the little dog that I befriended and then had to leave behind when my mother and I were on the run . . . and the bombing that I witnessed. . . . I only reconstructed the story my mother told me. . . .

However, the stories my mother told me and the knowledge of all that happened were a constant unwanted, uninvited presence in my life."[75] Thus Katin's double, her imagined self in the narrative, becomes the visualized figment and extension of memories that she imaginatively recalls. Thus both child survivor and second-generation accounts attempt to establish the grounds for memory and also their uneasy relation to the memories they illustrate. In doing so, both graphic artists draw themselves into the stories they narrate as an ironic measure of their efforts to control and arrange such memories. Both writers are on the edges of the stories they tell: Katin "witnesses" and recounts her own memories from a limiting distance; Lemelman introduces himself into the narrative only at the opening of the memoir and then departs after handing the story over to his mother, the authentic witness. Lemelman's "departure" from the narrative then suggests his tangential and fragmentary relation to the events he can only draw into life.

Lemelman returns to many of these moments in what is something of a sequel or follow-up to his first graphic narrative, *Mendel's Daughter*. In *Two Cents Plain: My Brooklyn Boyhood*, Lemelman draws a coming-of-age narrative that depicts his early years in the family store in Brooklyn. *Two Cents Plain* is the story of a Jewish boy growing up in Brooklyn in the 1950s and 1960s, but it is also the immigrant's story, the story of his parents, who, after the war, met in the Neu Freimann displaced persons (DP) camp located in the American occupied zone in Munich. Lemelman's story, in which he is a central player, reflects the imagined possibilities for those coming to America from a ruptured Europe, those Jewish refugees who, as both his parents put it, were "finished with Poland," a landscape responsible for the death of their families and communities and that would always remain inhospitable to Jews.[76] His parents set sail for America and eventually relocated in Brownsville, where they reinvented their lives. His parents' lives and his own are set against a portrait of the richness and vitality of his early years but also the decline of Brooklyn's neighborhoods and, ultimately, their own security there.

Generically, *Two Cents Plain*, unlike *Mendel's Daughter*, is Lemelman's story, the story of his education on the streets, at home, in the candy store, and in school. But after a brief prologue, the narrative returns to his mother's story, which, in condensed form, is the story she has narrated in the longer, extended form in *Mendel's Daughter*. Lemelman draws upon a similar structure and page layout in the second volume, fusing drawings, reproductions of documents, photographs, and text, including some of the same images and dialogue from his earlier graphic memoir. And as we revisit some of the traumatic episodes in his mother's past, we see once again the collage of photographs of her family taken before the war, the scantest details of their lives and deaths. Once again, Gusta narrates the past that precedes her son's birth. It is thus, in the survivor's own words, "my mother's voice," that Lemelman draws the story of her Holocaust history: the death of her family, hiding with her surviving siblings in a hole dug in the ground, her discovery and survival, and her return to their former home in the town of Germakivka, "in a hope," she reveals, "to settle again in my father's house." There, Gusta is confronted by neighbors who appropriated the family home and belongings after their forced departure and who, upon her return, barred her entry: "You are supposed to be dead.... You don't belong here no more." Made acutely aware that in Poland "they was murdering Jews—even after the war," Gusta leaves her home forever.[77] Her story of devastation, survival, and further disillusionment is followed by that of Lemelman's father, who served as a sergeant in the Soviet Army and who, after the war, returned to Poland to see what had become of his family. Recognizing the destruction of the Jewish community in the aftermath of war—"All the Jews... erased"—he too abandons the country that betrayed him.[78] Lemelman begins his boyhood memoir with his parents' voices, with their stories of what is now the remote past, because, as he acknowledges, to "know where I come from... to understand my boyhood in Brooklyn... I would have to first travel back to a dark time—a time before I was born... to wander the muddy roads... inhabited by ghosts."[79] Lemelman will leave them for his own story; he will allow their Holocaust voices to recede, but not their memory. For it is those "ghosts" whose lives become a measure of his own.

3

"Replacing Absence with Memory"

Bernice Eisenstein's Graphic Memoir *I Was a Child of Holocaust Survivors*

His past followed him like a shadow.
—Michel Kichka, *Second Generation: The Things I Didn't Tell My Father*

I felt his voice reach into me.
—David Bezmozgis, "An Animal to the Memory"

I inherited a suffering to which I had not been subjected.
—Alain Finkielkraut, *The Imaginary Jew*

"I have inherited the unbearable lightness of being a child of Holocaust survivors. Cursed and blessed."[1] So concludes Canadian graphic novelist Bernice Eisenstein as she draws to a close the 2006 graphic narrative *I Was a Child of Holocaust Survivors*. This semiautobiographical/biographical narrative is the story of Eisenstein's parents, Polish-born Barek (Beryl, Ben) and Regina

Eisenstein, survivors of Auschwitz and Birkenau, and the defining influence of their individual histories on the making of the author's own identity, an inheritance and lineage both "cursed and blessed." The graphic narrative examines the intersection of her parents' collective past with her own early life lived in the shadow of those memories. Eisenstein's attempts to come to terms with her parents' Holocaust history highlight the ways in which their experiences came to shape her own developing identity in the uniquely situated context of the children of survivors, those for whom, as second-generation writer Eva Hoffman puts it, such essentializing, "formative events of the twentieth century have crucially informed our biographies and psyches, threatening sometimes to overshadow and overwhelm our own lives."[2] Eisenstein's graphic narrative reveals her attempts to structure and make coherent the narrative of her parents' past, that unknown, "dark topography of the Shoah."[3] As Eisenstein reveals, she began her journey into the past without a sufficient road map, with the barest of directions: "I had no chronology, no laid-out sequence of events, in order for me to hold a newly found fragment and place it where it belonged."[4] At the conclusion of this process of discovery, Eisenstein admits, "I will never be able to know the truth of what my parents had experienced. It is beyond my reach, and perhaps even theirs, to know the full extent of their loss."[5] Despite her recognition of the limitations of such knowledge and the inadequacy of her ability to express the magnitude of such loss, Eisenstein, by the narrative's close, has created a mosaic of memory, a testimony to survival. In her graphic memoir, the enjoining of past and present speaks to both the "weight" and illumination of the past, its "unbearable lightness," thus "cursed and blessed" by an inheritance just beyond her reach. Her admission, as the narrative draws to an end, of the unreachability of the "full extent" of knowledge available to her and also the limitations of representation is less an acknowledgment of defeat than it is an expression of the acceptance of her own inability to "somehow make up for such sorrow."[6] In drawing and narrating her parents' stories as something of a necessary appendage to her own, Eisenstein inserts a place for herself in the interlocking continuity of generations bound by remembrance and an obligation to the past.

Memory is the central trope in Eisenstein's second-generation graphic narrative. As the graphic artist acknowledges in an interview about the book's origins, "My book is about a process of memory into not only my past, but the past of my parents and their friends.... Memory—going to another terrain—was the propelling influence, and from that, feelings of compassion and loss helped shape the drawings."[7] In Eisenstein's graphic narrative, memory stands as witness to the past but also as custodian of the future. The book's final pages include a reproduction of the passage from Deuteronomy inscribed in the Hall of Remembrance in the Holocaust Museum in Washington, DC: "Only guard yourself and guard your soul carefully, lest you forget the things your eyes saw, and lest these things depart your heart all the days of your life, and you shall make them known to your children, and to your children's children" (Deuteronomy 4:9). The words are centered against a blank page and suspended above a row of muted black-and-white etchings of the faces of survivors. Their ghostly presence at the very bottom of the page is a measure of the obligation of future generations to commit themselves to memory. The receding faces, diminished in size and faintly drawn in soft, pale lines, stand as a cautionary warning of the erasure of memory. Located at the bottom margin of the page, these faces are dwarfed, shadowed by the enormity of their history but also by the vicissitudes, distractions, and truancies of memory. In transmitting and extending the memories of the past—in "replacing absence with memory"—Eisenstein creates a collision of histories, voices, and stories catalyzing at the point of origin of the Shoah.[8]

Characteristic of second-generation Holocaust writing and especially the genre of the graphic narrative, Eisenstein has created a hybrid work that blurs autobiography, memoir, biography, and testimony. Loosely structured, the book moves back and forth in time between the past and the present, intersecting Eisenstein's and her parents' lives. Rather than a sequential, chronological narrative progression, the book unfolds in a latticework of narrative perspectives and portraits as one story gives way to another to accommodate different forms of testimony. As Hillary Chute argues, "The print medium of comics . . . offers opportunities to place pressure on traditional notions of chronology, linearity, and causality," thus challenging "the idea that 'history' can ever be a closed discourse, or a simply progressive one."[9] Navigating among the overlapping interstices of time, space, and action, such graphic narratives enact a traumatic imprint by imposing the past on the present. These overlapping structures and literary conceits reflect the complexity of the experience of the transmission of memory. Because, as Miriam Harris suggests, "traditional chronologies, in their linear sequencing of time, possess a rational logic that seems unsuited for the expression of incomprehensible horror," Eisenstein has created instead "a poetic stream of consciousness . . . that endeavors to grab hold of childhood memories and penetrate their mysteries."[10] At the same time, the erratic progression of the narrative, as it moves back and forth in time and place, suggests the graphic artist's inability to enter her parents' history, to bridge the experiential and affective gap in her understanding of her parents' past. Thus as Jean-Philippe Marcoux suggests, "The temporal and spatial dislocations that characterize the graphic novel are . . . indicative of the difficulties of the second generation to negotiate the burden of memories they do not share."[11] Their graphic representation and extension of memory is, after all, not their own but rather a secondhand, mediated memory. The indirect access of the past for the second generation is, by necessity, fragmented, stories pieced together through a variety of competing sources to represent disjunctive, cross-temporal, and spatial affect.

The past, however camouflaged, guarded, and concealed, is also undefended, contingently approachable. Through the graphic medium, the past is materialized in the narrative landscape, the past, as one of Ehud Havazelet's characters admits, "no longer something to be recalled from a distance—it was there in front of him, to walk into if he dared."[12] It is easy, however, as Eisenstein says, to get "lost in memory. It is not a place that has been mapped, fixed by coordinates of longitude and latitude, whereby I can retrace a step and come to the same place again. Each time is different."[13] Thus Eisenstein's graphic novel shifts time as well as location in its surrender to the differing shapes of testimonial articulation—both text and image. As Hoffman explains, as the daughter of survivors, "I was the designated carrier for the cargo of awesome knowledge transferred to me by my parents, and its burden had to be transported carefully. . . . Moreover, there was a kind of prohibition on the very quality of coherence. To make a sequential narrative of what happened would have been to make indecently rational what had been obscenely irrational. It would have been to normalize through familiar form an utterly aberrant content."[14] Thus in an attempt to be ever conscious of and faithful to the historical realities and the tangled threads of memories unspooling, second-generation narratives, as we see in works by Art Spiegelman, Martin Lemelman, Bernice Eisenstein, and others, create the conditions of rupture and dislocation through narrative interruptions, disruptions, sideways diversions, and spatial and temporal shifts. Such art forms, as Jill Bennett suggests, "endeavor to find a communicable language of sensation and affect with which to register something of the experience of traumatic memory."[15] Holocaust graphic writers/illustrators thus combine text and image to create an art form that performs "a kind of visual language of trauma and of the experiences of conflict and loss."[16] The language of trauma, thus achieved through the temporal disjunctions, shifting modes of discourse, and the exchange of narrating perspectives characteristic of the genre, contribute to the living shape, the experience, of memory and testimony. The past, thus materialized, shaped through the intersections of text and image in Eisenstein's work, becomes the material stuff of art, which, as viewed through the stories of her parents' past, "sculpted the meaning of loss and love" for the artist.[17]

Accompanied by the author's voice-over at various stages of her maturity and the images that form part of the scaffolding on which these discursive moments are framed, Eisenstein's graphic memoir loosely takes the following shape: (1) Ben Eisenstein's story as told by his daughter, the author, who draws herself into the narrative; (2) a found fragment of the father's family's past as revealed in a memoir indirectly handed down to the author, a memoir written by a landsman from her father's hometown of Miechow, providing information about the death of Ben Eisenstein's sister Binche, who was murdered by the Nazis, an account, as the author says, "leaving me without distance";[18]

(3) Regina Eisenstein's transcribed story, videotaped in 1995 as part of the Shoah Foundation's Archives of the Holocaust Project, that she "tells herself"; (4) an account of the author's maternal grandparents, who survived the Shoah; (5) the story of Eisenstein's aunt and uncle (her mother's sister and father's brother), both survivors who married each other; (6) a depiction of the "group" of survivors, friends of her parents, who form their own circle, bound to one another; and (7) concluding with the promise of generational continuity and the birth of the author's son, named in memory of her deceased father. In describing the book's structure, Eisenstein explains that, rather than proceeding "in a chronological, a linear form, with time movement forward, I... found the freedom to move back and forth through time.... This allowed me to sometimes speak through my own voice . . . and then also integrate and write about someone else."[19] The elastic, expanding movement among narratives is held together by interludes, commentary, and digressions that open up the life of the author as she gives voice to those whose stories formed and continue to shape the contours of her own unfolding narrative, her sense of self and place in that history. As Eisenstein's autobiographical narrator establishes early on, "Even though the past was something my parents tried to keep at a distance from their children, out of harm's reach, it inevitably shadowed the landscape in which we would grow."[20] Stories open up into other stories as the past erupts into the present.

While *I Was a Child of Holocaust Survivors* is purportedly the story of Eisenstein's parents' lives as well as the lives of the other survivors within the orbit of her family, this is also a coming-of-age story for the author, who moves in the course of the narrative from the anxious, self-conscious, and uncertain child of survivors, infantilized by the enormity of her parents' history, to a mature, rooted guardian of the past, as if the very process of discovery is aging. As the narrative—or rather the compilation of narratives—progresses, we see her shedding the illusorily protective skin of innocence and ignorance that has prevented her from bridging the gap between her parents' experience and her own limited and limiting knowledge of the events that shaped their characters and, ultimately, her own. As she admits, "I have never found for myself the right distance from the time when their lives had been so damaged."[21] In describing her parents, survivors of the Holocaust, refugees and immigrants arriving in a new country and unprepared for the radical upheaval of their lives, Eisenstein anticipates the transformation that she will experience in her own life as innocence is increasingly undercut by dawning awareness of her "surroundings." In a section titled "Growing New Skin," she describes the condition of transition for the émigré: "Watch the passing of a life and the moment strips the skin of the observer. . . . Nothing is familiar. How is one able to regain connection, belonging, when all that was as innocent as being alive has been taken away.... In time, memory is soothed, if never fully healed.

A second skin covers over and they become familiar to themselves once more."[22] In effect, in describing what she imagines to have been the experience of her parents, newly arrived émigrés to Canada, Eisenstein metaphorically maps the course of her own "exilic" experience as she departs the "country" of her childhood and enters the unknown terrain of the Holocaust, "the winding road of their sketched-in pasts."[23] There is a kind of loss that accompanies gain in the acquisition of such knowledge. She can no longer see the events from the same vantage point of self-protecting distance.

The problem initially for Eisenstein is not so much a lack of knowledge of the Holocaust per se, since, by her own admission, she describes herself, early on, as being obsessed with the subject of the Holocaust. She is powerfully drawn to its detailed historiography and images: "The way it makes me want to dive into its endless depths, sending me out of my home alone to the cinema, to the library, where I can see every movie and read every book that deals with the Holocaust."[24] Like others of the post-Holocaust generation at her time in history, Eisenstein has grown up with access to an increasing plethora of information: archival materials, documents, literature, films, monuments, museums—all artifacts of memory preserved, recorded, and memorialized. Ironically, as Hoffman argues, "even as our fascination intensifies, we inevitably contemplate the Shoah from an ever-growing distance—temporal, geographical, cultural—with all the risks of simplification implicit in such remoteness."[25] Thus what Eisenstein wants, like others of the second and third generations, is not the "academic," distanced abstractions—the remoteness of numbers, maps, images, documents, and recordings of victims and survivors unknown to her. Rather, she wants that which she has been unable to locate, the specifics of her own family, the experiential, affective moments of their lives and their individualized loss and grief—in other words, the lived experience of memory and trauma. In an interview, Eisenstein comments on the design of her graphic narrative: "The book is not an autobiography of my life, but more to the point, it is a memoir of a sensibility, a relationship to the Holocaust that integrally formed that sensibility. And that means it is not one thing, not based on facts and numbers, but on individual lives and my understanding and feelings for them."[26] And it is with regret and longing that she fears such knowledge has only come to her belatedly, as she says of her father, "Dead not for longer than a decade. . . . He is no longer here for me to discover his past, to ask him about the war, about Auschwitz, or what life was like growing up in Poland. About his family, his parents, my grandparents. Though from early on, I knew that the past was something not to be ventured into."[27] It is as if those members of her extended family whom she never knew were not only lost once but lost again, eclipsed from the narrative of her family's severed lineage. Thus as Eisenstein writes, "Death leaves a hole that grows covered with longing," the longing for recovery.[28]

This anxiety about absence, both physical and narrative, is articulated in Daniel Mendelsohn's third-generation memoir *The Lost: A Search for Six of Six Million* as a response to his fears that his unknown relatives "vanished not only from the world but—even more terrible to me—from my grandfather's stories."[29] If the transmission of stories perpetuates the memory of those who have perished, then the lack of a narrative is a definitive signpost of closure. In an attempt to mitigate or compensate for the absence of a personalized narrative, Eisenstein will try to visualize her father in the context of the Holocaust. She is drawn to the photographed images of concentration camp inmates in order, finally, to locate her father within the frame of that moment: "I searched to find his face among those documented photographs of survivors of Auschwitz. . . . I thought that if I could see him staring out through barbed wire, I would then know how to remember him, know what he was made to become, and then possibly know what he might have been. All my life, I have looked for more in order to fill in the parts of my father that had gone missing."[30] Such a sought connection functions as an aide-mémoire, a mnemonic aperture to understand her parents' history and thus her own, to give a "face" to that history and thus draw herself into this picture, even if it means seeing her father in extreme suffering, in death.

Speaking to this same impulse to visualize her unknown extended family against the background of actual footage of Holocaust victims, Arlene Stein, in *Reluctant Witnesses: Survivors, Their Children, and the Rise of Holocaust Consciousness*, explains, "Because I don't have any scrapbooks of family pictures, every face could be a face of a relative. Even though the number of my mother's family is finite, when I see pictures of hundreds, they all become related to me in a sense because any one of them could be a true family member."[31] The conditional "could" here reveals the way in which the child of survivors imagines her mother's family in the wider collective scope of suffering, but it is also suggestive of the failed realism in the endeavor. As a second-generation "coaxer of stories," as Stein characterizes the relationship of the descendants of Holocaust survivors to their relatives, the association and identification of her own family members *in the face* of those victims captured in the still of the photograph—that is, caught in the historical moment—stem, in part, from the projection of her own, unarticulated desire to have "been there," to have participated *in* that defining history. In superimposing the unknown faces of her relatives onto the equally anonymous faces in the documented photographs of victims, Stein, by extension, places herself in the image. As Susan Sontag writes in *Regarding the Pain of Others*, "Photographs objectify: they turn an event or a person into something that can be possessed . . . a species of alchemy, for all that they are prized as a transparent account of reality."[32] Belgian-born Israeli cartoonist Michel Kichka, in the graphic narrative *Second Generation: The Things I Didn't Tell My Father*, describes his fixation on the few remaining photographs of his father's family, all of whom perished in the war. He is particularly drawn to the last of the three photographs, the "one of the whole family taken in Brussels right before the war."[33] As Kichka's autobiographical narrator admits, "I used to look at it a lot as a kid, in secret, crying my eyes out."[34] There is something seductive yet clandestine and transgressive in the child's fascination with the photograph, as if he possesses something that he should not see, as if he fetishizes the object of his desire. The child's desire to enter the narrative of the photograph is a kind of wish fulfillment or wishful thinking in which he imagines himself into another history.

There is something irresistible in photographs of suffering, and one's empathetic identification forces the gaze inward. The fantasized object becomes the focus of traumatic identification and an unconscious form of exaggerated, self-aggrandizing narcissism, the failure to distinguish oneself from others or, in this case, the desire to see oneself in the image of the other. The projected desire to have participated in the suffering of others is a common trope among the children of survivors. Spiegelman's second-generation autobiographical narrator in volume 2 of *Maus*, for example, at a moment of not unironic critical self-exposure, admits, "I somehow wish I had been in Auschwitz with my parents so I could really know what they lived through! I guess it's some kind of guilt about having had an easier life than they did."[35] Significantly, Spiegelman imagines himself not alone in Auschwitz but rather *with* his parents, to have shared, alongside them, their suffering. The response to trauma is to keep the family together, to put the family back together (and, of course, the desire to return to the unbroken family is even more complicated for Spiegelman given his mother's suicide). In part, Spiegelman's anxiety locates itself in a form of survivor guilt, but this projection is complicated for the second generation, who were not, in actuality, survivors. At a very telling moment in Kichka's *Second Generation*, the cartoonist draws a reproduction of the iconic image of the young boy in the Warsaw Ghetto, arms raised in fear and submission. Here Kichka projects his own image onto that of the frightened child, saying, "I thought I looked like that little boy." His desire to insert himself into the image, to see himself in the image, suggests the kind of split identity that results from being the child of survivors, of identifying with the *other*, an identity and a history with which the child of survivors cannot compete. His identification with the child in the ghetto, a German soldier pointing a weapon at him, a look of terrible fear and sorrow on his face, suggests his desire to have participated in the events that he narrates as a means of projecting himself into the past. However, such a desire is constantly undermined, thwarted by reality: the second generation did not live through the events that they now guardedly resurrect, and thus, as Sidra DeKoven Ezrahi suggests, "the urgency of representation, then, unfolds in continual tension between desire and its limits."[36]

Both second- and third-generation narratives are preoccupied with visualizing memory *in the image*. Kichka, not unlike Eisenstein, combs over the recorded photographs of Auschwitz in search of his father among the faces of the victims. As he explains, "It's like I need to see him to believe it."[37] There is enormous power in the image. In providing a historical record, the image, as Georges Didi-Huberman suggests, both addresses and refutes the unimaginable.[38] It creates an opening for ethical witnessing through the remote vantage point of a distanced spectator, one who observes, if not the events themselves, then the afterimage of atrocity. The image thus testifies to both presence and absence. For, while the image plants one in place and time, it also reflects that which is no longer present, an image ever receding as it is rendered intelligible. The desire to see the image—that is, to find the familiar face in the image of historical reality—is ambivalently portrayed by the dread of what one finds in the image. As Kichka confesses, in scrutinizing photographs of concentration camp inmates for the visage of his father, "I was afraid I wouldn't recognize him. I was afraid I would."[39] After all, his father's presence among the victims ominously portends his absence. Thus Kichka will draw an image of himself as a young child looking down from the scrim of dreams to the image of his father's skeletal body splayed against the background of Auschwitz, directly underneath the smokestack billowing the ashen faces of the dead (fig. 3.1).

Above the caption that reads, "Ghosts haunted my nights. I had nightmares in which I saw my dead father," Kichka projects his worst fears realized on the image. As Marianne Hirsch explains, "Children of those directly affected by collective trauma inherit a horrific, unknown, and unknowable past that their parents were not meant to survive. Second-generation fiction, art, memoir, and testimony are shaped by the attempt to represent the long-term effects of living in close proximity to the pain, depression, and dissociation of persons who have witnessed and survived massive historical trauma. . . . Loss of family, home, of a sense of belonging and safety in the world 'bleed' from one generation to the next."[40] I would suggest that Holocaust graphic narratives, in the complex hybridity of the genre—fiction, art, memoir, and testimony—construct a language that captures both personal and collective trauma in the immediacy and urgency of its performance.

There are ultimately, however—as Eisenstein, from her position of secondary witnessing, acknowledges—limitations to the imagination, limitations that prevent her from the kind of complete, unhampered entrance to the past that she desires. The conditions of her time and place in history, however fortuitous, will forever keep her, metaphorically, on the other side of the barbed wire. There are some things that are finally off limits, as we see visualized in the following concentration camp image (fig. 3.2).

Against a blank, white page, Eisenstein draws an image, unmediated by text, of the long-since deserted grounds of Auschwitz and the barracks

FIGURE 3.1. "Ghosts haunted my nights." Michel Kichka, *Second Generation: The Things I Didn't Tell My Father* (France: Dargaud, 2012), 8.

where her mother was imprisoned. This is an image that captures the quality and texture of distance that Eisenstein and other post-Holocaust writers imaginatively attempt to navigate. Contained within the larger frame of the page is situated another frame of swirls of gray and white, an impressionistic representation of what might be interpreted as whirls of smoke or metonymic contortions of figures dissolving into smoke and ash. Set against that blurred hazy backdrop is another frame within which Eisenstein has drawn

FIGURE 3.2. On the outside of experience. Bernice Eisenstein, *I Was a Child of Holocaust Survivors* (New York: Riverhead Books, 2006), 115.

a seemingly simple, minimalist, black-and-white etching of barracks. From a distance, the buildings appear to be deserted, remote, melancholic artifacts of the past, emptied of those who once inhabited them. Our gaze, however, is drawn to the rectangular windows and doorways that are dotted against the brick background of the buildings through which Eisenstein has sketched indistinct figures, faces of those once interred within.

This is a disturbing scene, set against a silence that anticipates absence. The indistinctness of the faces, drawn huddled together with crude, child-like features, is all the more unsettling because of the implied and understated expression of loss and the diminishment of life conveyed. Standing before the buildings are stark, skeletal trees, stripped of foliage, whose branches reach upward, extending beyond the margins of the frame into the cloudy, ashen sky above—metaphoric arms, emaciated fingers extended, imploring, beseeching. Finally, moving figuratively outward (in something of a simulacrum of three-dimensionality), Eisenstein has drawn an image of barbed wire that extends beyond the frame within the frame, barbed wire that stretches across the entire image. The barbed wire is extended horizontally as the barren branches of the trees extend vertically; the one constrains, restrains, while the other stretches upward in supplication. The barbed wire prevents egress, but it prevents entrance, as well. While the distorted figures—in a sense defigured—claustrophobically are contained inside the barracks that are inside the barbed wire, we as viewers are outside the barbed boundary that encloses them. Such an image reflects not only the receding range of distance from which (through which) we view the Holocaust—temporally, spatially, experientially, affectively—but also the layers of trespass through which subsequent generations must penetrate to enter that imaginative space. It is through the understated simplicity of the drawing that Eisenstein paradoxically expresses the complexity of the endeavor to reanimate history and to project the past into the present.

Eisenstein's recognition that she will always remain necessarily and profoundly on the outside looking in is part of the process of maturation that takes place over the course of the graphic narrative. The knowledge she ultimately gains enables her to reframe her own position within her parents' history, all the while negotiating the terms of that distance. The initial fraught conditions of the author's attempts to unearth and piece together her parents' stories and to find her place in the ongoing narrative of the past are ultimately resolved by the book's conclusion. By the memoir's close, Eisenstein achieves that which has been her quest all along: not only, as she says, "to step into the presence of absence"[41] but also, to borrow a phrase from Berel Lang, to create a "telling place in its shadow."[42] But the initial, uneasy conditions of the author's attempts to construct a narrative out of the past and to find her voice in that "shadow" set the stage for the diminishment she fears under the weight of that history.

The cover of the book immediately introduces and exposes the author's uneasy sense that her own life has been eclipsed by her parents' past and establishes the tension between innocence and knowledge that directs the unfolding of the narrative that follows (fig. 3.3). The cover illustration depicts Eisenstein as a young girl dressed in childhood attire and holding a doll in her arms. Her expression, however, belies her childlike stance. Her eyes tell a different story from that of the youthful naïveté suggested by her clothes and carriage. In commenting on her graphic style, Eisenstein explains, "I'd like my drawings and paintings to have . . . both a lightness and a weight."[43] This juxtaposition between "lightness and weight," innocence and awareness, youth and maturity, and naïveté and experience suggests that the process of uncovering

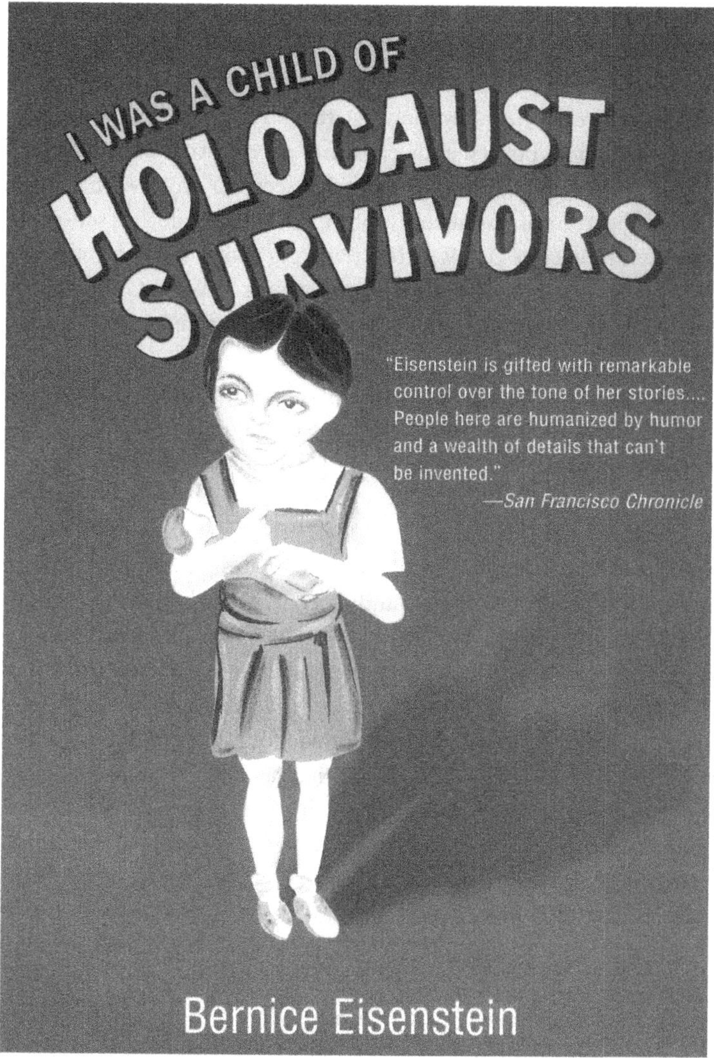

FIGURE 3.3. In the shadows of the Holocaust. Bernice Eisenstein, *I Was a Child of Holocaust Survivors* (New York: Riverhead Books, 2006), cover image.

such knowledge is both an aging and an infantilizing experience. Characteristic of Eisenstein's artistic style throughout the memoir, in this cover image, the focus is on the figure's eyes. Her head is disproportionately larger and more pronounced than the rest of her body. We are drawn immediately to her eyes. Instead of looking directly outward, her gaze is turned to the side as if she sees something beyond the reach of the book's cover. She is not looking at the reader; her focus is elsewhere, and her eyes convey a kind of knowledge incompatible with or unsuited to the childlike qualities of her dress and comportment, emphasizing the juxtaposition of innocence and the weight of inherited knowledge. Her gaze is disconcertingly suspicious, knowing, the eyes reflecting in their weighted gaze, as Harris suggests, that her "childhood innocence had already been profoundly affected by awareness of her parents' suffering," affected and overshadowed by her parents' traumatic past.[44] While the foregrounded figure on the cover would seem to promise that this book will be autobiographical, Eisenstein's for the most part colorless self-portrait is contrasted with the large yellow letters towering above her: "Holocaust Survivors." The first part of the title, the prefatory words "I Was a Child of," appears in a reduced, far less formidable font, its subsidiary white letters subordinated to the main focus of the title.

Against a deep-red background, Eisenstein's self-portrait, drawn in shades of black and white and gray, as Harris suggests, "does not cast its own shadow against the vivid red background, but rather is shadowed by the silhouettes of her parents . . . a strikingly vivid metaphor" for the way in which Eisenstein has believed her identity to have been eclipsed by that of her parents.[45] Indeed, instead of casting her own shadow, the young Eisenstein projects the shadowy outlines of her parents, standing together, while she, foregrounded on the cover, stands alone. While this cover image, as Harris rightly proposes, "testifies to the haunting influences of the past, and to the extent to which her parents' trauma consumes her own identity," it also reflects her isolation from her parents, separated by the traumatic impact of her parents' past, a distance that is the source of her discomfort and insecurity.[46] The book's cover thus promises the complexity the narrative produces. It is not, therefore, just that Eisenstein, as the child of survivors, lives under the shadow of the Holocaust, a recurring trope in second-generation writing. Rather, as we see in this image, the shadows extend behind her. Significantly, she is the one who casts their shadows, which suggests the indelible ways in which her parents' trauma has been grafted upon and subsumed by the author. As Samantha Baskind proposes, "The book's cover vividly demonstrates the extent to which her parents' ordeal informs her identity. Against a blood-red background, a black-and-white rendering of Eisenstein as a child does not cast a shadow; instead, the dark figures of Eisenstein's parents metaphorically provide the shadows behind her tiny body."[47] Curiously, the illustrated figure of the second-generation child, as we are introduced to her on the book's cover, is not dwarfed by the ghostly shadows of the past, but rather, it is she who looms over her parents' silhouettes. As Eisenstein's autobiographical narrator says, in the absence of tangible memory, "I have had to create their shadows for myself."[48] She will imagine them onto the page. It is she who is at the center of this narrative; she will compete for her own place, both in the spatial "time" of the narrative and in the projected future. Locating her place in the ongoing narrative of the past has been a central issue for Eisenstein, as she admits, "I have never discovered the Holocaust's vanishing point, have never been quite sure where to stand on its horizon."[49] Thus she will position herself—albeit a little off center—at the focal point of the book's cover, laying claim to her "standing" on the "horizon," both distanced by and from the events that have shaped her life.

This sense that the Holocaust has left a defining, ineradicable imprint on the children of survivors is a recurring pattern in the literature of the second generation, one that crosses genres. Second-generation writer Thane Rosenbaum, for example, has, at the center of his novels and short stories, children of survivors for whom the legacy of the Holocaust, as one character puts it, "was passed on through the genes. . . . My DNA . . . forever coded with the filmy stuff of damaged offspring."[50] As Hoffman says of her own experience growing up as the child of Holocaust survivors, "I absorbed my parents' unhappiness through channels that seemed nearly physical."[51] The materiality of their affective inheritance is a continuing trope in second-generation narratives. Their parents' trauma shapes their vision of the world they apprehensively and tentatively inhabit, as another of Rosenbaum's anxiously figured characters reveals, "Their own terrible visions from a haunted past became his."[52] The Holocaust is, for the second generation, their own origin myth, one that links them to others of their generation in defining ways, an "'imagined community' . . . based not so much on geography or circumstance as on sets of meanings, symbols, and even literary fictions that it has in common."[53] For the second generation, the Holocaust becomes, achingly, the moment of conception, that from which all things emerge. As second-generation writer Melvin Bukiet acknowledges, for the children of survivors, "In the beginning was Auschwitz,"[54] as Hoffman puts it, the "dark root from which the world sprang."[55] Similarly, for Eisenstein, Auschwitz is the beginning of her parents' lives together and thus the imagined origins of her own beginnings.

Her parents' introduction in Auschwitz took place shortly before the liberation of the camp as the Russian Red Army was approaching, and as Eisenstein's self-appointed narrator says, "This is when my father and mother's life together began. Like Adam and Eve, ousted from a perverted Eden, they were cast out to find another home."[56] This is an origin myth that begins well after the fall, a traumatic, undiminished focal point of both beginnings and departures that would seem to define the lives of the "hinge generation"—as Hoffman puts it, those who, in a generational lineup, maintain a "living connection" to survivors. It is thus from survivor to child, as Hoffman suggests that "the legacy of the Shoah was being passed on to . . . its symbolic descendants and next of kin. We were the closest to its memories" and thus to the obligatory heft of such an inheritance.[57] Bukiet defines the obligatory relation of the second generation to their parents' history as "a cosmic responsibility," one that shapes the contours of their lives.[58] As Henri Kichka, the sole survivor of his family, very simply informs his son in the graphic narrative *Second Generation*, "You are my way of getting back at Hitler," anxiously interpreted by his son in terms of his responsibility to make up for—despite the impossibility of doing so—his father's enormous loss.[59] The controlling trope in second-generation literature, the fundamental conceit that creates the conditions for these narratives of loss and the strains and fragments of memory, is that the identities of the second generation are, to a large extent, mortgaged to that past; their lives are defined by their parents' traumatic experiences and the memories that outlive the events of the Shoah.

Thus Eisenstein, on the book's cover, will stand against the backdrop of the shadowy figures of her parents, reflecting the formative influence that they exerted upon her identity and her sensibilities as the child of Holocaust survivors, a responsibility to the past that carries itself into the future. Simply put, as Bukiet explains, as a way of discharging this obligation, "if you were a writer, you wrote."[60] Because of the deeply interlocking and mutually dependent connection between the survivor and the second-generation recipient of that legacy, there is very little distance between the events of the past and their implications for the present. In other words, most, if not all, of the work of the second generation has a significant autobiographical component. The stories of extended trauma exert themselves on authorial issues of identity. The second-generation writer/artist, in this regard, can't quite separate himself or herself from the traumatic experience shaped by the events of the Holocaust. In his discussion of authenticity in autobiographical comics, Charles Hatfield fittingly proposes that "if autobiography has much to do with the way one's self-image rubs up against the coarse facts of the outer world, then comics make this contact immediate, and graphic."[61] Such self-exposure is doubled in the graphic narrative through the conjoined media of comics and story line. Thus second-generation graphic artists can't quite take themselves out of their narratives, even if the story they tell "belongs" to someone else. It is no surprise, then, that these graphic narratives are narrated and drawn from a first-person perspective, even when that first-person voice shifts or merges with other authorizing, telling voices, blurring the boundaries of author and character, object and subject. There is a kind of immediacy, intimacy, and thus urgency to these works, one that exposes the fraught identity of the author/narrator as it navigates the traumatic conditions of the survivor's past.

The title of Eisenstein's graphic narrative suggests her complicated relationship to and discomfort with her ability to locate an appropriately measured distance in relation to the subject of the Holocaust. The title *I Was a Child of Holocaust Survivors* focuses on the "I" and thus makes emphatic, from the very beginning, the author's privileged position in the narrative. The iconic evocation of the title, however, suggests the position the graphic memoirist takes toward the narrative that will follow. The title's melodramatic tonal quality recalls the faux-confessional genre of 1950s teen horror films: *I Was a Teenage*

Frankenstein (1957), *I Was a Teenage Werewolf* (1957), *I Married a Monster from Outer Space* (1958). The pop cultural reference is juxtaposed jarringly to the history it references. While the "I" positions the graphic novelist at the forefront of the narrative that promises to be about her, the stock locution "a child of . . . ," the pop cultural reference, undercuts her privileged status. Given the enormity of the subject and her parents' lived experiences, her own position is on shaky ground. At the same time, however, as the younger incarnation of Eisenstein's narrating self acknowledges, "Without the Holocaust I would not be who I am. It has seared and branded me with its stippled mark on my forearm and pulled me into its world, irrevocably, as its offspring. The collective memory of a generation speaks and I am bound to listen, see its horrors, and feel its outrage."[62] While Eisenstein may feel conflicted by and uncertain about the appropriate expression of distance from the subject of the Holocaust, what the retrospective voice of the graphic artist does have distance from is herself. Eisenstein, through the course of the narrative, thus establishes two voices: the self-absorbed, immoderate, and insecure younger persona and the retrospective voice of the older, judicious, and measured narrator, who looks back with no little self-irony on the younger hyperbolized and as-yet-to-be-formed version of herself.

Looking back on her younger self, Eisenstein maintains a critical authorial distance from what she describes as her obsession with the Holocaust and her exaggerated self-importance in putting herself at the center of the family drama. Admitting to her excessive and largely self-focused preoccupation with the Holocaust, Eisenstein ironically and self-parodically confesses to her addiction to the Holocaust, as she, as the child of survivors, is in search of a fix: "The Holocaust is a drug and I have entered an opium den. . . . I will discover that there is no end to the dealers I can find for just one more hit, one more entry into a hallucinatory world of ghosts. . . . My parents don't even realize that they are drug dealers. They could never imagine the kind of high H gives."[63] Her self-parodic, self-critical pose is emphasized by the cartoonish caricatures with which she, at times, draws herself. As Hatfield suggests, such "autobiographical comics make . . . seeing happen on a quite literal level, by envisioning the cartoonist as a cartoon. This is the auto-biographical comic's most potent means of persuasion: the self-caricature. . . . Prerequisite to such caricature . . . is a form of alienation or estrangement, through which the cartoonist-autobiographer regards himself [or herself] as *other*, as a distinct character to be seen as well as heard."[64] In humorously satirizing and ironizing herself and what she now knows to have been her muddled, obscured motives for the obsessive preoccupation with all things Holocaust related, Eisenstein, the more distanced author, recognizes in retrospect that which she could not see at the time: that being the child of Holocaust survivors gave her a kind of currency; her connection to the Holocaust and thus to suffering and victimization became for her a kind of capital of exchange, exchangeable both socially and psychically as identity formation. Eisenstein only recognizes in hindsight, with the passage of age and experience, what she could not see at the time: "I would trade on its cachet, shamelessly it seems to me now, with a mixed bag of reasons and emotions—in order for the attention to be paid to me. It was a way of staking claim to my position in the world."[65] Such a critical, retrospective assessment of her immaturity and unexamined motives exposes a genuine complication for this child of Holocaust survivors: that her preoccupation was a deflection from her sense of inadequacy and isolation from her parents' most shattering moments and thus a projection of her fear and disempowerment onto her generational claim to a history and memory that, in truth, are not her own. As she only now, years later, can admit, "My life was not cursed, theirs was."[66] Nonetheless, Eisenstein, the child of survivors, simply put, has grown up against a backdrop of loss. As Hoffman has said of the children of survivors, "The Shoah pursues us and demands something from us. It ambushes us . . . even when we thought we were done with it. It is, after all, our past."[67] Up against such a legacy of loss, the ghosts of the past accompany Eisenstein throughout her life as she attempts to negotiate the complicated family dynamics that stem from such loss. As she acknowledges, "While growing up and trying to discover my own way into the world, I sometimes found it impossible not to wander off course, with a different aim in mind. Knowing that the Holocaust happened was not enough, I needed to know what it had done to my parents."[68] She needs, in other words, to know the particulars of the emotional DNA that has been passed on to her, beyond her control, in an almost material way.

Such found if opaque knowledge is even further complicated by Eisenstein's initial misdirection. Against her parents' silence about the Holocaust, she sought sources outside the immediacy of their memories: documented histories, films, literature. It is only after her father's death that she "was left to find the pieces of his past, led by the wish to have more."[69] Thus the subsequent search for her father's story and the acquisition of her mother's taped testimony creates the necessary conditions for her to start piecing together the fragments of the past. But this is a winding and fraught process of transition for the child of survivors, complicated by, as Hoffman suggests, the need "to separate our voices from the spellbinding, significance-laden voices of the survivors, to stop being ventriloquists for our parents."[70] This process, however, is hard won, as Eisenstein illustrates in the graphic narrative, demonstrating the transition from immaturity to responsible telling through the juxtaposition—revealed through both text and image—of innocence and knowing, knowing, that is, when to step out of the narrative of her own life and let the survivors "speak." Such a surrender to the authorizing voice of the survivor, the primary witness, involves giving up her own, already unstable, sense of agency.

For second- and third-generation indirect witnesses to the Holocaust, knowing when to yield to the testimony of the survivor and thus surrender one's own defended and wished-for "translation" of events is complicated by the difficulties of narrative agency but also by the gap between the fantasy of knowing and the acquisition of such knowledge. For example, Kichka, in *Second Generation*, poses his autobiographical narrator in the uncomfortable position of relinquishing the story to his father, who, only after years of studied silence and only after the suicide of his youngest son, cannot stop talking about his experiences during the Holocaust. With a feverish and repetitive compulsion to talk, Henri Kichka, survivor of Auschwitz and Buchenwald, once unsilenced cannot arrest the flow of words. It is only when his father begins to speak and speak and speak that Michel Kichka—the child of survivors, who for so long wanted to know his father's experiences and the fate of his father's family—retreats in ambivalence. Of his father's experiences, Kichka explains in an interview, he and his siblings knew "almost nothing": "We knew in general that he was arrested on September 3, 1942 in Brussels, and taken to different camps. We knew that he was liberated from Buchenwald on April 11, 1945. But we didn't know the details of all the work camps he passed through. I hardly knew the names of his younger sisters. We were simply told as kids not to enter this field—it was like a minefield. I was not sure whether I would get answers, or whether asking would be too painful for my father. Silence was the rule of the game."[71] One traumatic episode, however, gives way to another, and the death of the younger son takes Kichka's father back to the originating trauma of the Holocaust (fig. 3.4).

Standing in a pile of eyeglasses, a yellow star stitched on his jacket, the young Henri, whose likeness resembles that of his son the graphic artist, only now will speak. On the top of the page is a represented stream of sound: a litany of "and he talks talks talks talks talks talks talks talks talks . . ." in seemingly endless rows of silence shattered. As the son of the now unquieted survivor admits, however, "So what's better? Silence or words? Honestly, I couldn't say."[72] These are words, once unleashed, that can't be taken back; neither can they be unheard.

Kichka represents the moment in which his father begins, finally, to speak without the specificity of the actual words that make up the story of his capture, deportation, and incarceration. He signals that the story is being told by the repetitive referent "talks." The graphic artist cannot give words to his father's speech, cannot, that is, fill in the interstices, the shape and texture of the story he tells and tells again, in large part because it is not his to tell. The words are not his; he cannot give actual language, the precision of language, to those words spoken by the primary witness. The potential unrepresentability of the survivor's narrative, however, is made up for by the illustrations that underlie—that exist under—his story. The survivor's eruption into memory,

FIGURE 3.4. Words unleashed. Michel Kichka, *Second Generation: The Things I Didn't Tell My Father* (France: Dargaud, 2012), 54.

however, is articulated for the graphic artist, who admits that when his father "began to tell, I was not ready to listen."[73] Knowing, "hearing" the testimony of the primary witness requires a posture of responsible listening—that is, being open to the ambushes and betrayals of history and also being receptive to the inadequacies and limitations of representation.

In *I Was a Child of Holocaust Survivors*, Eisenstein initially draws herself as a young child, who in her embryonic self has yet to develop the kind of consciousness that enables her to negotiate the legacy of her parents' past. The book's opening image, following the cover illustration that appears on the title page, is of the author, as a young girl, perched atop an unevenly arranged stack of books (fig. 3.5). Here we are introduced to the narrator in her unformed, nascent state. In a parody of Auguste Rodin's *The Thinker*, Eisenstein draws herself, chin resting on hand, seemingly deep in thought as she gazes into the distance. She is naked, her body undeveloped, fluid. Her expressive facial features are juxtaposed with her developing, not fully formed body. Again, as on the cover, her expression belies her apparent youth. Her nakedness here, as elsewhere, suggests at once her vulnerability—she is unclothed—and also her exposure. As Marcoux suggests, "The child's nakedness indicate[s] that . . . she is, at that point, devoid of *a* narrative about her identity as second-generation witness."[74] She is her own blank canvas, poised to be filled in. But at this early point in the book, she is still very much a work in progress as a subject of understanding and awareness. She is unsteady; the top two books on which she sits are angled so that her position is precarious. Memory is, after all, slippery. She is in danger of sliding off. Significantly, on the two angled books on top, Eisenstein has inscribed the title of the graphic memoir, *I Was a Child of Holocaust Survivors*, as if this is the very condition of her instability. Indeed, as we will soon discover, she is not, initially, in control of the narrative that

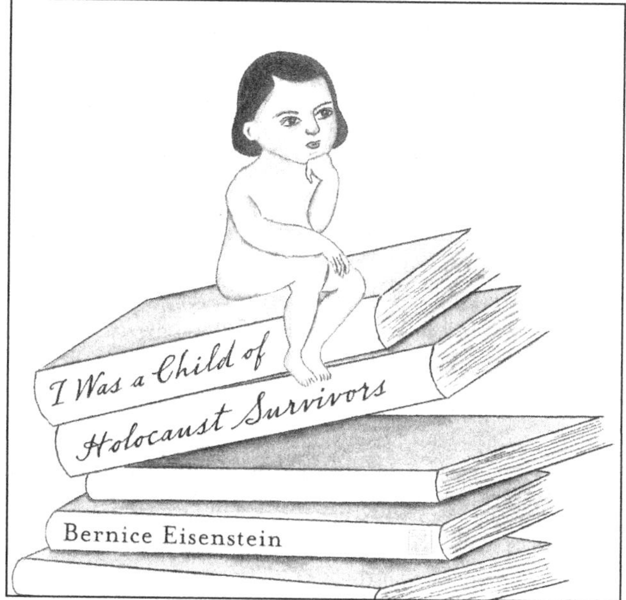

FIGURE 3.5. Perched atop a pile of books. Bernice Eisenstein, *I Was a Child of Holocaust Survivors* (New York: Riverhead Books, 2006), title page.

will follow. Here Eisenstein, from the very beginning, establishes the tension between knowing and not knowing, seeing but seeing into the distance as if searching for something that she cannot as yet make out. In doing so, the graphic cartoonist calls attention to "the problematic of knowing and not knowing that is so essential to the transmission of traumatic history."[75] From the very beginning, then, Eisenstein problematizes the condition of knowing, of grasping hold of and arranging—structuring a coherent narrative—of her parents' memories in terms of the intellect. Her pose suggests that hers is an existential, ontological problem that she might resolve through words, the stuff of the intellect. Her unsettled position on top of the pile of books, however, presages the difficulty she will encounter in trying to wrest control of the narrative of the past. The intellect alone is insufficient in both mining the intricacies of memory and also transmitting that history. At the same time, however, the book is a kind of touchstone, totemic of both the problem and the sought-for resolution. Thus as Harris proposes, "Eisenstein uses images and text in combination to restore some degree of wholeness and tangibility to the indeterminacy that each medium in isolation generally exhibits."[76] In other words, the materiality of the book is a surrogate for the absence and loss to which the graphic artist attempts to give voice.

Eisenstein will return to various iterations of this figure of herself as a naked child in the mature pose of *The Thinker* as a way of emphasizing the tension between innocence and experience, knowing and not knowing, and the weight of history that both anchors her and threatens to topple her. Her nakedness is significant. Not only does it represent her innocence and inexperience, her developing, nascent self, but also it figures her unguarded, exposed condition. Unclothed, she has nothing to conceal. As Hatfield suggests, "There is something radical about the intimacy of graphic self-representation," and we see such undefended, intimate self-exposure in Eisenstein's self-images.[77] Early in the memoir, on the verso side of the page that introduces the text of her narrative, Eisenstein again draws herself perched on top of a rock-like structure. Unlike the first iteration of this drawing, in this second image, her thoughts are materialized. In a self-reflexive moment of metanarration, she calls attention to the complexities and challenges of her project. As a means of establishing authenticity, the graphic artist draws herself into the narrative as she ponders—and considers again, thinks through again—her way into and out of the maze of fragmented memories. Below the speech bubble that begins with the line "I am lost in memory," Eisenstein's figure is barefoot, naked, again in *The Thinker*'s pose.[78] The base on which she sits is inscribed with a chorus of Yiddish words, the language that the young Eisenstein grew up speaking, "the soul and substance of the life in our home."[79] The mosaic of Yiddish words that constitute the edifice upon which she sits stands in contrast to the intellect. Yiddish evokes for her the emotions, the "sound" and expression of home, of her own childhood, "the way the past and a language are fastened together."[80] Through the literary device of backshadowing, here as elsewhere, the graphic artist shows the way in which the past influences and coexists with the present. Both distant and more proximate memories confound temporality as they continue to inform the present. Yiddish represents the diasporic language of loss, her parents' "mother tongue, their *mamaloshn*, filling every step they had taken from one country to the next" and constituting the remaining fragments of that world (fig. 3.6).[81]

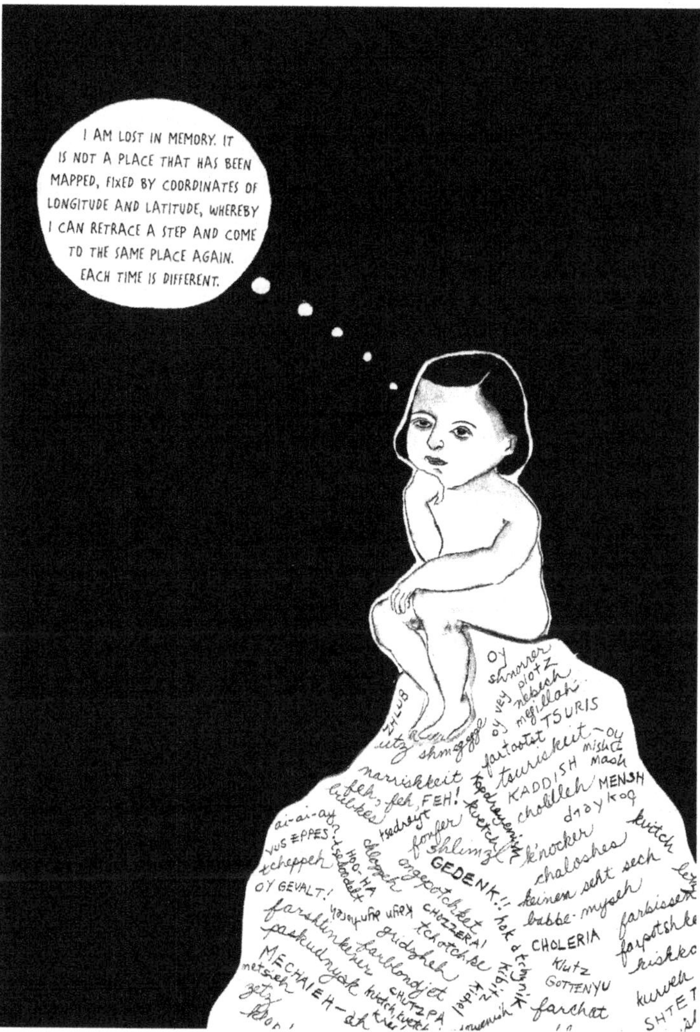

FIGURE 3.6. A Yiddish legacy. Bernice Eisenstein, *I Was a Child of Holocaust Survivors* (New York: Riverhead Books, 2006), 10.

Here we find the creation of the relation between that which is depicted by the artist and that which is perceived by the reader, a characteristic conceit of the comics form.[82] What is missing in this image, of course, but what is implied are the figures of the dead as represented by the language of *Yiddishkeit*, a culture all but eradicated by the Holocaust.

The recurring drawings of the young artist sitting atop symbolic representations of the Holocaust, in both their figurative iconography and their metaphorical diagnosis, are not unlike Art Spiegelman's drawings in volume 2 of *Maus*. Here he self-reflexively reveals his deep anxiety and guilt about the critical and popular reception of the graphic depiction of his father's experience in Auschwitz. The awareness that he has inadvertently capitalized on his parents' suffering is infantilizing and paralyzing for Spiegelman, who fears losing control of his own agency. At the beginning of chapter 2, "Auschwitz (Time Flies)," we find the cartoonist, in mouse mask, sitting at his drafting table below a pile of naked, dead bodies of Jews. This panel is accompanied by a text bubble with the understated disclosure made by the author/narrator, "Lately I've been feeling depressed."[83] Spiegelman's debilitating anxiety (in the final panel on this page, he is slouched over, his head in his hands) stems in large part from his knowledge that, through the "critical and commercial success" of the two-volume narrative of his father's traumatic ordeal, he has unintentionally capitalized not only on his father's suffering but on the collective suffering of millions. The weight of such knowledge has an infantilizing and disempowering effect on the artist. Subsequent panels show him regressing to a childlike state, diminished in size and crying for his mother. His childish tantrum—"I want . . . absolution. No . . . No . . . I want . . . I want my Mommy . . . WAH!"—is symptomatically complicated.[84] Not only does he want his mother—a victim of the Holocaust who later committed suicide—to exonerate him, but, very simply, he wants his mother. He is, after all, the abandoned child fighting against the absent mother, which complicates, if not impedes, the "work of mourning."[85] The absence of the mother is, in some ways, the threatened absence of the self. "Sometimes," Spiegelman's autobiographical protagonist ironically confesses, "I just don't feel like a functioning adult."[86] The only relief he gets is when he takes himself to a psychiatrist—also a survivor—who validates Spiegelman's testimonial project, despite its inevitable inadequacies. Such therapeutic approbation allows him to regain both maturity and agency. We see the graphic artist with renewed resolve as he leaves the psychiatrist's office regaining, in a set of three panels, his stature, growing larger and larger with each self-affirming step. Thus as I have suggested previously in relation to Eisenstein's graphic novel, an awareness of the complexities of accumulating and transmitting memory is, for the child of survivors, both an infantilizing and an aging, maturing process of discovery. Ironically, knowledge here is not empowering but depleting, disempowering. Thus ironically, addition leads to subtraction; the obsessive pursuit of the unknowable, the irrevocably lost, diminishes the pursuing subject by the sheer weight and magnitude of suffering.

Such self-referential moments—the calling attention to craft and to the ethical complexities of self-representation—enact the material extension of trauma and memory. In doing so, as Chute proposes, "against a valorization of absence and aporia, graphic narrative asserts the value of presence, however complex and contingent."[87] Drawing oneself into the narrative of the past is a way of attempting to keep terror at bay by engaging with it, by imagining (inserting) oneself in the ongoing dialogue with that past and thus keeping watch over it. Thus Eisenstein, if not to rewrite history then to ward off its debilitating mantle, will at a later point in the narrative return to this image of her naked body sitting atop a stack of books. Again, she draws herself unclothed, unformed, and as yet uninformed (fig. 3.7). In this image, however,

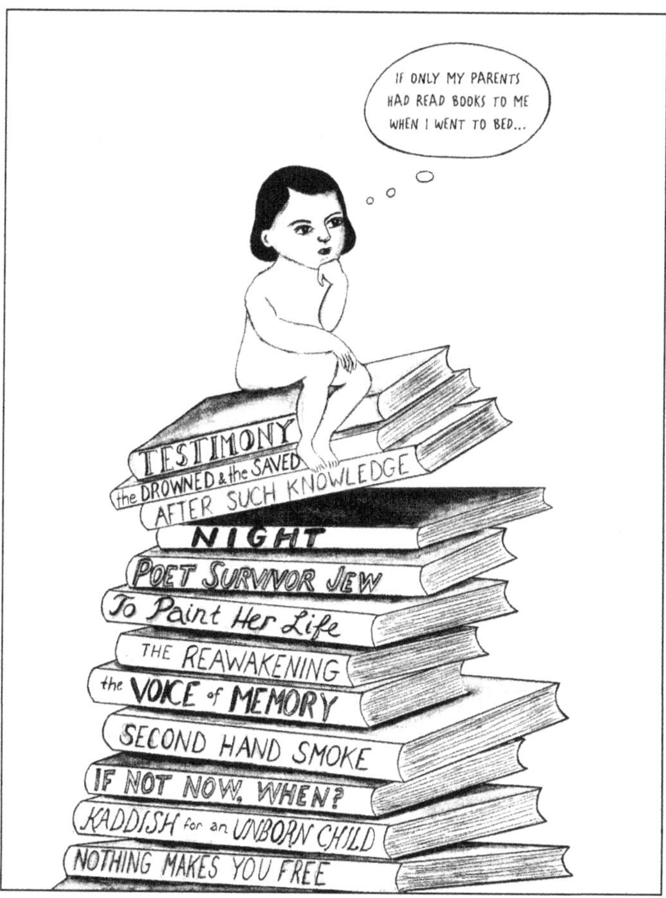

FIGURE 3.7. Voices of memory. Bernice Eisenstein, *I Was a Child of Holocaust Survivors* (New York: Riverhead Books, 2006), 88.

the books she sits atop are written by "authorized" literary figures, including both survivors (such as Elie Wiesel, Paul Celan, Primo Levi, and Imre Kertész) and canonized second-generation writers (such as Eva Hoffman, Thane Rosenbaum, and Melvin Bukiet).

Here once again, Eisenstein is drawn precariously perched, uncertain of the legitimacy of her voice and of her standing among recognized "witnesses" to and spokespersons of the Holocaust. She has yet to establish her voice. She is still infantilized by her limited knowledge and by the immense scope of her project. And as the speech bubble projected from the top of her head—"If only my parents had read books to me when I went to bed"—ironically acknowledges, she was unprepared for such "bedtime stories," fairy tales that do not bridge the divide between the imaginary and the real.[88] She is, as yet, displaced, lacking the authority to speak. Thus sitting on top of books written by survivors and other second-generation writers is a matter of "reestablishing and renegotiating the dialogic potential between first and second generations of the Holocaust experience."[89] At the same time, however, her position atop the pile of books suggests that no amount of reading the work of others, however authentic, will fill in the gaps in her family narrative. She sits unaccompanied and forlorn atop this mount of information. The intellect alone will not—cannot—answer the questions that consume her. Nonetheless, this recurring image metaphorically calls attention to her attempts to carry forth the cultural legacy of the Holocaust. Eisenstein, as the child of survivors, sits atop history, its weight propping her up, the foundation on which she rests. She is in the process of defining her place in the ongoing transmission of the memory of the Shoah. She will add her voice to those who came before her.

Thus Eisenstein, though precariously perched herself, constructs the graphic design of her parents' Holocaust experience and the way that experience shaped their lives and characters as well as her own. In doing so, Eisenstein draws upon a variety of artistic and narrative styles and structures. Primarily, her book is controlled by large sections of text interspersed with drawings, a different design than that of Martin Lemelman's *Mendel's Daughter* (see chapter 2) or that of Spiegelman's and Kichka's second-generation narratives. In Eisenstein's account, there are some pages that consist only of sustained blocks of text and others that include drawings that complement the narrative. For the most part, however, image is subservient to text. There are moments when the narrative reads in some ways more like an illustrated book than a graphic novel. There is one exception to this pattern: the interruption of an eighteen-page interlude of comics that appears not quite halfway through the book and that graphically recounts the basic story of what Eisenstein has narrated thus far. In drawing upon a variety of expressive styles—at times there is a kind of stark simplicity to the drawings, for example, and at other times the images are cartoonish—Eisenstein suggestively would seem to be trying out different forms in an attempt to get the expression right. That is, the assemblage of fluctuating genres, voices, and accredited artistic styles—the influence of van Gogh, Ben Shahn, Saul Steinberg, and Chagall, for example—create different representational modes and discursive forms as a way of both arresting and extending the movement of memory as well as bringing the characters to life in their complexity.[90] Such moments, achieved through both text and image, enact the fragmented and disjunctive expression of trauma and memory. They also speak to the representational difficulties in transmitting the stories of the Holocaust for a generation connected by birth to those who survived but a generation that nonetheless remains on the outside of the experience that the graphic artist attempts to articulate. There is a distinctly performative aspect to the genre of the graphic narrative, which, in the case of Holocaust representation, uniquely re-creates a "living connection" to that history through its visually voiced performance. As Eisenstein puts it, "The drawings are intended to have that past come to life, just as the door was opened for me to remember them; the drawings are there for their life to be seen."[91] There is also a performative aspect to autobiographical graphic narratives, which, as Martha Kuhlman suggests, "have the unique potential to exploit the possibilities of comics form to express an evolving sense of identity . . . self-reflexive in their depictions of the narrator/protagonist . . . calling into question claims of authenticity or ironically reinforcing them."[92] Such performative aspects of the genre broach the space of memory and its discursive, therapeutic possibilities.

I would suggest that the prominence of text in Eisenstein's graphic memoir draws our attention to the book's images all the more. While her drawings are influenced by a variety of styles, they are defined primarily by the juxtaposition of distinct, expressive faces—sometimes rigid in their expressiveness—and more fluid, even rubbery representations of bodies. Her "lush, sensuous style" of drawing, as Michael Kaminer puts it, gives texture to the amorphous shapes of memory and loss.[93] The faces of Eisenstein's characters are more realistic, more detailed than their bodies, which together embody an abstract fluidity that represents the changing shape of memory as it is passed on generationally. We are drawn to the eyes of Eisenstein's characters throughout the narrative. In her self-portraits, Eisenstein typically shows herself looking off the page, eyes askew, cast to the side, her gaze in the distance as if she is searching for something that she cannot as yet see clearly. Consistently, however, her gaze—the expression in her eyes—belies her youth, illustrating throughout the jarring paradox of knowledge and innocence and the representational difficulties those oppositional positions signal. Significantly, in contrast, the eyes on the faces of the survivors tend to be focused outward, facing the viewer, as they look straight ahead. As Malcolm Lester suggests, "What you notice most of all in [Eisenstein's] drawings is the alert gaze on the faces of the survivors—whose eyes have seen horrors beyond imagination, and whose lips are invariably closed, as if the unimaginable should not be spoken."[94] The disparity between Eisenstein's self-portraits and the images of the survivors suggests, as I have argued, the complexities in representing through images the differing positions from which the generations "witness" and "remember" the events of the Holocaust. The images hope to fill in the gaps in the narrative. As Eisenstein's narrator says of her attempts to reign in and give shape to the imagination, "It's difficult enough to discover the right words for what is to be remembered, but even harder when each word longs to shelter and sustain the memory of a generation aged and now dying."[95]

Thus Eisenstein both textually and visually mediates the past through the juxtaposition of text and image. There is a moment a little more than halfway into the memoir in which Eisenstein reproduces a drawing of a photograph of her mother, her grandmother, and her aunt, "posed as [she] had wanted to draw them."[96] The photograph was taken after the end of the war, the three women finally reunited. In the photograph, Eisenstein's mother, grandmother, and aunt are sitting together, the grandmother flanked on either side by her two daughters, whose images are set slightly in the foreground (fig. 3.8).

Leaning forward, the eyes of the three women are looking outward, not at each other, but somewhere outside the image on the page. The looks on their faces are knowing ones, having witnessed that for which Eisenstein has no clear referent. However, at the center of the photograph, their three arms are outstretched, tattoos exposed, providing her with the material referent that

FIGURE 3.8. Eyewitnesses. Bernice Eisenstein, *I Was a Child of Holocaust Survivors* (New York: Riverhead Books, 2006), 112–113.

anchors her to history. The foregrounding of the tattoos corresponds to the direction and directness of their gaze, which, while directed outward, seems to encompass, to "take in," a panoramic outside the limitations of the page. As Chute suggests, second-generation texts "do not conceal or cloak trauma, but rather put its elements on view."[97] We are drawn to those numbers, whose sequential numbers mark the arrival and incarceration in Birkenau of Eisenstein's mother, aunt, and grandmother. The tattoo here serves as both signifier and referent and helps Eisenstein mediate her mother's experience. That is, the tattooed numbers both signify the experience and stand as a striking material icon of that experience. On the facing page, Eisenstein draws herself as a young artist, ink pen, pencil, and dripping paintbrushes in her arms, as one would hold a child (not unlike the pose on the cover with the doll in her arms). Her own image is significantly smaller than that of her mother, grandmother, and aunt. In contrast to the image of the photograph that takes up most of the page, bleeding into the right-hand page of the spread, Eisenstein's image is much smaller, diminished in size compared to the images in the photograph. They are the primary witnesses; she is secondary. She is, the juxtaposition suggests, diminished by their knowledge and their experience, which extend well beyond the enclosed time of their incarceration and, as suggested by the way in which the panel spreads onto the next page, intrude into the life of subsequent generations. The bleeding of the panel from one page to the next is a way of signifying, as Scott McCloud suggests, the extension of time, that "time is no longer contained by the familiar icon of the closed panel, but instead hemorrhages and escapes into timeless space," in the instance of the child of survivors, collapsing past and present, visually moving the past into the present, a spilling over of one story onto another.[98]

The indexical "I" here shifts from the title's "I" of the child of survivors to the "I" of the witness, the firsthand account of the Holocaust from one who was there. At the same time, by drawing herself self-referentially as the artist, Eisenstein inserts herself into the narrative of her family's past, the effect to "double the act of witness."[99] Indeed, in these two images, the one bleeding onto the other page, their eyes all resemble one another's, and Eisenstein too is looking somewhere off the page, catching the reader's gaze. All eyes are looking to the future, as Eisenstein says of the image in the photograph of her mother, aunt, and grandmother: "I briefly saw something I'd never seen in them or recognized—a kind of innocence, a lightness, as if their arms don't even carry the mark of the past."[100] Yet the referent here is inscribed on their arms, made visible as the embodied, materialized past. Ironically, the innocence of the women that Eisenstein imposes onto the image is not reflected in the drawing; their innocence refers to a condition before the camps, before awareness. In this way too, Eisenstein projects her own inexperience, her own innocence onto her wished-for projection of her mother's past. This two-page spread makes emphatic, as Chute has proposed of the genre, that "witnessing and memory can be treated as a creative interlocutionary process, rather than something anchored in the unfaceable."[101] Here three generations are brought together on this two-page spread, faced and faceable, suggesting the dialogic nature of bearing witness and the intergenerational or transgenerational extension of memory. Thus the figures, though divided temporally, are spatially aligned on adjacent pages, an imbrication of past and present.

In the attempt to mediate the past and present, the literary and artistic challenges of representation that Eisenstein encounters are complicated by the resistance she experiences in her attempts to return imaginatively to the time of the Shoah. Early on in the narrative, Eisenstein includes an image drawn in shadowy swirls of black and gray, of the ghosts of the dead, a chorus of voices who, she imagines, stand in her way. Their haunting presence prevents her access, her trespass into a past she cannot fathom; instead, in words sprinkled with Yiddish, they enjoin her to move into the future, thus avoiding the dangers inherent in the backward glance. As one voice, they warn her, "Oy, will we never get any rest? . . . We're ghosts. Dead, fertig, toyt, finished. We know what was done to us. And this one now. We have no room here for her. Dahlink, go—dance, live. It's enough just wanting to speak our names. Can she hear us? Nu, what can we do? Don't ask us questions. Einekle, little one, we are the answer."[102] Eisenstein fears her persistent desire to know the past and to resurrect the lives of the victims, if only in the imagination, is an intrusion, an imposition, an unwelcome invasion into the private suffering of others. However, Berel Lang and others would caution us not to mythologize, iconize, or privilege the figure of impossibility or unspeakability in Holocaust representation. As Lang insists, "The Holocaust is speakable . . . and, most of all, ought to be spoken. Virtually all claims to the contrary—in those variations on the unspeakable that cover also the indescribable, the unthinkable, the unimaginable, the incredible—come embedded in yards of writing that attempt to overcome the inadequacy of language in representing moral enormity at the same time that they assert its presence; certainly they hope to find for their own assertions of such inadequacy a useful—*telling*—place in its shadow"[103] The invocation of inexpressibility, in other words, becomes a useful trope of discursive self-authorization. Furthermore, the unacceptable alternative to the ongoing attempts to bear witness to the Holocaust, of course, is silence—the eradication of memory and the absence of responsible reckoning. As Chute proposes, "Graphic narrative, invested in the ethics of testimony, assumes . . . the risk of representation. The complex visualizing it undertakes suggests that we need to rethink the dominant tropes of unspeakability, invisibility, and inaudibility."[104] Thus instead of silence, or absence, Eisenstein re-creates the conditions and prescriptions of memory—as limited and isolating as they may be for the child of survivors—as a measure of her own accountability. As the older, more aware narrator, by the book's close, acknowledges of her fraught journey through the memories of others, "I felt the bittersweet pull of *gedenk*, remember, and came to understand in a new way the breadth of its reach. It was as if the word had been silently spoken by a generation soon to be gone—Remember us," the call to memory, the mitzvah of *zachor*, remembrance.[105]

Try as she might, Eisenstein will always remain on the outside of the memories of those who experienced the trauma of the Shoah firsthand. The distance from which she, and others of a post-Holocaust generation, by necessity, views the past is complicated for the child of survivors by the paradoxical position of being both insider and outsider to that past. On the one hand, the child of survivors is the direct descendent of the direct witnesses of the Shoah; as Bukiet insists, "What the Second Generation knows better than anyone else is the First Generation."[106] On the other hand, the transmission of the experiences of survivors is often withheld from the second generation, as Eisenstein, yielding to the authority of their position, concedes, "The circumstances of my parents' lives had taught them to guard their stories."[107] When there are openings into the past, the memories are fragmented, fractional, and disjointed, often contradictory and incomplete. The recipient of such stories, then, must piece together a historical narrative, all the while deeply aware of the limitations of such knowledge but also acutely sensitive to, as Hoffman puts it, the "deeply internalized duty not to let diffusion, or forgetfulness, or imaginative transformation, dilute the condensed communications" of the traumatic, ruptured past.[108] Thus Eisenstein, characteristic of her limited position in the generational extension and expression of her parents' history, finds herself in the uneasily navigated position of insider and outsider, the past both remote and proximate, and she remains on the outside looking in from a hazy, concealed distance.

Such a rhetorical position is both paradoxically isolating and insulating. Standing outside the circle of her parents' circumscribed orbit, Eisenstein fears that she is separated from her parents' most intimate and private emotional space. Their "family," consanguineous insiders, consists of the "Group," those who shared the most traumatic moments of their lives, those with whom they identify: "All of them were linked to the same past, sharing the same history, an unbroken chain of survivors."[109] This is a community with which Eisenstein cannot begin to compete. This ongoing chain, if not familial then existential, is both comfort and manacle; they gain strength in their connection to the "Group", all the while being shackled to that past. As Eisenstein is acutely aware, "They were one another's home, their own having been confiscated and destroyed. My parents and their friends are inextricably linked, by the events in their shared past and by the future they came to build."[110] And although Eisenstein is the child of those who lived through the Shoah—in other words, the direct descendent of that lineage—she is not a link in that particular chain of suffering and endurance. That she is and always will remain an outsider to the "Group," those survivors who form an impenetrable community, exacerbates her own sense of loss, as if their collective history has eclipsed her own. Looking at a photograph album of her parents and their close-knit group of friends "huddled tightly," a chronicle of the many years of their mutual bond, Eisenstein remains on the outside looking in.[111] "Cursed and blessed," she will always remain an outsider to their history. Despite—or perhaps because of—her unbridgeable distance, finally, from the community of survivors, as Eisenstein says, "the pull of their history was irresistible."[112] She is both pulled to (by way of instinct and compulsion) and pulled away from (by time and circumstance) that history, a measure of the twin poles of distance and proximity that define her position in relation to the events of the past, an expression of her limited participation in the extension of memory and also what it means to stand alone against the backdrop of such traumatic history.

A significant shift in tone and comportment occurs at the moment in the graphic memoir when Eisenstein steps out of the narrative and transfers the agency of the telling to her mother. The chapter title signaling this shift is "My Mother on Tape." Eisenstein, now the stage director for the story that follows rather than a character actor in her own unfolding drama, reveals that in 1995, her mother gave a taped interview for the Shoah Foundation's Archives of the Holocaust Project. Eisenstein was given the tape by her mother, as she says, "a tape that I watched, and watched again in order to be able to write my mother's story as she told it."[113] Not unlike the literary conceit in Lemelman's graphic memoir *Mendel's Daughter*, the "taped voice" of the survivor narrates the story that follows, unmediated by the textual intervention of the second-generation author. However, whereas Lemelman compensates for his lack of narrative intervention by contextualizing his mother's words within the surrounding structure of his illustrations, Eisenstein, for the most part, turns the telling over to her mother's found voice, stepping into the background and thus allowing her mother, as direct witness, to tell her own story. There is one striking moment in this brief account in which the graphic artist introduces an image, a shadowy sketch of her mother's aunt, a teacher at the Bedzin orphanage, her arms sheltering the children under her care. This single image is sketchily drawn in outline for the simple reason that she can't see it. It is not her memory. Other than this one tentatively drawn image, the only narrative interventions are the bracketed questions sporadically interjected by the interviewer and a few explanatory notes. It is as if Eisenstein does not want to tamper with or break the flow of her mother's words. As she explains in an interview, "I had her story on tape, and it was hers to be told. So I struggled with finding her voice, unadorned by mine. There is a gravitas, a centre to be found in her chapter."[114] At the center of gravity, in other words, is the authority of the survivor, the authentic voice of experience and memory.

And thus, her mother's abbreviated story, only a snippet of her life, begins with the assertion of self set implicitly against a political regime and its machinery that would have silenced her: "I am Regina Eisenstein."[115] The introduction to her narrative significantly parallels the title of Eisenstein's memoir. Unlike the opening of her mother's testimony, however, Eisenstein does not name herself, since she believes her own agency to have been eclipsed by that of her parents' history. Eisenstein's *I Was a Child of Holocaust Survivors* lacks a referent for its "I." Her name is subservient to and subsumed by the fact of her immediate relationship to Holocaust survivors. The "I was" of Eisenstein's introductory title is thus contrasted to her mother's opening declaration of "I am." Eisenstein was and will always be the child of survivors, a status conferred to her by chance and the vagaries of birth and upbringing. Her mother's "I am" achieves what Eisenstein has been attempting throughout her narrative: to replace the specter of absence with presence. Her mother's voice—"I am"—will continue in its undiluted form both on tape and in the pages of her daughter's book. The mother's "I am" replaces the "I was" of the book's title. The change of verb tense suggests that Eisenstein has moved from being subsumed by her preoccupation with her parents' story to being responsible for its transmission. She is no longer defined solely by that singular inheritance. Her identity is no longer overshadowed by her parents' Holocaust past; she is free to move into the future, but only after she has yielded to the authority of the survivor.

Her mother's direct, unmediated address, however, is brief and truncated; it ends elliptically, her story trailing off. And it does so with the admission that she cannot continue her story because words fail her: "I cannot describe what it was like when I am reunited with my mother and sister . . ."[116] Despite the fact that the story remains unembellished, unfilled in, hearing her mother's words and her mother's self-imposed silence gives Eisenstein her own kind of narrative authority to join her voice to that of her mother and the other survivors who people her book. Such knowledge—the found awareness of the authorizing voice and the realignment of narrative agency—is humbling for Eisenstein but no longer infantilizing. Thus the tone in the remaining sections of the memoir will change. When Eisenstein reappears, she has adjusted her own graphic and linguistic comportment; her voice is no longer self-parodic, sarcastic, defensive, or insecure. Explaining the effect of her mother's words, the narrator reveals, "When I heard the precision and directness of her words I was transfixed. . . . There was something in her controlled objectivity that initially caused me to feel distanced, but as I listened to my mother, I discovered the courage she has always possessed. Her story, which she had told me only in pieces when I was growing up, was now sequenced as best her memory would allow. I watched her set the pace with a steady bearing and, with her, I was able to look straight ahead."[117] Hearing the voice of the survivor tell her own story makes all the difference for Eisenstein. Her mother's courage gives her the courage to proceed. From this point forward, Eisenstein's self-portraits, to a large extent, retreat from the narrative. When she does appear, her gaze looks straight ahead, no longer off center but focused outward, at the viewer, prepared to meet our scrutiny. Eisenstein "grows up" over the course of the narrative as she learns more of the facts of her parents' history but also as she learns to accept her limitations and her place in that lineage. Such knowledge is, for the child of survivors, empowering and maturing. And thus Eisenstein's autobiographical, second-generation spokesperson learns, through the course of the graphic exploration, to navigate the very distance that was the source of her anxiety and unease and to adjust her expectations, her misguided and impulsive desire not only to understand the totality of her parents' loss but to "somehow make up for such sorrow."[118] Despite this recognition of her limitations, she nonetheless has found "a telling place in its shadow," which, after all, as she comes to appreciate, is no little achievement.[119]

Thus at the close of her graphic memoir, Eisenstein ends with the future, the promise of continuity and the birth of her son, the third generation, to whom is bequeathed the legacy of the past. The emergence of a new generation signals the coming of the end of survivor testimony and thus gestures toward a shift in guardianship of that memory, from first to second and now, by the narrative's end, to the third generation. The final chapter, following the lines from Deuteronomy 4:9, establishes the ancient imperative, one commanded long ago, to continue the transmission of memory into the future, thus extending the past, made "known to your children, and to your children's children."[120] Fittingly, then, the text of Eisenstein's narrative concludes with the bris of her infant son, an event linking the generations to each other, "to their heritage, to their origins in an ancient world."[121] Here at the narrative's close, Eisenstein reconciles the unresolved tensions and contradictions that framed her identity as a child of survivors and that left her own life seemingly incomplete, leaving her "to find the pieces . . . led by the wish to have more": past and present, ordinary and extraordinary, distance and proximity, knowledge and concealment, presence and absence, belonging and trespass, participant and outsider, vigilance and inattention, order and disorder, self and other, and loss and creation all resonate as the narrative moves to closure.[122]

The book's final image is a drawing of a group portrait, generations of both the living and the dead as they are gathered around a table, Kiddush cups in hand (fig. 3.9). In this image, Eisenstein provides no mediating text or speech bubbles; instead, inscribed on the blank surface of the table, as if on a white tablecloth or a page of text, are lines from Romanian-born survivor Paul Celan's elegiac poem "There Was Earth Inside Them." Celan's poem, an evocative lament to the dead, through its repetitive cadence, is a call to memory reawakened at the site of a mass grave as it is dug. But in Celan's elegy, both the dead and the living, the buried and the unburied,

O you dig and I dig,
and I dig towards you,
and on our finger
the ring awakes.
— PAUL CELAN

FIGURE 3.9. Generations gather in memory. Bernice Eisenstein, *I Was a Child of Holocaust Survivors* (New York: Riverhead Books, 2006), 189.

dig—"O you dig and I dig, and I dig towards you"—until they meet, when "on our finger the ring awakes."[123] This closing epigraph harkens back to an earlier moment in Eisenstein's graphic narrative. Upon her father's death, Eisenstein is bequeathed the ring that was given to her father by his wife on the day of their wedding. The ring, an artifact of the past, comes, as objects of memory always do, with a story. As her mother discloses, when she was in Birkenau, she worked in the "Canada" unit of the camp, sorting the seized belongings of the inmates and those going to the gas chambers, "cataloguing the remnants of their dying culture."[124] Among the piles of items, stitched in the lining of an abandoned coat, her mother came upon a ring, whose anonymous bearer had perished in Auschwitz. This was the ring that Eisenstein's mother was able to keep hidden in her shoe for the remainder of the war, and it was the ring that she gave to her husband on the day they married. This ring, in its materiality, an icon of remembrance and commemoration, is a metonymic reminder of all that was lost, and as such, Eisenstein says, "I wear the ring as a bittersweet inheritance," not only in memory of her father but also in the memory of the unknown, original bearer of that artifact of the past.[125] The ring, as an object of memory, a tangible container for embodied memory, becomes the opening for narrative, for the imagined story of past lives lived. Such artifacts—photographs, maps, diaries, letters, found belongings, pieces of history—are fragments that speak to a past wholeness, a provisional stand-in for that which was lost and might be lost again in memory. Such objects speak to a history and a legacy that extends beyond one defining moment in time, and thus such artifacts transcend time through the imagination. The object thus figuratively takes the shape of the materialized past onto which is projected the fantasized completeness of the ongoing narrative.[126] Thus as the poet Celan wrote, "the ring awakes" in the hand of another who will carry it through history, across generations, carrying its weight into the future.

Through the genre of the graphic narrative and its juxtaposition of text and image, Eisenstein establishes a living voice at a time that marks the end of direct, unmediated survivor testimony. In the tradition of the second-generation memoirist, Eisenstein attempts to find for herself a critical and responsible distance from the events of her parents' past. At the same time, the graphic artist has attempted to find the means to enliven and revivify their memories, to reanimate that traumatic history in order to calculate to some measure that "undercurrent of loss" always present.[127] This attempt to negotiate distance is a recurring preoccupation among second-generation graphic artists and writers. Lemelman, in *Mendel's Daughter*, turns the telling over to his mother; the transliteration of her taped interview determines the text of the memoir. Lemelman introduces the narrative by insisting on his peripheral manipulation of her story: "This is her story. It's all true."[128] Whereas Spiegelman and Eisenstein insert themselves in the narrative, Lemelman essentially turns the telling of the memoir over to his mother's voice. But his mother's story is decoded through the interpretive lens of Lemelman's guiding illustrations. Spiegelman tempers distance and immediacy through drawing his characters as animals—Jews as mice, Nazis as cats, and so forth—although the expressions minimally sketched on the faces of those who figure in the ruthless labyrinth of predator and prey are all too human in their malevolence and their misery. In all instances, however, to one extent or another and in one "disguise" or another, all the second-generation graphic artists discussed here introduce their own narrating agency into their narratives. They all disclose a variety of modes and strategies of balancing distance and immediacy. In doing so, Eisenstein, through the course of the narrative, finally comes to evaluate the range of her own imagination, acknowledging that "over the years all that I have ever been able to imagine is chaos and sickness and exhaustion and the constant rediscovery that so few survived. But I was wrong. There was more. Life forces life to continue."[129] Thus Eisenstein's memoir deliberately looks ahead into the future as it looks back onto the tragic past.

The book's closure in part explains the function of one of its opening images. The second drawing, following the cover image, appears before the actual text of the narrative begins. It is both a dedication page (since it prefaces the second of two title pages) and also a prelude to the graphic memoir that will follow. Sitting around an unevenly drawn pentagonal table that resembles at once a game board as well as a roulette wheel, with a spinning arrow positioned in the middle, are five figures, all of whom are positioned differently in relation to the events of the Shoah: Eli Wiesel, Primo Levi, Charlotte Salomon, Bruno Schulz, and Hannah Arendt. Extending from each figure is a respective text bubble, words of advice given to the graphic memoirist on how to proceed through and measure the effects of the labyrinth of memory before (and behind) her. The game at which these "authorities" on the Holocaust are at play, however, remains unfinished; there is no discernable winner of this contest of chance and correct counsel, yet this is a "game" whose stakes are high. The arrow seems to hover in its at least temporary resting place between the figure of Primo Levi and Charlotte Salomon—between, that is, the intellectual and the affective: in Levi, a clinical assessment of the human condition, and in Salomon, a self-exploratory, autobiographical imprint of the self set against the backdrop of history. And it is also Salomon, as Ariela Freedman suggests, "who points Eisenstein toward . . . the work of witnessing as also a work of recollection."[130] The one looks outward, the other inward. Because of the indeterminacy of the arrow's final resting point, there is, among this host of players, no "final word," no single authorizing experience that guides the artist on the path by which she must proceed to procure the answers.

Directing the arrow between these two authorizing figures speaks to the twin poles of distance and proximity that Eisenstein navigates, and it is in the counsel given by the scientist Levi and the artist Salomon that Eisenstein navigates this tension. She will take to heart the advice both from the heart and the intellect, the personal and the historical, that which is internalized and that which is external to individual desire and impulse. Levi's "fear that . . . language has become inadequate, that you need to speak a different language today," combined with Salomon's conviction that "you must first go into yourself—into your childhood—to be able to get out of yourself" together jointly inform and structure Eisenstein's graphic narrative.[131] Thus through the intersections and juxtapositions of text and image, Eisenstein finds a "new language" with which to access and adjudicate the past. Together, as Harris suggests, "words and images [are] potent symbols of presence in the face of absence, and . . . keys to enable the unlocking of secrets."[132] The juxtaposition of words and images and the blurring of genres, characteristic of the configuration of Holocaust graphic narratives, create a language of trauma, a mode of bridging the space between presence and absence through a dialogic exchange of temporalities, if only for the moment of the narrative instant.

In *Correspondences*, a book-length poem by poet/novelist Anne Michaels, Eisenstein joins with the poet in creating a textured work of memory, one that combines image and words, framed by poetic tropes of lamentation and loss. *Correspondences*, published in 2013 by Eisenstein and Michaels, author of the Holocaust novel *Fugitive Pieces*, is an accordion of memory. The pages of the book are hinged together, pleated, so that when you open the book, the pages expand and contract, as an accordion, suggesting the way in which time as memory extends and retreats, moves forward and returns to its source, closing the gap between language and loss, re-creating, as Michaels writes in *Fugitive Pieces*, the way in which time collapsed into itself, bended, "buckled, met itself in pleats and folds."[133] The book is thus a material extension of time and memory, the symbolic weight of the book, a material form of testimony, of voices fused in an elegiac response to history—as the poet writes, "the burnt book, the drowned book/the buried book/the typewritten record, the handwritten/witnessing."[134] *Correspondences* is an elegy to Michaels's father, Isaiah Michaels (1918–2009), but it is also an elegiac testimony to those who lived during the fraught era of the mid-twentieth century, Holocaust survivors such as Paul Celan, Primo Levi, and Charlotte Delbo but also those writers, artists, and intellectuals such as Franz Kafka, Nelly Sachs, and Charlotte Salomon whose lives orbited that of her father, those who shared the same historical and intellectual landscape. The book-length poem thus intersects the personal and the historical, situating Michaels's personal loss within the larger context of historical rupture.

On one side of the book's pleated pages is Michaels's lengthy, extended poem; on the other side of the book's pages are portraits drawn by Eisenstein. The portraits appear on the right side of the page, and centered below each portrait is the name of the figure captured in Eisenstein's simple but elegant drawings. On the left-hand side is a caption, words attributed to the figures whose images occupy the pages of the book. These are the words that remain, voices that speak "to one another" so that, as the pages unfold, "a layered kinship is formed, a touch across the pages."[135] Together their words and faces speak to the treacherous and unstable age in which they lived. There is a kind of minimalism to the pages of Eisenstein's images, an uncluttered, unadorned expression of humanistic concerns, individual expressions of worlds both lived and imagined against otherwise blank, white pages. The book is meant to be read from different directions; turned one way, we read Michaels's memorial poem to her father and to those whose lives, if only in the imagination, intersected with his own; flipped over, we read the book as witnesses to the unfolding portfolio of faces and adjacent lines arranged in verse, in a kind of haiku minimalist rhythm (without its formal structures).

To unfold, as Michaels and Eisenstein explain, is to "extend . . . to remove the coverings from; disclose to view . . . to reveal gradually by written or spoken explanation; [to] make known." Correspondingly, to enfold is "to envelop . . . to hold within limits . . . to embrace."[136] Reading the book from one end to another and then, turning it over, reading it again from the other side of the pages creates a layering and overlapping of lives and elegies. Beginning again at the end, which of course is the beginning, creates a variation of a Möbius strip, itself a metaphor for the way in which memory is transmitted. Such overlapping and pleating of lives and words create an extended, unfolding dialogue that carries over throughout time, "just as a conversation can become the third side of the page" (lines inscribed on the back cover of the book). The words on the dedication page, *Es hot undz dos lebn gerufn*, transcribed from Yiddish, simply read, "Life called for us," or "Life called to us." As Eisenstein said, "It is a phrase of the *mamaloshn*, the 'mother tongue,' that resonates and expands, stemming from its place in the past and reaching forward to the generations to follow, to those who will inherit the knowledge of all that was once done to extinguish its breath. . . . And it is one that addresses us with a request, accompanied by the awareness of a debt to be paid: 'Remember us.'"[137] Thus just as the pages of the book stretch out and expand, so do memory and testimony extend beyond the borders of time and space.

Cover to cover, the side of the book devoted to Eisenstein's soft, muted drawings begins with the image of Paul Celan, whose words—"We / don't know, you know / we / don't know, do we?"—invites the reader into the memorial to memory that will follow. The final image is that of the German-Jewish poet and playwright Nelly Sachs, whose final lines—"If I only knew / On what your last look rested"—echoes the internal structure of lamentation and longing that fills both sides of this book. Together the words of Celan and Sachs (whose correspondence lasted for years following the war and, as written on the opening flyleaf of the book, "in giving something to each other, they made a place beside them for others") bookend this stunning collection of words and images. Both deeply affected by the Holocaust, together they lay the groundwork for the expression of longing and lamentation that motivates the ongoing extension of testimony and also mourning. Celan's words create an opening, inviting the reader to enter the space of memory with the sure knowledge that one who was not there, who was not a direct witness, cannot, with any authority and particularity, *know*. On the other hand, this invocation ends with a question:

"Do we?" is a caution but also a challenge, an invitation to enter the text of history. The concluding line from Sachs—"If I only knew"—in some ways answers Celan's question, but the conditional "if . . . only" makes imperative the obligatory, urgent responsibility to continue the quest, the legacy, the discovery and transmission of such knowledge that extends, as we see in these graphic narratives, to self-knowledge. In the words of the caption aside the portrait of W. G. Sebald, "What would we be without memory?"[138]

Thus in *I Was a Child of Holocaust Survivors*, guided by her own autobiography, through the exploration of the self, Eisenstein will reach back into history, steered through memory ultimately by all the found voices of her experience and her imagination, providing her with a "compass with which [she] could find [her] way."[139] All the presences, the voices, around the opening table, in concert, provide Eisenstein with a context, a "language," for approaching the subject of the Holocaust. Their different perspectives do not represent different notions of truth but rather different approaches to the calculation and evaluation of evil. Eisenstein here engages together—joins at the table—not necessarily contradictory responses to the Shoah but rather through the voices of the survivor, the writer, the artist, the scientist, and the philosopher ways of thinking about and forming a coherent narrative about the "truth" of the historical moment. These spokespersons from the past thus sit as sentry to responsible telling, vigilant guardians of testimony.

The opening and closing parallel images in Eisenstein's graphic memoir together create a wholeness out of the fragments of narratives. The opening scene at the table contrasts and complements the book's final image of the gathering of generations seated at a different table. Instead of the game of chance, however, this final collection of survivors and their descendants cast their lot with the words of the poet Celan, whose voice calls upon future generations to continue to "dig" and "dig" and "dig" into the past, into memory. In contrast to her absence among the congregation of survivors posed in contending corners of their asymmetrical table in the opening scene, Eisenstein is present at this table. Seated at the table, perhaps—if only in memory—awaiting the fabled arrival of the prophet Elijah, they represent together the mediated connection of past and present, generations connected by and committed to the continuity of testimony. These two tableaux thus frame the narrative, bookends to the legacy of the Shoah: from direct eyewitness testimony to the intergenerational extension of witnessing, different if paired voices of "authority." The narrative ends with the naming ceremony for the writer's newly born infant, who will carry his grandfather's name into the future. Thus the concluding image, generations gathered together, "entwined" in remembrance, is less an ending and more a beginning, an invitation to enter the space of the past and bear its weight into the future.[140] Both assemblages of linked inheritors of the Shoah sit as sentry—one at the book's beginning and the other at the end—faithful guardians of memory.

4

Flying Couch

A Third-Generation Tapestry of Memory

The origin of a story is always an absence.
—Jonathan Safran Foer, *Everything Is Illuminated*

The albatross of my conscience.
—Paul Auster, *Mr. Vertigo*

There is no way around it: you enter history through my history and me.
—Philip Roth, *The Counterlife*

In Amy Kurzweil's third-generation graphic narrative, *Flying Couch*, the Deuteronomic imperative "teach your children" provides the backdrop against which the autobiographical narrator, "in the tradition of curious and dutiful sons and daughters before [her]," will fulfill her inherited obligations to memory.[1] Kurzweil, the grandchild of a Holocaust survivor who fled the Warsaw Ghetto, re-creates her grandmother's personal history by transcribing and illustrating her story. She will, in Deuteronomic tradition, performatively "immortalize it, fashion it into those stories to be imprinted upon our homes and on our gates, as we lie down and as we rise up." Not only is her grandmother's past bequeathed to her as a narrative, but the obligation to perform her grandmother's memory, to perform her stories, is part of her inheritance and her identity: "Maybe," the granddaughter admits, "it's in the blood."[2] As Eva Hoffman, the daughter of survivors, suggests, the continuing effects of trauma, "the deep effects of catastrophe, the kind that are passed on from psyche to psyche and mind to mind, continue to reverberate unto the third generation."[3] This is a story that, as Lisa Appignanesi writes, is "uncontrollable," a legacy that "cascades through the generations."[4] Thus in contextualizing her project in a shared cultural framework, Kurzweil gestures toward a history larger than herself, recalling a covenantal scaffold for the development of identity, instructions taken "to heart": "Impress them upon your children. Recite them when you stay at home and when you are away, when you lie down and when you get up. Bind them as a sign on your hand and let them serve as a symbol on your forehead; inscribe them on the doorposts of your house and on your gates" (Deuteronomy 6:6–9). Situating her endeavor "to write and illustrate her [grandmother's] life" with this long-standing cultural and textual framework gives the graphic novelist literary license to "translate" and fashion her grandmother's stories and to place herself in the narrative of her grandmother's life.[5] Thus Kurzweil draws herself into the text of her grandmother's story in a posture of calculated reckoning, a measured, critical view of her role in the transmission of another person's stories, one that is both performatively self-reflexive and explicit about its felt obligations. Characteristic of third-generation Holocaust narratives, Kurzweil's account performs her own participatory role in the telling of her grandmother's history as part of the process, as Alan L. Berger poses, of the third generation's "working through the burden of their inheritance."[6] This "working through," I will argue, becomes a matter of deconstructing the anxiously figured fears of third-generation writers of their place in and responsibilities to that inheritance and its history.

Kurzweil thus re-creates through her graphic memoir a psychoanalytic journey through her own life. That life is informed by an expanding, parallel engagement with her grandmother's history. The act of telling both her own and her grandmother's stories increases her understanding of her grandmother's past but also of her own fraught maturation. The images she draws help her to see that history but also, to some extent, control the story. Thus Kurzweil creates an elaborately constructed, self-conscious temporal and spatial hybridity in the visual juxtaposition of words and images. The text echoing the lines from Deuteronomy is followed at the bottom of the page with an image of a computer screen—an implied contrast to sacred text—on which we see what we are meant to assume are the writer's hands on the keyboard typing the elliptical words as they trail off: "meta-narrative, third generation inheritance, transcription of oral-history, making the unseen visible, framing stories."[7] This gesture toward explicit self-reference calls attention to her awareness of her own dramatized self-representation and to her fantasized projection of her grandmother's story on the screen of her imagination and on the page. Not unlike the second-generation graphic memoirist Bernice Eisenstein (whose memoir *I Was a Child of Holocaust Survivors* is the subject of chapter 3), Kurzweil makes no pretense that this is not a narrative also and not insignificantly about herself as well as about the survivor. *Flying Couch*, like other second- and third-generation graphic narratives is thus an amalgam, to one extent or another, of direct testimony (re-created through an artifice of mediated forms of communication, including diaries, letters, interviews, and tape and video recordings) and autobiography. The autobiographical "I" of Holocaust graphic narratives, as elsewhere in Holocaust literature, conflates writer and character, but in the comics form, this relation is complicated by the visual embodiment of the author/illustrator/character. As Charles Hatfield suggests, autobiographical comics focus "everything on the question of . . . identity."[8] In those semiautobiographical comics narratives that navigate the subject of Holocaust memory, the question of identity becomes all the more elastic, slippery, and unstable because of the competing weight of the presence of the original bearer of and direct witness to the story that is being transmitted by someone else. Thus we find a blurring of voices (that of survivor mediated through that of writer/illustrator), of genres (biography, autobiography, memoir, fiction), of boundaries of identity, and of authorizing sources. Thus the autobiographical "I" of these narratives implicitly asks the following: "Where does one story end and the other begin?" "Where am I in relation to this text?"

The kind of self-reflexive intrusions that we find throughout Kurzweil's graphic narrative call ironic attention to its own artifice and also to the performative aspects of her project. In this way, Kurzweil also calls attention to the performative nature of self-invention. As Philip Roth's recurring character Nathan Zuckerman would have it, the performance of the invented self is a matter of "impersonating one's selves," those "artificial" (created) selves that at once expose and conceal one's motives and character. The art of self-invention is a matter of narrative construction, "the kind of stories that people turn life into, the kind of lives that people turn stories into."[9] To the immediate right of Kurzweil's drawing of the computer on which the artists' hands are poised in the process of writing, encased in a corresponding circular frame, is a self-portrait of the graphic artist looking askance at her own words even as she types them. Her apprehensive gaze is turned toward the text box rather than toward the computer on which she types as she looks with some trepidation at the words she has just typed yet is reluctant at this point to accept ownership of them. She is hesitant, that is, to enter the text of that history (fig. 4.1).

These adjacent, twined images, the one of the computer screen and the other of the writer, exist as separate and thus separated containers rather than as a singular panel of the writer as she authorizes her text. Such positioning

FIGURE 4.1. Transcribing testimony. Amy Kurzweil, *Flying Couch: A Graphic Memoir* (New York: Catapult / Black Balloon, 2016), 51.

suggests Kurzweil's anxiety about her relation to the narrative that she writes, the position of the third-generation inheritor of the story to that history. Such a self-reflexive, critical pose is a reminder that this is merely a motivated representation of her grandmother's memories and thus not only a reminder of her and our distance from the experience she will incompletely and imperfectly present but also a projection of her own "narrative" as writer, as potential bearer of testimony, and as moral voice.

Significantly, Kurzweil draws herself enclosed within a circle. This framing device shows her contained and constrained within her own orbit as a way of signifying that we are viewing the interior subjective position that she uneasily inhabits. The artist's ego is at stake here, confronted by the magnitude and seeming impossibility of the task before her. Thus there is an abrupt shift from this scene of the writer at work on the text of her grandmother's story to Kurzweil's own more proximate history at her bat mitzvah. The reference to the moment of coming of age, of Jewish adulthood, and thus of assuming the duties and responsibilities of *mitzvot,* of performing the commandments, signals that she is conscious of the moral obligation of participating in the transmission of her grandmother's story. Yet the tension that Kurzweil suggests by the distinct images that separate writer from text reveals that assuming responsibility for the legacy bequeathed to her is both as potentially dismantling of the ego as it is potentially empowering. As psychoanalyst Adam Phillips provocatively suggests, "The ego in the Freudian story—ourselves as we prefer to be seen—is like a picture with a frame around it, and the function of the frame is to keep the picture in tack."[10] Kurzweil, in this third-generation narrative, calls attention to the allied processes of writing and drawing her grandmother's stories and also to her own ego investment in the story. In doing so, she calls into question issues of authenticity and representation—both representations of history and self-representation—as they intersect. Interestingly, as Rocco Versaci proposes in a discussion of Art Spiegelman's similarly represented self-construction in *Maus,* "The inherent self-consciousness of the form is the means by which . . . distortions become a 'truthful' representation of this history insofar as they communicate the inadequacy of any representational strategy."[11] And thus here the "truth" of Holocaust reinvention in the graphic mode is the truth of the necessary inadequacy of the testimony to atrocity.

The performance of such secondary or tertiary witnessing involves the slippery art of ventriloquism, voices projected onto other selves telling others' embodied stories. As Kurzweil explains in an interview, "My grandmother was literally running from Poland to Germany, the memory of Nazis fresh, when my mother was a fetus. My mother was raised by two parents who had lost everyone in their respective families. . . . My grandmother's fragmented memories of hunger and loss echo in my early childhood memories. . . . We all grow up either hearing the stories of our parents, or at least feeling their effects. . . . I say these stories are inherited like DNA, because the emotions of these stories live in our bodies."[12] Kurzweil's *Flying Couch,* subtitled *A Graphic Memoir,* is both a rendition of her grandmother's story of escape and survival—as her grandmother insists, "I survived. I don't know how. . . . My parents, my family, my life, would not"—and a coming-of-age narrative that charts Kurzweil's own chronology from childhood into early adulthood and maturity.[13] Part of her maturation process involves coming to terms with her grandmother's history and her place within that legacy. Thus she attempts to construct a bridge[14] between her limited knowledge and lack of affective understanding and the paradox of her grandmother's experience of suffering and survival: "The way it happened . . . it was a terrible miracle for me. God's watching over me. I don't know why. What did I do so good in the world? Or so bad?"[15] Through a shifting back and forth in narrative time, made emphatic by textual and pictorial juxtapositions, Kurzweil voices her grandmother's intervening, mediating stories, a chronology made to parallel her own more proximate history. For it was her grandmother's survival that ushered in her own place in that history: "It was 1951," Kurzweil's grandmother tells her. "We went first to New York, to an island, you know, the place where the newcomers come . . . the happiest day of my life."[16] It is thus within the context of her grandparents' safe passage into their reinvented lives in America that Kurzweil credits the making of her own identity. But in particular, it is through the image of her grandmother and mother that she views herself; it is, as she writes in the book's dedication, "for the women who made me."

Thus, although to a lesser extent, this book is also a gesture toward Kurzweil's mother, born in Germany in a DP camp at the end of the war and who, as a young child, immigrated to the United States with her parents, both Holocaust survivors. Kurzweil thus creates the entwining narratives of three generations of women, whose histories both inform and are formed by each other's lives and their preoccupations, anxieties, and memories. In doing so, Kurzweil merges the voices and perspectives of multiple generations as they interact: survivor, second generation, and third generation, a heteroglossia of voices in response to the Holocaust. This multivoiced narrative is structured largely chronologically. Beginning with her own fraught childhood, shaped by fears that were, admittedly, "mostly imaginary," Kurzweil describes her movement through her own life: from early childhood to adolescence, her bat mitzvah, her ambivalence toward her Jewish identity, college, a birthright trip to Israel, early adulthood, and the beginning of her career as a graphic artist. But her own chronology is interrupted by her grandmother's story that runs in a loosely parallel structure to her own years, for as Kurzweil explains, "I think about my grandmother all the time."[17] Set in between her grandmother's developing story—drawn from the transcription of her oral testimony—and Kurzweil's own coming-of-age narrative is her mother's abbreviated life story. We learn of Sonya Kurzweil's birth in a DP camp near Heidelberg, in Bensheim, Germany, where she and her parents lived for two years—"Eight families in one room"[18]—their relocation to America, where, as her grandmother editorializes, "We didn't know nobody . . . to sponsor us, and we didn't want to go to Israel. Dear God forgive me, I did not. I said, I lost enough,"[19] and Sonya Kurzweil's eventual training as a psychotherapist. While the details of Kurzweil's mother's life are sketchy—having "grappled with the immigrant status . . . the lack of homeland, the inevitable identity crisis"—she functions in the narrative as a kind of mediating presence and as a measure of comparison to her daughter's unease: "Her fears and memories," as Kurzweil acknowledges, in contrast to her own, "are real."[20] Her mother is an imposing character as seen through her daughter's eyes: exacting of herself and others, precise, authoritative in her professional role, seeming in control—that is, everything that Kurzweil fears she is not. Each woman's story interrupts the others, and events are retold through the distinct lens of the individual storyteller who has a personal and often idiosyncratic investment in the story she tells.

Such narrative interruptions and reiterations are less a matter of competing narratives than they are a chorus of different postures and relational perspectives. They emerge in the work as different modes of distancing and immediacy that together create a kind of wholeness. They constitute an attempt by the graphic artist to authenticate the representation of her grandmother's experience in the Holocaust but also to portray the direct and extended aftermath of the Holocaust the way it casts a shadow over extended generations. Kurzweil's graphic narrative is also a narrative about the making of character: the formation of self in response to the influences of others; the construction of the ego as a seemingly self-made defense for negotiating the exigencies of one's times; and the graphic novelist's attempt to shape and give voice to those who become characters for the moment of the unfolding of the narrative. Kurzweil interweaves her mother's story, her grandmother's, and her own, the story of a third-generation bearer of history who fears that her life will be subsumed and overshadowed by those who came before her. This assemblage of narrating voices in Kurzweil's graphic narrative pieces together events from the past, present, and future. As Andrés Romero-Jódar, in *The Trauma Graphic Novel*, points out, such an assemblage composes "both visually and narratively . . . a constellational representation of memory that may produce the 'plausible feel' of the sense of traumatic history that affects not only the survivors, but also the following generations."[21] In Kurzweil's graphic narrative, we find distinct yet mutually dependent personae whose stories participate in creating a picture of the multiplicity of effects of the Holocaust on both the survivor and her descendants, whose lives and identities, we are meant to understand, are shaped by this catastrophic moment in history. Furthermore, as Versaci suggests, "the very nature of the medium—the fact that the images are drawn, the details arranged within panels, the panels arranged within a page—foregrounds . . . an active reconstruction of the past . . . the ideal medium in which to explore how 'truth' is constructed."[22] Thus through the blending and blurring of voices, narrative perspectives, and temporalities through individual testimonies arranged graphically and spatially on the page, Kurzweil creates immediacy through narrative contiguity, moving the reader into the gap between historical reality and the traumatic imaginary. That is, the imagination's desire for an ordering response to the generational chaos of trauma re-creates this gap through the conceit of trying to suture it.

These are stories that are passed down generationally, stories that "build a house," a foundation and space for identity. The opening pages of the memoir graphically depict a layering of histories that create the domestic space that "houses" the developing ego of the granddaughter, who narrates the intersection of three generations. The memoir's dedication—"For the women who made me"—is an inscription immediately followed by the visual construction of a house, a home built from the originating stories of Kurzweil's grandmother (fig. 4.2).

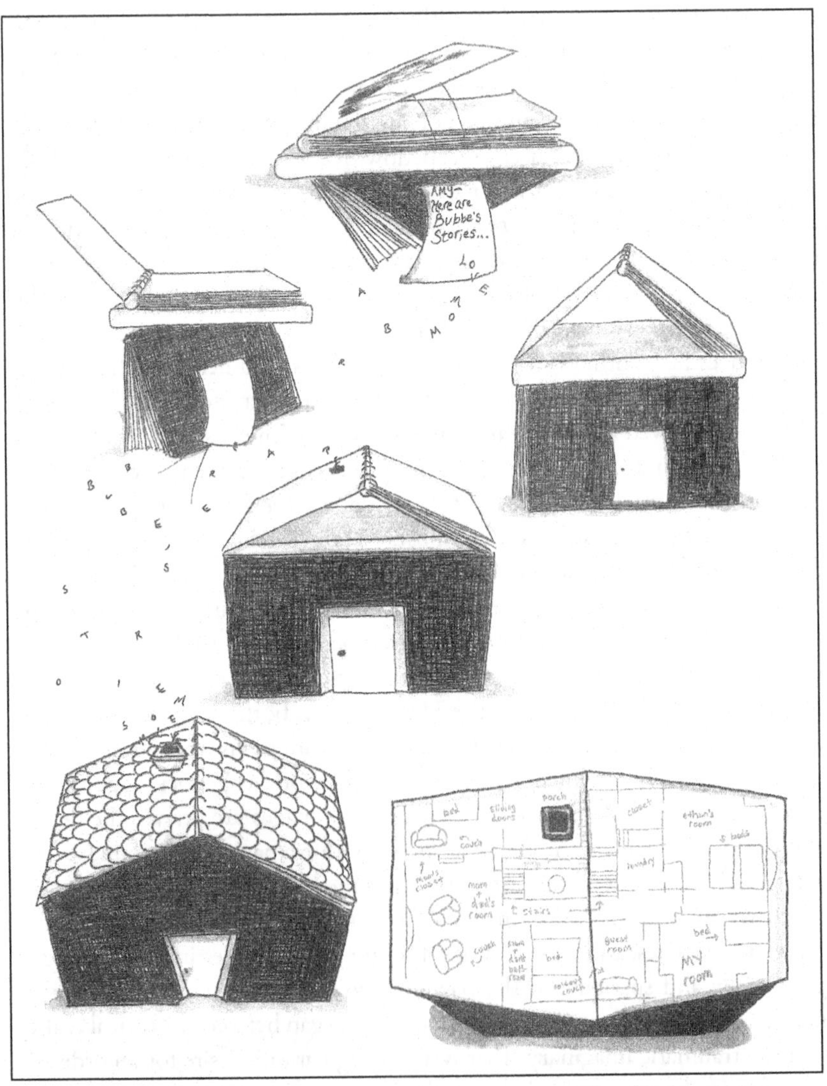

FIGURE 4.2. Stories that build a house. Amy Kurzweil, *Flying Couch: A Graphic Memoir* (New York: Catapult / Black Balloon, 2016), 1.

The image at the top of the page shows a blurred photograph of Kurzweil's grandmother on the cover of a book, given to the artist by her mother, along with her accompanying note: "Here are Bubbe's stories."[23] This is the same, if less distinct, image that appears on the bottom left of the preceding page. Her grandmother, drawn as a young woman on the book's cover, is the authorizing source of the narrative that will follow. These are stories that wind their way down the page as their words spiral and tumble through the generations. As they do so, they become the foundation for the graphic artist's family home, a dwelling erected upon the stories of the past, a history that shapes the psychic space that Kurzweil inhabits.

The image of the open book introduces the tropes of concealment and memory contained within, but much like the metaphor of the house, it also serves as a physical embodiment of testimony from a subjective position, one of projected interiority. There is thus a parallel here between the materiality of the house, as a metaphor of subjectivity, and the materiality of the book. As Hatfield, in discussing the function of such referential symbols, suggests, "The reader's awareness is called to the materiality of the book itself . . . in such a way as to inflect her understanding of the narrative."[24] Furthermore, grandmother and granddaughter are both writers and characters in their own stories. Later in the graphic narrative, Kurzweil will create a similar layout in which her grandmother, now older, appears on the pages of the book from which her story emanates in speech bubbles. Such a conceit, as Dana Mihăilescu suggests, "signals the metacritical dimension of Kurzweil's narrative, one which draws attention to the artist's conscious act of framing the family members as characters in her graphic novel . . . represented as both a physical book and a house from which the characters are surfacing."[25] In the case of Kurzweil, the figured materialization of the book—images of her grandmother's book within the covers of the granddaughter's book—calls attention to the process and artifice of storytelling, directing the reader to the value inherent in the transmission of the word as a foundation for continuity and identity formation. Thus her grandmother's stories, her past, serve as a forecasting blueprint for the present and the future, a structuring frame within which present and past interact, the present formed from and informed by the past, by the histories of those who laid the foundation for the future. Indeed, the initial image of the book of "Bubbe's stories," drawn to represent the process of opening its pages, becomes in the final image on the page a home, a scaffold filled in with rooms, closets, stairs, and furniture, metonymic accoutrements for those who inhabit the home. We see the home built on words, stories that flow from their originating source. What begins with a collection of stories becomes a fully framed and furnished home. This completed, inhabited drawing of home significantly never loses its connection to its origins in Kurzweil's grandmother's stories.

The small reproduction of the photograph of Kurzweil's grandmother on the cover of her book of stories, drawn at the very bottom-left corner of an otherwise blank facing page, represents in miniature the importance of the book within the book. On this book's cover, Kurzweil's grandmother is facing directly at the reader, a signal that the following story is initiated by her. In other words, we are invited into her past by her open, welcoming gaze. We can compare the image on the cover of her grandmother's book with the cover of Kurzweil's framing book, the memoir that contains the inner text of her grandmother's story. On the cover, Kurzweil draws herself as a young woman, suitcase in hand, as she is poised on a journey. Standing on a platform, as if waiting for a train, she overlooks the landscape before her, an indistinct terrain of uneven, rolling peaks and valleys, the outlines of uninhabited dwellings in the proximate distance. She is looking, in other words, to the future, to a future that is as yet unformed, uninhabited. Her back is to the viewer. Unlike the image of her grandmother on the cover of her own book of stories, Kurzweil's character is as yet not an "open book"; her visage is concealed. Unlike her grandmother, she is uncertain of the outcome of her own "history." While her grandmother's narrative looks back, her granddaughter's looks ahead; both, however, look into the distance, one whose pages are filled and the other in the process of writing her life. Her grandmother's story—her very survival—is the foundation for the home that emerges as Kurzweil's place of becoming but also the home she will leave of her own free will. Her departure from the home "built upon" the foundation of her grandmother's history is shown as a positive consequence of Kurzweil's maturation and autonomy. This point of departure is sharply contrasted to her grandmother's leave-taking of her demolished home at the age of thirteen, ironically the age of adulthood in Jewish tradition. Her grandmother's flight from her family home may be equally necessary, but having returned home from the hospital where she was treated for the wound caused by shrapnel fire, she finds her own grandmother dead, and thus her "home is gone."[26]

At the end of her memoir, Kurzweil will show herself filling her own home with objects, with the "stuff" of living, its "effects." Arranging the material accoutrements of a life—as she puts it, "to order the objects of real life, the things I can feel and name"—gives her a hard-won agency over her own life.[27] She begins with a blueprint of the home in which she grew up, an architectural framework that grounds her spatially and temporally. Chapter 1 of Kurzweil's memoir is introduced by an image of her mother locking the door of her home from within, an effort perhaps to prevent both entrance and also exit, a defensive measure keeping out that which would threaten the containment of the family within. This image is followed by a two-page spread of a blueprint of the home, the young Kurzweil and her mother separated by floors. We have an aerial view of the interior of the house, and the book must be turned in different directions, from one side to another, in order to orient the viewer. Thus the terrain is altered by the perspective from which the landscape is viewed. Maps are, after all, unstable; their landscape changes over time, as does the interiority of the domestic space as well as the subjectivity of the developing self. Kurzweil has thus constructed a temporal map, her memoir a cartography of interior structures, of foundational stories. This interior map of the home in which she grew up will later be contrasted to the two-page spread of the map of Poland as her grandmother, disguised as a gentile, flees the Warsaw Ghetto and traverses her way through perilous and uncertain terrain. This is a narrative in which maps serve as diasporic points of departure and points of arrival. As Mihăilescu suggests, "These maps underline how the acts of seeing and being seen depend on one's vantage point or positioning in space and time which become, in turn, ways of mediating one's understanding of others."[28] Such psychological mapping provides the graphic artist with the means for visualizing the intersections and crossings in the familial and interlineal relations among generations as they extend from the defining influence of the Shoah.

Thus in terms of the matrilineal line of descendants, her grandmother's originating story is the beginning of the generations whose lives play out together within the covers of Kurzweil's memoir. But also, and more significantly, her grandmother's written story is the platform on which her daughter and granddaughter have fashioned their own lives—both in defiance of her history and in tribute to her memory. Her history has been subsumed in the complex, partially repressed unconscious workings of their own personalities and temperaments, their dispositions toward place, self, and other. As Kurzweil's autobiographical narrator explains, her growing-up years were predicated on "a persistent conviction that something black and invisible dwelled in *my* bloodstream."[29] Such projection shows itself in the young Kurzweil's conviction that the space she inhabits and the "ordinariness of life" were both ruses. Perilous dramas "hid under the surface of everything."[30] At an early moment in her graphic memoir, Kurzweil shows her younger self awakening in the night from uneasy dreams to pull aside the curtains of her bedroom window only to see a scene nightmarishly distorted temporally and spatially. Rather than looking out upon her own terrain, she sees instead a scene from the past, one recounted later, of her grandmother in 1939, a young girl herself, hit by shrapnel as she attempts to flee the Nazi assault on their lives. These are nightmares brought about by a persistent dread of impending disaster—as she puts it, the something "black and invisible" dwelling in *her* "bloodstream." Her fears may be inherited, but they are also self-imposed, reinforced by her obsession with catastrophes—both real and imagined. Prior to the nightmare, she draws herself obsessively watching the news and films of the Holocaust, fascinated by—both drawn to and repelled by—violence and death. As Kurzweil explains in an interview, "The extent to which I, as a younger person, was curious and afraid of very particular things, most notably, leaving home and leaving family, in particular my mother, and the way I sometimes feared, often irrationally, for my physical health and safety, yes, I think this is the remnant of grief and fear related to the Holocaust."[31] In an unconscious act of transference, she fears that her own life, as measured against the reality of her grandmother's history, is fraudulent, her own troubled childhood, adolescence, and early adulthood eclipsed by her grandmother's genuine misery and suffering under the Nazi terror. Thus she will impose on herself—inflict upon herself—the disasters that befall others, so much so that she cannot separate herself from the imagined real of her fantasies.

Kurzweil's grandmother's past becomes part of her unconscious terrain, but she is largely unable to distinguish between actuality and fantasy. Thus her grandmother's stories provide the road map she will follow as they guide her further and further into the traumatic past. She admits of her own upbringing, "In my tranquil New England suburb, our greatest privilege was our greatest ignorance."[32] For the young Jewish girl, growing up in the safety and security of America, antisemitism was a distant and somewhat "academic" concept in direct contrast to her grandmother's life in Europe. As her grandmother cautions, "Oh I could tell you so many stories, I have stories and stories. A thousand and one stories."[33] Kurzweil cannot separate her grandmother from the stories she tells; both are enthralled by the possibility of stories as having a restabilizing effect, by biding time, on traumatized lives. Neither can she trust herself to distinguish between her imagined fantasy worlds and the actualities of her grandmother's history. She fears, however, losing her grandmother to history, losing, that is, her grandmother's individual story of loss and survival to the larger, abstract historical ramifications of the Holocaust, for, as she admits, "I spend more time with figments than people. What's more real, a person or a symbol?"[34]

This is a very intimate narrative constructed largely through the intersection of Kurzweil's cumulative interior monologue and her grandmother's unfolding oral testimonies. In large part, Kurzweil establishes such intimacy through stream of consciousness. Her narrative takes the form of a confessional. As she does so, she opens herself up—"a child of strange preoccupations"—to a self-reflexive and often self-parodic critical self-assessment. Characteristic of the graphic narrative, the intimacy and immediacy established draw upon the intersection of text and image. As Versaci explains, such intimacy and, I would add, urgency are established to a significant extent through "the directness of an author appearing amid the panels . . . looking us in the eye, and delivering heartfelt testimony about him- or herself."[35] Such direct address, the first-person narrative "I," is both an assertion of Kurzweil's dominant, orchestrating place in the narrative and also the limited, restricted lens through which she filters the events of her own and her grandmother's lives. Thus Kurzweil establishes both narratively and visually two distinct subjectivities, two interior positions of the "I": granddaughter and grandmother. However, as her older, more self-aware persona ironically discloses, "I'm always mining life for a good story, but all I ever see, I fear, is just my own reflection."[36] Her own confessional, intimate, and immediate narrative movement is, as I've suggested, interrupted by her grandmother's equally personal testimony. In allowing her grandmother to narrate her own life events, Kurzweil compensates for her lack of knowledge of her grandmother's Holocaust history: the fabric of her prewar life in Poland and the household she shared with her parents, her four sisters, and her own grandmother; her family's upheaval and displacement in the Warsaw Ghetto; the erosion and loss she experienced—"Sometimes a whole world is one person. My worlds were disappearing, one by one";[37] her escape from the ghetto through a small hole in the wall, sent forth by her father—"Go, he said, you gonna tell the free world what they did to the Jews";[38] and her subsequent flight and attempts at refuge and survival. Kurzweil's cumulative interior monologue is thus imbricated with her grandmother's unfolding oral testimonies. The effect is to foreground simultaneously past and present, traumatic events and their retrospective interpretation.

Kurzweil constructs the fictionalized conditions for her grandmother to tell her own story, a constant reminder that only her grandmother can be the author of her own testimony. Yet at the same time, we see her grandmother through the lens of her granddaughter, the graphic artist who arranges and draws the experiences and emotions described. In calling attention to the layers of storytelling, Kurzweil makes emphatic the limitations and different levels of distance intrinsic to such representation. Kurzweil's grandmother's survivor testimony was originally part of an oral history archive, a series of interviews conducted through the University of Michigan. Her oral testimony, transcribed onto the pages of a recorded document that Kurzweil received from her mother, is introduced initially by a drawing of the book of interviews: "The following is an interview conducted with Mrs. Lily Fenster at her home in Bloomfield Hills, Michigan on the morning of November 8, 1994" (fig. 4.3).

The book is opened to the grandmother's transcribed interview with a note from Kurzweil's mother attached to the facing page calling attention to the artifice of the design of the memoir but also to the imperative of the generational transmission of the story. The circularity of the frame within the panel signifies the encircling of the text within the text. Significantly, the circular frame is set atop a shelf of books by recognized writers (Kafka, Morrison, Sebald, Kraus, etc.). This juxtaposition allows Kurzweil to make claims for the authenticity and legitimacy of her grandmother's narrative. It also allows her to place her grandmother's book in the literary canon and her history in the historiography of the Holocaust.

The subsequent shifts into Kurzweil's grandmother's narrative are signaled by a change in typeface and design, the script resembling font from an old

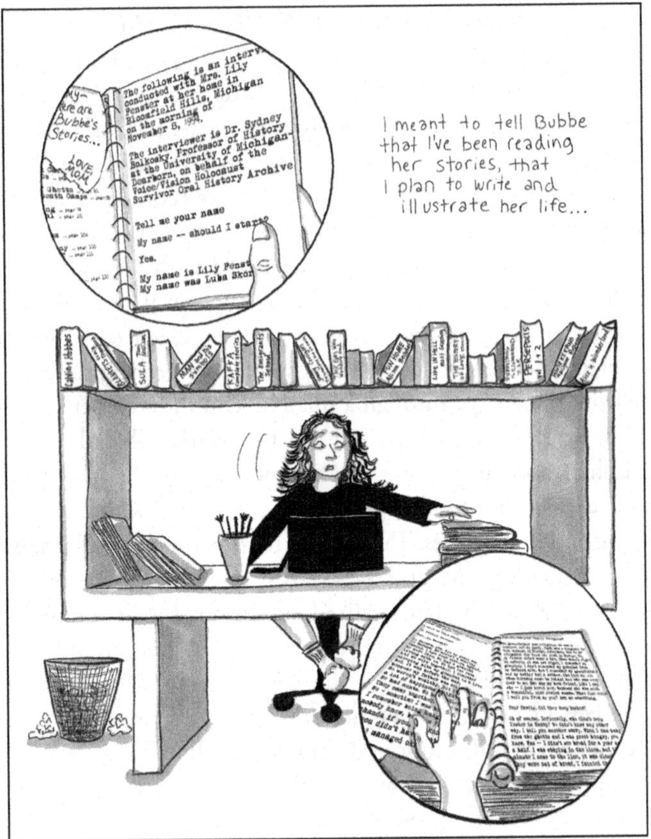

FIGURE 4.3. Stories handed down. Amy Kurzweil, *Flying Couch: A Graphic Memoir* (New York: Catapult / Black Balloon, 2016), 50.

manual typewriter, some of the letters smudged with black. This style is set in contrast to Kurzweil's own narrative, the text printed by the hand of the granddaughter, calling attention in both cases to the limitations in self-authorship and thus the reconstruction of memory. The visual juxtaposition between the typewriter font of her grandmother's words and Kurzweil's hand-printed lettering calls attention once again to issues of authenticity and testimony. While the typewriter font signals a kind of documented evidence, a realistic marker of recorded memory, the hand-printed letters of Kurzweil's narrative signal a text in the making, one as yet to be authenticated. So too the introduction of different fonts signals temporal shifts in the narrative. The anachronistic lettering of the typewriter takes us back both temporally and geographically. When Kurzweil's grandmother speaks in the "real" time of the narrative—that is, in the narrative present—her words are printed in speech bubbles unlike the documented text of her story as recorded in the book of interviews. In the previous image, the graphic artist draws her own hand holding the book, calling attention to representational issues of authorship and, at the same time, to the generational "handing down" of the narrative, her grandmother's stories transferred to Kurzweil by her mother. Such self-reflexive representation, the book within the book, the story within the story, calls attention to the differences in generational testimony and the distance between witness and second- or third-hand recipient of the stories, a witness to the witness's memories. Such self-conscious, self-referential metanarration is a constant reminder throughout the memoir of the distance between subject and viewer as well as of the gap between experience and coming to such knowledge belatedly.[39] Kurzweil thus "hears" her grandmother's testimony, not from her grandmother's own mouth but from her own voice once removed. Her grandmother "speaks" to her through the distanced lens of the recorded oral testimony, words initially spoken to someone else that, years later, she reads, repositions, and visualizes. Kurzweil thus speaks not only to the limits of representation but also to the limitations of third-generation "witnessing." The third generation must contend not only with limited information and absent experience but also with its own desire to bring the experience of others into sharp relief, to allow that experience to speak its "truth."

The intersection and juxtaposition of Kurzweil's more proximate past and her grandmother's increasingly distant history put her own life into perspective. The "translation" of her grandmother's past is the means by which the graphic memoirist is able to resolve and work through the chaotic and ambivalent conditions of her own life. Kurzweil titles the memoir *Flying Couch*, seemingly in ironic deference to her mother, the psychotherapist, but also to the therapeutic flight of fancy the graphic novelist has taken in drawing the memoir and to her self-parodic self-analysis in "taking the couch with her" wherever she goes. Kurzweil's autobiographical narrator is never free of affectionately deprecating self-analysis. With characteristic self-parody and comically ironic self-portraiture—"Humor is mortar. It binds the bridge between the real and the unimaginable"—Kurzweil assesses the way in which her preoccupations, her insecurities, and her unformulated but very real fears shaped her developing sense of self and place within the scope of her mother's and grandmother's histories.[40] After all, as Versaci suggests, "retelling one's personal history is, in part, an act of invention."[41] It is so in the articulation and thus the making of self. Throughout the narrative, at moments of ill-defined anxiety, Kurzweil shows herself to react with infantile regressive flight, a return to a state of infancy. She wants to be protected from the past—that is, from the projected obsession with a history that overwhelms her (fig. 4.4).

Ironically, her mother's middle-of-the-night therapeutic recommendation is "to try reading a book," which is what, of course, brings on the "monsters in the window."[42] She finds herself torn, pulled in many different directions. In one

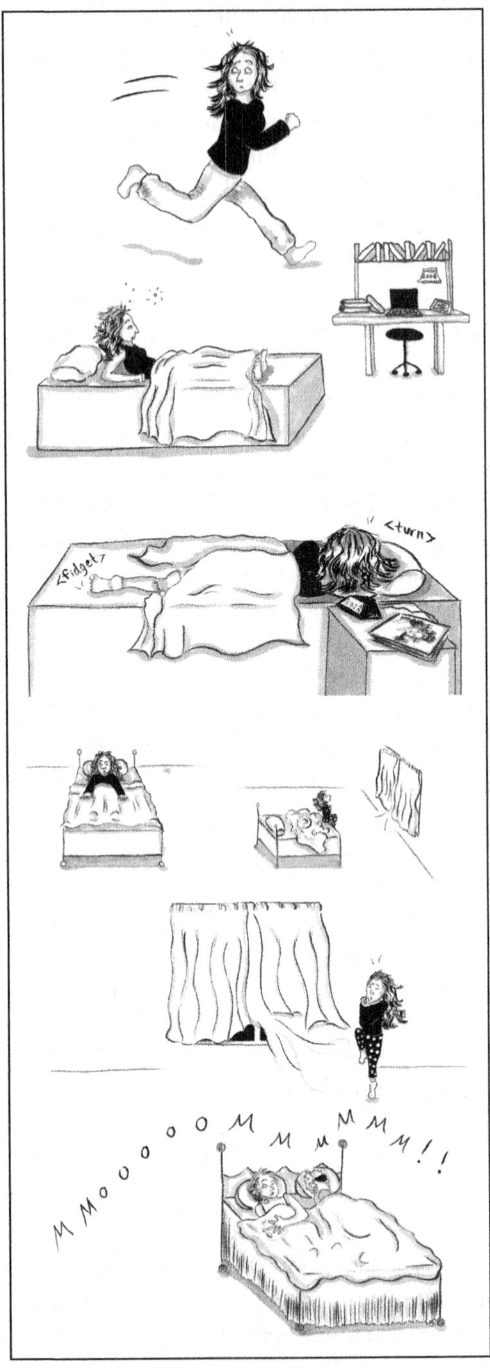

FIGURE 4.4. In flight. Amy Kurzweil, *Flying Couch: A Graphic Memoir* (New York: Catapult / Black Balloon, 2016), 116–117.

particularly comic moment, Freud, Marx, Theodor Herzl, and the patriarch Jacob all gang up on her, all making demands on her fraught psyche.[43] Comic as these scenes are, such indecision is debilitating, preventing the intervention and catalyzing influence of the superego. Chased by unresolved anxieties (in the form of these historical figures), Kurzweil shows her ambivalence to be paralyzing and regressive. Interestingly, it is through her identification with her mother and grandmother—the very identification that has been at the root of her unease—that she is able to resolve her insecurities and arresting anxieties about her place and her developing personhood as autonomous from but acceptingly indebted to the women who came before her. Kurzweil's memoir thus foregrounds the complicated nature of identity and identity formation, the "shifting self" created through the blurring and blending of voices and generic indistinctness of the graphic narrative.[44] The graphic narrative's juxtaposition of word and image creates this indistinctness, an indistinctness exacerbated by the redoubling of modes of self-authentication. In foregrounding her own changing postures and the various phases of her identity, Kurzweil draws the elastic, fluctuating stages of her developing ego, different "versions" of the self, especially as she reduces in size, reverting to childhood fantasies and terrors.

A product of her mother's and her grandmother's apprehensions and directives, Kurzweil's identity is formed by the shape of this developing legacy. Kurzweil displaces their anxiety onto herself. When traveling with her mother in Germany in an attempt to reconstruct her mother's early life, Kurzweil writes, "I felt strange, disembodied. Was this the alienation I'd read about? The legacy of diasporic peoples forever displaced from the homes of their parents? Or was this some kind of narrative shame," the sense of being displaced from—outside of—her own narrative?[45] After all, while Kurzweil is the artist/author of this book, this story is and is not her creation. In large part, she has assumed their fears and the weight of their history; her identification with both her mother's and her grandmother's pasts manifests itself, as she admits, in an "unconscious desire for suffering."[46] That she recognizes this transference with good humor suggests the trajectory toward her developing sense of self and place in the mutating shape of ancestral, familial, and generational histories. Locating, for instance, the source of her anxiety is the first step in resolving it. She sees her own fears of abandonment and separation as part of a continuing legacy of trauma, which she attributes to the reality of the death of her grandmother's mother. In portraying an ongoing conflict she has with her own mother, Kurzweil explains, "I never know exactly what we're fighting about, but it usually has something to do with leaving each other."[47] That which they argue about is that which they share, that which connects them, anxieties about abandonment, separation, absence, and loss. Their intangible but no less consuming fear is rooted in their mother's/grandmother's trauma, the death of her family in Treblinka. As Kurzweil's grandmother laments, "I try to picture a face. My mother's face. If I could draw, I would draw her. Just to bring her back to my eyes."[48] While her grandmother has the authority of memory, Kurzweil will assume artistic license. In opening up a space for the extension of memory, the graphic artist, in her grandmother's stead, will draw the past and those who inhabited it back to life, if only for the moment of the memoir, in an attempt to stabilize her own fraught identity.

Like other writers of the third generation, Kurzweil begins her project with a felt sense of absence. French third-generation graphic novelist Jérémie Dres, in *We Won't See Auschwitz*, recounts his journey to Poland in search of his grandmother's home in Warsaw, before the Nazi occupation, in order "to find her again."[49] Dedicated to his grandmother Tema Dres, née Barab, who left her home in Poland in 1930, Dres explains that his "journey wouldn't just be a personal one. It'd bear witness to the future of an entire people . . . to life before and after, over the course of my research into my family."[50] In chasing the stories of the past, Kurzweil and her mother, in mutual collusion, participate in the quest to reanimate the past, to locate, as Daniel Mendelsohn has put it, "the lost." The quest narrative, a characteristic conceit among third-generation writers, structures the reinvention and reanimation of the past, "return narratives" that, as Marianne Hirsch suggests, hold "the promise of revelation and recovery" but inevitably "defer any possibility of narrative closure."[51] As Kurzweil admits, "I wonder about roots. If my mother could complete our family tree, would it matter. . . . All we know about those missing relatives is that they are gone."[52] Dres's autobiographical character in his graphic memoir too seems to suggest that the quest for discovery and recovery, the "tangible presence of our roots," a reclamation of his family's personal history, has value not only in the awareness and transmission of his grandparent's stories but also in terms of his developing appreciation for his Jewish identity and his place in a long and enduring lineage.[53] As he comes to recognize, their tragic lives single them out as "worthy heirs to the Jewish legacy, and its rich, complex history." In returning to the prewar Poland of his grandmother's life, Dres and others of his generation locate "that broken hidden part of our identity . . . found . . . at last."[54] Thus this is a generation invested in understanding not only that period of the Shoah but also pre- and post-Holocaust life in order to see the Holocaust as a singular but not the *only* marker of Jewish identity. As Dres's persona in *We Won't See Auschwitz* asks, "The real question is: what does it mean to be Jewish?"[55] For a largely secular generation of Jews coming of age in the twenty-first century, this is a complicated and fraught question, especially if weighed against the defining event of the Holocaust, "a trauma so present," as Dres fears, "as to overshadow all the rest."[56]

Characteristic of third-generation narratives is the uneasy sense that the stories of the past have been withheld or that the value in such testimony has been recognized by the grandchildren of survivors too late for recovery. Israeli comics artist Rutu Modan, in speaking of her graphic novel *The Property*, the story of a granddaughter and grandmother's fraught journey back to Poland, the country of her family's past, acknowledges, "Growing up, my parents and grandmothers never spoke about Poland. They never spoke about the families that were left behind either. If Poland was mentioned at all, they called it 'the land of the dead' or they'd refer to it as 'one big cemetery.' . . . It was not just that everybody they knew and loved died, the country they knew also vanished."[57] As a result of the silence and reticence surrounding the past for so many of the third generation, Kurzweil admits of her interactions with her grandmother, "Our conversations are always in fragments, like my knowledge of her life."[58] For her grandmother, such memories are labored, too painful to remember: "My mother's face. Such a thing I have to recollect. A lot of things you block out."[59] Born too late to "remember," subsequent generations increasingly must rely on written accounts, accumulated data, and archived documents, material objects at a receding distance from both the bearer and recipient of such knowledge. Thus they "return" geographically or in the imagination to the originating sites of rupture and trauma. Such memories may be difficult to tell, but they are also hard to hear, "reminding us," as Kurzweil says, "of things we'd rather have forgotten . . . or couldn't understand."[60]

Thus the three generations here create a kind of tag team, participating in a relay race in which memory in the form of the story, or even simply the anecdote, is the material artifact that is passed along. Kurzweil depicts the story as a material object by visualizing it as an artifact, a *Yizkor* book memorializing the past through individual testimonies. The individual story, the point of traumatic origin for the survivor, both frames and contextualizes the lives of subsequent generations. Once unleashed and made available, the survivor's stories become both the catalyst and medium for intergenerational participation in the continuation of memory. Here Kurzweil makes clear the interdependence of the generations, the dynamic by which the three generations choreograph and navigate their way through history and their commitment to it. In one revealing moment, Kurzweil will ask her mother, "Who can we rely on?" Her mother's comically nonplussed rejoinder is "Anyone reliable!"[61] The mother's tautology evokes in disturbing ways Nathan Englander's "What We Talk about When We Talk about Anne Frank," with its deadly game of "who would save us now?" While humorously undercutting and dismissive of Kurzweil's question, the mother's response suggests their shared anxieties and suspicions in defense of a legacy of "such knowledge."[62] This is, for all three generations, a shared project of recovery and transmission.

The opening of memory begins with the survivor's firsthand testimony. In participating in the project of remembrance, Kurzweil's grandmother explains, "I met other survivors but we didn't really talk about it. . . . But lately now we talk more. Since people began to say never again. Never again. Now we want to talk because we don't want for it to happen again, not to anyone."[63] However, for the granddaughter to become the bearer of that history, the child of the survivor figures as the intermediary; she gives her daughter the book of stories that contain her grandmother's stories. The intercession of the second generation in the process of recovery is seen as an active, conscious choice in response to a felt sense of loss:

> When my children grew up, they didn't know my stories, but they were all very sort of sad. Why don't I have an uncle, they say. Why don't I have cousins? Why don't I have grandparents? Why? Why? I said, I'm sorry, if I could buy you an uncle I would buy you an uncle! Now my children, they understand. . . . They say, you never told us. . . . So much time I spent alone, in a prison with myself, holding on to a secret like a bomb, then keeping inside more memories and pain like sinking stones in the stomach. No more. I want all my children to hear my stories, for everybody to hear it.[64]

Kurzweil, in the burgeoning tradition of the third generation, will carry this history into the future, a three-generational, three-dimensional foundation built upon her grandmother's stories, her mother's stories, and her own. But this history, this "secret," is also a "bomb," one that unleashes fear, anxiety, and fragmentation with it, not unlike the box of horrors handed down from the second generation to the third in Spiegelman's "A Father's Guiding Hand," an excerpt from *Breakdowns: Portrait of the Artist as a Young %@&*!* (discussed in chapter 2).

The anxieties of discovery and authorial transmission, the narrative "handling" of the stories of the past, are balanced by the compulsion to know, to wrest some meaning from the past, and to carry that memory into the future. The graphic telling of these narratives is in large part mediated through the graphic artist's self-awareness not only of the artifice involved in transmission but also of the insufficiency, the limitations, and the intrusiveness of such intervention. While the obligation to memory, to fulfill the Deuteronomic imperative, is motivating, the formal constraints of the genre, of any mediating form of invention, expose its own limitations. In what is a recurring conceit in Holocaust graphic narratives, third-generation comics artist Leela Corman, in the brief comics episode "The Book of the Dead," calls attention to the artifice of her project, the artificial and artful nature of drawing her grandparents' war experiences. Poised in the act of creation, Corman shows herself at the drawing table, directly beneath her a swirl of black that spirals downward to a body as it is engulfed in flames (fig. 4.5).

The act of creation is thus contrasted to one of destruction, calling attention to the paradoxical character of the artistic creation of annihilation—that is, the antithetical disposition of creating absence—that is, negation. As she

FIGURE 4.5. The act of creation. Leela Corman, "The Book of the Dead," in *We All Wish for Deadly Force* (Philadelphia: Retrofit Comics, 2016).

puts the paintbrush to paper, she comments on her precarious position, "War is a hole I sit on top of. I sit here, distant from it, in my place of privilege, because a few of my family members managed to survive the holocaust, barely, and lately I've been wondering if I'm doing their memories any favors by being an artist."[65] Corman's self-conscious, self-reflexive autobiographical narrator, like other Holocaust graphic artists of her generation, simultaneously constructs and deconstructs two parallel narrative thrusts: the story of her grandparents' Holocaust experiences and the artist's attempts to mediate and animate the memory of past trauma. These twin conceits at times run as parallel lines of development and, at other moments, inform and intersect with each other. The juncture of the point of overlap—both visually and metatextually achieved—suggests the inseparability of these concerns.

Thus we see a recurring image of the artist in the act of drawing contiguously placed on top of an image of the dead: Art Spiegelman perched atop the towering piles of dead beneath his feet in *Maus* volume 2; the young, unclad

Bernice Eisenstein sitting on top of a rock on which is inscribed the Yiddish voices of the dead; and Corman's fraught meditations on her craft. All these graphic artists depict their vulnerability in the process of creation, their undefended, naked position in relation to the task before them. However, it is not only a matter of drawing *what* their relatives experienced during the Shoah that poses the greatest challenge but rather accessing the emotional immediacy and imprint of such experiences, as Mihăilescu suggests of Kurzweil's graphic memoir, ever conscious of "inherent tensions between the grandmother's lived experience and the limited extent to which the granddaughter can access and faithfully represent it in her narrative."[66] It is thus the felt, *lived* experience that these artists, through the graphic form, illustrate through the widening lens of time and distance. As Jessica Lang poses, third-generation narratives, largely defined by characteristically "emotionally laden textual interactions," self-referentially exhibit "a fascination bordering on obsession and often include a deeply personal brand of interest and investment."[67] For the third generation in particular, who did not grow up, as did the second generation, under the direct influence of the survivor, the stories of the Shoah are seen in relation to the more proximate circumstances and tragedies of their own personal lives and the geopolitical conditions of their own time. In other words, the Holocaust is the final measure, the moral register and standard against which other disasters—both imagined and real—are felt and measured.

The Holocaust thus often becomes the point of comparison that provides a language for trauma but also for survival. In, for example, the short graphic sketch "Drawing Strength from My Grandfather, Who Carried His Losses from the Holocaust," Corman introduces the narrative with her own more proximate tragedy, the death of her first child. "Staring into" the dark "tunnel" of her child's death brings her to Poland, September 1939, and her mother's father who spent the war in hiding after his parents and young sister were murdered by the Nazis. As the graphic artist writes, "I have thought of him often over the years. How he didn't have time to be afraid or to mourn. How he carried his losses. I draw strength from him." In articulating the extent of her own tragedy, Corman contextualizes it within the devastation of her grandfather's loss and the enormity of the Shoah, a measure, though again insufficient, of her own devastating loss. As she writes, "We trudge forward, carrying the weight of our dead."[68] Her grandfather's survival, his ability to continue to refashion a life, situates her in a language and a discursive, anecdotal "history" of suffering.

Corman's identification with her grandfather's loss gives her a context in which she can articulate her own suffering, a shared grief in which she is in the imagined company of one who knows what they both know all too well: that "there is really no safe place to be when you have experienced a grave trauma. The hole does not close."[69] Thus in "Bearing Witness at Buchenwald," an excerpt from her forthcoming graphic novel *Victory Parade*, Corman evokes the voices of the dead in their nightmarish haunt of Sam Arensberg, an American soldier present at the liberation of Buchenwald.[70] In restless, dream-filled sleep, Arensberg is summoned by the silent voices of hands descending from red clouds hanging over his bed. In these opening panels, there is no text because the myriad of hands outstretched, beseeching, imploring, speak for the ghosts of the dead, who tug at Arensberg as he sleeps, pulling him into a hellish scene of dismembered and piled bodies.[71] He recognizes the dead; they are his own, since literally or figuratively, he belongs to them: "Boychik, you're one of us," a beheaded man in prisoner garb gruesomely reveals to him.[72] The autobiographical narrator in Corman's "The Book of the Dead" insists that "the dead don't speak in our world." But of course they do. Their voices are reanimated, their felt presence materialized through the persistently figured interplay of text and image in the graphic genre.

There are many forms of drawing absence, of giving voice to that which is no longer present. Emily Steinberg's economical, nineteen-panel graphic narrative "Berlin Story: Time, Memory, Place," for example, takes us back to the Wannsee Conference, held on January 20, 1942, in Wannsee, a suburb of Berlin. It was here that Reinhard Heydrich, along with Adolph Eichmann, disclosed to a group of leaders in the Nazi Party the plans for the Final Solution. In detailed black-and-white drawings, Steinberg captures the pastoral serenity and lushness of the grounds of the neoclassical villa where the luncheon meeting took place—its exterior fountains and gardens, its elegance and opulence. The dense crosshatching and attention to detail, however, stand in direct, unswerving contrast to what is so obviously and eerily not there. In graphic understatement, what is missing, what is absent from these panels is any sight of life. There are no human beings depicted in these drawings, no sign of the fifteen "high ranking Nazi officials, all men, between the ages of 32 and 52," nor of the millions of Jews and other victims of the Shoah whose fates were being adjudicated with alarmingly dispassionate contempt as they "discussed various methods of execution." Here the understatement of the scene reflects the matter-of-fact, pragmatic negotiations that took place around the table. It is through absence, what is not drawn, that evokes, simultaneously, presence and its antithesis. In a prelude to the retrospective portrayal of the meeting that ushered in the Final Solution, the graphic artist, born on September 8, 1964, as she wonders, "Twenty years before . . . this unbelievable shit was going down," explains her motivations for traveling to Berlin, "the belly of the beast, the epicenter of all things Third Reich." As she confesses, "To say I'm obsessed with Nazis and the Holocaust is a gross understatement."[73]

Similarly, aware of her preoccupation and predisposition toward such strong identification with the Shoah and with her familial past, Kurzweil asks, "Why does it feel like I'm not the protagonist of my own life?"[74] And while she wants, as she puts it, a kind of comforting narrative closure to her own story—"Something tougher than myself, something with edges and corners, something with a beginning, a middle, and an end"—she comes to recognize the value in the open-endedness of the story.[75] Despite the propensity to define oneself solely in terms of this legacy and to see the shape of the world determined by the atrocities of the past, the shared stories of the Holocaust are transformative for both the bearer of such stories and the recipient. The opening of Spiegelman's traumatic box of horrors—that is, the extended legacy of the Holocaust—is seen in Kurzweil's graphic memoir as disruptive but also curiously reassuring. Kurzweil seems to have achieved something of a working through of her ambivalence and apprehension, her lingering qualms about autonomy and self-formation, through the course of the memoir. As the narrative grows to a close, Kurzweil shows her image and that of her mother as shadows, the outlines of figures that pull apart, each leaning in a different direction as they board flights headed to different destinations. Both mother and daughter—the child and grandchild of survivors—seem to have conditionally resolved the separation anxiety that is a response to an originating loss, the point of traumatic origin. Thus Kurzweil shows this long-embattled and deeply ambivalent struggle for self-containment to be, if not resolved, then for the moment provisionally disentangled. Kurzweil draws on a two-page spread the three generations of women each separated from the other in distinct circular panels, each contained, encircled, by her own "made" world but "in sight" of and beholden to the other.[76]

This image is reminiscent of the earlier drawing of Kurzweil isolated, alone in the circled panel, and separated from her words as she warily watches herself type them.[77] But in this later image, something has been resolved. Kurzweil has moved beyond the text into the lives of the other women, recognizing her indebtedness and consanguinity but also her distance. Yet such movement is not without its occasional regression. Immediately following this scene, Kurzweil draws herself, as in her childhood, awakened by fears and unable to sleep. Her mother's admonitions notwithstanding—"You're a big girl"—Kurzweil reverts to her childlike, infantilized state as she climbs into her mother's bed for comfort and security.[78] There is no easy resolution to the family drama, but Kurzweil's humorously portrayed awareness of her continuing anxieties goes a long way in navigating them. If sleep is a metaphor for the unconscious, then in the memoir's final scene, Kurzweil shows herself controlling her fears. Once again, she draws herself now in her own domestic space unable to sleep. Her immediate response to the ambush of unrestrained, recurrent anxieties is to regress. Crying out, as she did as a child, for her mother, Kurzweil draws herself, once again, going back in time, morphing into her preadolescent state. Yet in this final episode, Kurzweil is able to talk herself back into sleep by invoking the relaxation techniques taught to her by her mother. It is thus the soothing incantation of her mother's words—"You start to reeelax . . . your neck and your head . . . until everything is safe . . . your mind is calm . . . your breathing is slow . . . and deep"—that lull her into sleep.[79] In some ways, unsurprisingly, part of the humorous, self-parodic resolution to the family drama is the recognition that we inevitably, to one extent or another, become our mothers. But her indebtedness here is taken with good-humored surrender rather than being the source of arresting infantilization or regressive defiance. The final image is one of Kurzweil asleep in her own bed, for, after all, as the American Jewish poet Delmore Schwartz famously said in his own coming-of-age-story, "in dreams begin responsibilities."[80]

Finally, at the narrative's close, the grandchild of survivors is able to erect her own home and fill it with her own self-fashioned artifacts, creating her own space in the narrative of her life, which, as she puts it, "reminds me that my life is my own, and it has not, although at times it might seem otherwise, been prewritten."[81] Thus the memoir concludes with the third-generation graphic artist looking to the future, her life not mortgaged to nor eclipsed by the past. Neither is it defined solely by the past, by an arresting trauma. Leela Corman's autobiographical narrator in the short piece "The Blood Road" travels to Buchenwald, the site of the "family legacy," where, rather than being felled by the magnitude of the experience, she feels "defiantly alive."[82] Characteristic of third-generation narratives, Corman will make a future. This forward movement reflects, as I've suggested elsewhere, Amir Eshel's argument that "as contemporary literature engages modernity's man-made catastrophes, it also moves toward the future"—that is, "by expanding our vocabularies, by probing the human ability to act, and by prompting reflection and debate," modes of contemporary literature may engage with history, even its darkest moments, and at the same time resist a future overshadowed by the events of the past.[83] This is accomplished, in large part, by refiguring both language and genre, through a fluid, elastic bending of traditional forms and structures, as we find in contemporary graphic literature. Acquiring and structuring found knowledge of the past, as we find in Kurzweil's graphic memoir as elsewhere in the literature, enables the grandchild of survivors to recognize and to a significant extent resolve her own fears, locating her comportment and disposition within a legitimate context of suffering. While her grandmother's stories interrupt the narrative of her own life, they also give shape to it. And while neither she nor her mother "want[s] to seem like some . . . victim of history," each is acutely aware of the responsibilities inherent in living in a post-Holocaust world.[84] As her grandmother urgently and generously acknowledges, "Ohh! My stories! Tree times I read your book. I say, my granddaughter, she listen, all dis time she listen! My stories are not in vain!"[85] Storytelling thus binds them to each other, locates them in a history larger than themselves, defines the present, and gives meaning to the future.

The Deuteronomic imperative to graft the covenantal bonds onto the future, bearing witness to subsequent generations, is midrashically reinterpreted in response to such fractures in ongoing testimony. The long-standing tradition in Jewish law and text to transmit the narrative of the past, words imparted and carried into the future, is foundational to the legacy of Holocaust memory and testimony. The resonant injunction to remember creates the conditions for continuing the transmission of personal narratives of lives lived and lost in the Holocaust. The obligatory call to perform memory thus sets the stage for literary and graphic representations of the Shoah, the foundational conceit for the opening of personal stories. As Berger suggests, the literature of the third generation reflects a "paradigm shift in literary representation of the Shoah for two basic reasons: it appears near the era of 'after testimony,' and it concerns itself with intergenerational transmission of a story that is both chronologically remote yet deeply personal."[86] These are, indeed, very personal narratives that represent the individual shape of suffering within the broader context of Holocaust historiography. Their scope is limited to individualized, personalized experience rather than to represent the Holocaust as a remote historical event. Thus these graphic narratives focus on a metonymic part of the whole, a piece of the puzzle that is the Holocaust. These are individual and individualizing narratives that create immediacy and urgency in their hold on specificity, in giving character to the extended if remote shape of history. The graphic comics form provides a new venue, a new opening for such exploration. The very shape of these graphic renditions is personalized, a personification of memory, individuals brought to life for the moment of articulated personhood.

Miriam Katin's child-survivor memoir *We Are on Our Own* (discussed in chapter 1) discloses one year in the life of a mother and child as they flee the Nazi invasion of their homeland and the concurrent antisemitic threats to their safety. Martin Lemelman's biographical memoir, *Mendel's Daughter* (the subject of chapter 2), is a singular portrait of his mother's hiding and survival as her family's lives are capsized. Bernice Eisenstein's *I Was a Child of Holocaust Survivors* (that frames chapter 3) unveils the coming of age of the artist as she attempts to locate her own agency in her parents' past. Amy Kurzweil's memoir, as I've discussed in this chapter, focuses on three generations of women who together attempt to negotiate the legacy of the Shoah. Joe Kubert's *Yossel*, the subject of the following chapter, presents a different approach to Holocaust history and memory that we have discussed thus far. Kubert, in his graphic novel, creates a fictionalized historical account of the Warsaw Ghetto Uprising as he imaginatively sketches the brief life of one orphaned adolescent boy who dies in the resistance and who serves as a surrogate for the graphic novelist and illustrator. While Katin's, Lemelman's, Eisenstein's, and Kurzweil's semifictionalized memoirs move back and forth in time and location, blurring and overlapping past, present, and future, Kubert's graphic novel, as I will go on to show, freezes time, remaining rooted in the past. Kubert is interested not in the present but rather in the past, in a particular moment in Holocaust history.

5

Yossel: April 19, 1943

Possible Histories

History is amoral: events occurred.
But memory is moral.
—Anne Michaels, *Fugitive Pieces*

History claims everybody, whether they
know it or like it.
—Philip Roth, "My Uchronia"

In the graphic novel *Yossel: April 19, 1943*, the late comics artist Joe Kubert (1926–2012) creates a self-referential counternarrative in which his alter ego, sixteen-year-old Yossel, is a resistance fighter in the Warsaw Ghetto Uprising.[1] The narrative, while fictionalized, is less counterfactual, however, than it is an overlay of fictional characters and imagined dialogue and action onto a distant historical event, a midrashic reinvention of responding to, animating, vivifying, and extending the narrative of the Warsaw Ghetto Uprising. In doing so, Kubert peoples the increasingly remote event with sound, with an interpretive, fantasized rereading of events and the people who participated in the resistance efforts. Through this graphic representation, Kubert has created a midrashic extension of this historical moment, one that opens the "text" of the Warsaw Ghetto Uprising and the Holocaust to further amplification. Midrash is, after all, an interpretive process of unraveling texts—texts of history and of received and recorded testimony—as a means of fleshing out the inconsistencies, the impasses, the confusions, and the uncertainties that create a chasm in the narrative, an opening for further explication, expansion, and amplification. As Sandor Goodhart suggests, midrash is a responsive, interpretive story, a "material extension of [an] earlier text," responding to "a gap or tear or hole or discontinuity of some kind; a wound, or silence, or absence, or lack. The prior text is broken in some fashion; it lacks wholeness or completeness. Something is missing from it, and midrash is a response to that hole."[2] Significantly, then, midrash "does more than just respond to a perceived gap in the text; it performs that dislocation itself; it echoes the dislocation that is already a part of the primary narrative to which it is responding."[3] That is, a midrashic reading both addresses and repeats textual dislocation and absence. Such midrashic moments create the interpretive space for the mediating perspective of the narrating voice through whose imagined filter the meaning of experience is explored and extended.

Midrashic openings thus create a historical hiatus, a matter of arresting the "texts" of history in order to reshape and unravel experience, to offer alternative readings—if not an alternative history, then an alternate angle of seeing, the position from which one witnesses and mediates events. History here becomes a motivated narrative, an interpretive extension of and response to a posited historical moment. Midrash is thus a kind of intervention of sorts, an interruption in the narrative, an interpretive aside. But such gestures of the imagination are reined in by the necessity to remain faithful to that history, thus eliding the gap between distance and proximity, between unfamiliarity and recognition, and between an uncanny condition of awareness and a vicarious participation in those events beyond one's reach. As Sara R. Horowitz suggests, through such midrashic mediations, "Holocaust fiction intercedes to fill in cognitive and psychological absences in history and memory while also reproducing gaps . . . that require of readers not distance but moral and emotional engagement."[4] Midrash creates the conditions for a kind of secondary witnessing and testimony, an active participation in those historical moments—events, textual gaps, and opacities—that preceded such mediated engagement. Thus as Horowitz explains, "By imagining oneself into these seminal events in history, one collapses temporal distance and acknowledges the traces of those events in one's present life. At the same time, the very need to imagine reinforces the experiential distance between the personal memory of the imaginer and the events recollected. Midrash thus represents an ongoing effort and an ongoing failure of memory."[5] In an attempt to bridge the gap between distance and proximity, absence and presence, midrashic engagements call attention to those occasions that invite further openings in a narrative, possibilities for the undermining of a sharp distinction between past and present in the continuing attempts to engage with that history, with that story.

Thus with the Warsaw Ghetto Uprising as the historical frame of his graphic novel, Kubert imagines a congruent, parallel narrative—as Brad Prager puts it, an "allohistorical space between what was and what might have been."[6] In introducing the narrative, Kubert writes, "This book is the result of my 'what if-?' thoughts. It is a work of fiction, based on a nightmare that was fact. There's no question in my mind that what you are about to read could have happened."[7] The conditional "could have," contingent less on temporality and more on circumstance, creates an amalgam, not only of genres—fantasy, journalistic memoir, historical fiction, comics novel—but of perspectives through which we witness the events as they unfold, underscored by the cacophonous collage of images on the book's ashen-toned pages. Against the backdrop of the Warsaw Ghetto, Kubert creates an alternative history, an account of the uprising in which he constructs a doppelgänger, an alter ego who narrates the events as he participates in them. While "allohistorical" refers to an "other" or alternative history, it also suggests the creation of the "other," a second self that exists as a marker of difference. Psychoanalytically, one identifies the other *in* oneself in order to distinguish oneself *from* the other. That is, we identify ourselves in part from what we are but also from what we are not, what we might have become, save the contingencies of history and character. Thus the "other" exists alongside the constituting, identifiable self as a kind of restraint, a measure against which the ego is kept in check, but it is also figured as an imagined, "possible" self, an aspirational ideal of the struggling ego. Aware of the fortuitous nature of his own history and the contingencies and instabilities of chance, Kubert fashions an "allo-self" as a means of mediating his fantasized fears and his identification with an "other" self. The existence of this other self, then, is a validation of self, a created identity against which one measures the capacity for vigilant self-formation and self-assessment. In other words, the imaginary other provides an opening for the exploration of possible selves.

Thus Kubert fantasizes himself as an "other" existing in an alternative history in order to vicariously—safely, belatedly, and from a distance—experience the trauma of the Shoah. The creation of an "allohistory"—an "uchronia," as Philip Roth calls the result of this imaginative, projective psychic gesture—is a matter of "disarranging the historical past."[8] In doing so, Kubert imagines himself in—literally and figuratively draws himself into—the traumatic episode of the uprising. In doing so, Kubert enters into what Alison Landsberg describes as a "transferential space" constituted by "experiential relationships with events through which [one] did not live."[9] For his ego ideal, Kubert constructs his projected self as a courageous resistance fighter in the Warsaw Ghetto, taking action on the side of good, precisely what the young Kubert, living in safety and security in New York, could not have been. In his introductory remarks to *Yossel: April 19, 1943*, Kubert outlines his own family history as the inspiration for the design of the book. In 1926, at the age of two months,

Kubert, along with his parents and older sister, fled Europe for America. Of his life growing up in Brooklyn, Kubert says, "I was lucky":

> I've given thought to the idea of what might have happened if my parents had decided not to come to America in 1926. In 1939, I was thirteen years old, attending the High School of Music and Art, in New York City. In 1939, Hitler invaded and conquered Poland. . . . The elimination of all Jews in Europe and Russia had begun with a vengeance. . . . Between 1940 and 1942, I was still in high school. Wonderful things were happening to me. . . . At the same time in Europe, people were being led into the gas chambers and fed into the ovens.[10]

Kubert's position in relation to the events he describes speaks not only to his individual family history but to his position as a Jew at a fraught time in Jewish and world history. He acknowledges the haunting chasm between what his life was and what his death could have been, and he envisions this gap as a way to reenter the register of historical feeling that the disparity between the two invites.

Kubert thus envisions his own life through the lens of a proximate, parallel history. While he and his family were enjoying the relative freedom of their reinvented lives in America, Jews were being systematically murdered throughout Europe. Kubert thus sees his and his family's lives as contingent on an auspicious turn of fortunes. As Andrew Gordon suggests, "Alternate history . . . derives from the universal human tendency to speculate about the random and arbitrary nature of existence, and about how our lives might be dramatically altered if one small event in the past were to change. We do it to congratulate ourselves on our good fortune, or to express our fear of the huge role chance plays in human existence, or to wish that our lives had gone otherwise."[11] Such motives are complicated, however, for Kubert, whose "place" in and in relation to the fictional conceit of his allohistorical graphic novel suggest a complex web of impulses and responses rather than the simple choice implied by "or" in Gordon's equation. Kubert's admission of fortune exists alongside his fear of the events that did not happen to him but that happened to others on a vast, collective scale, those whose histories, if not fates, tangentially touched on his own early origins. As Kubert acknowledges, "If my parents had not come to America, we would have been caught in that maelstrom, sucked in and pulled down with the millions of others who were lost."[12] The significance of Kubert's imagining of this alternative set of events is not only a matter of recognizing the "luck" of his fortunes but also on seeing his own originary relation to the events proximate to his own history.

Moreover, what perhaps might be considered, to a certain extent, "survivor guilt" is complicated for Kubert by the knowledge that his family was initially deterred at the port crossing in England because his mother at the time of their attempted crossing was pregnant with him. This deterrence represents to him the kind of anxiety-producing historical contingency that might have resulted in their never having left Poland. Indeed, it was only after Kubert's birth that the family, "a persistent lot," was granted permission to set sail for America.[13] At any number of points, their departure might have been aborted, resulting in the parallel history that Kubert constructs. Kubert's sense of "what might have been," more felt because a factor in his own received origin story, creates the conditions for "an exchange of existences." Kubert, in other words, takes up the narrative position of Philip Roth's recurring character Nathan Zuckerman, a position that Roth ironically identifies as foregoing "the artificial fiction" of a fixed, essential self "for the genuine, satisfying falseness of being somebody else."[14] Thus as a means of playing out the fantasy of his participation in an alternate history, this counterreality, Kubert creates a fictionalized narrative in which the narrator/protagonist is the constructed double of the artist/writer. In this way, *Yossel: April 19, 1943* enters into the transferential space of the past. He projects himself onto the character of his young narrator. In an interview, Kubert makes his relation to his protagonist very clear:

> Over the years I had been thinking off and on what would have happened to my family, to me and my siblings if my family hadn't come to the United States at that time. I heard all these horror stories going on. The concentration camps and so on. So, Yossel is a story about what if. "What would have happened if we stayed in Europe?" "What would have happened to me?" I would have still been drawing pictures, no matter what I know I would be drawing pictures. So the character in the book is me. Yossel in Hebrew is Joseph, that's my name. That's the reason I did the book.[15]

While the Hebrew name Yossef translates as Joseph in English, the diminutive Yossel corresponds to Joe. Kubert gives his protagonist his name as well as his penchant for drawing, a process of shaping his fantasies and providing the means by which to disappear into the text of his imagined history.[16] As Yossel explains, "When I was drawing, everything else disappeared. Only my drawings existed. Only the characters and the settings. Only they were real. . . . I sketch roughly at first. . . . Then, I build my drawing. Layer on layer. Watching, judging, correcting, as my drawing grows with each successive darker line . . . into a finished drawing. . . . It felt good to draw."[17] As Yossel comments on the artistic method, Kubert draws Yossel in the act of sketching his characters onto the scraps of paper that are given shape and depth on the page of Kubert's graphic novel. We thus see an image of a page of paper on the page and a hand drawing the picture on the page. Thus Kubert self-referentially conflates artist and his creation in the mutual act of creating their comics art. In transferring his imagined self, the self he escaped, as it were, onto a character whose actions, whose emotions and reactions, and whose fate he can control in the moments of the narrative, Kubert participates in a mediating midrashic intertextuality, a midrashic intervention into the text of history by creating another coexisting visual and textual narrative.

While the fictionalized protagonist Yossel tells the story of "what happened," the counternarrative that exists alongside the imagined events, as Kubert insists, "could have happened"—could have happened, that is, to Joseph, the self he did not inhabit.[18] Thus "what might have been" (in terms of the Kuberts' actual lives), "what actually occurred" (the events of the Warsaw Ghetto Uprising set against the wider scope of systematic murder), and "what if" (the invention of the double, Yossel) become conflated. Kubert thus constructs a "might-have-been" narrative, a fantasized "what-if" tale in which the graphic artist imagines himself as someone he might have become but for the accidents of history. Kubert inserts himself *inside* the events of history as well as *inside* the covers of his book as a means of asserting his place in the context of lost memories, lost because they exist beyond the reach of lived experience. As Prager proposes, "The author may be responding to the sense that he ought to have certain memories, yet does not—that he should have partaken of a particular fate, yet did not."[19] Thus through the creation of a fictional counterpart who lives a parallel existence, Kubert "is addressing his own absence of memories, a lack for which he compensates . . . by way of his alter ego."[20] In doing so, Kubert, as I've suggested, exposes at once a desire to have been that young resistance fighter, his fear that it could have happened, and his projected apprehension that, had he been the subject of this historical narrative, he would not have had the resilience and fortitude of his doppelgänger, his imagined other. Kubert thus turns an "if-only" conceit into a "what-if" hypothetical, with all the attendant anxieties and self-punishments implied by meditations on loss. As Samantha Baskind suggests, "As a child who just barely escaped Nazi tyranny, Kubert occupies a unique position—not a Holocaust survivor nor a second-generation witness but still closely attuned to the War's disastrous consequences. . . . As such . . . Kubert . . . has taken the burden of the Holocaust on as his own."[21] The relation between actuality and imagined reality thus stages the unfolding of the narrative, blurring genres and complicating the shape of memory. Kubert creates the conditions, the space in which to control the otherwise unconscious process of orchestrating and resolving—of acting out—the fulfillment of a wish. In psychoanalytic terms, it is through the symbolic structures of the dream, as Cathy Caruth points out, in relation to discourses of trauma that "unconscious, conflictual desires . . . find expression."[22] Kubert's graphic novel in this calculation is like the traumatic dream or the daydream through which the graphic artist might satisfy and find some relief in the fulfillment of his wish to have been that brave and anguished boy incarcerated in the Warsaw Ghetto, a dream that "turn[s] the psyche itself into the vehicle for expressing the terrifying literality of a history it does not completely own."[23] Thus the graphic novel as symbolic dream reveals also the graphic novelist's fear that, were he someone else, he could have been, instead, that boy who lost everything.

Neither a survivor nor the relative or descendent of someone immediately affected by the events of the Shoah, Kubert is, in Geoffrey Hartman's terms, a "witness by adoption."[24] In creating a spokesperson so clearly aligned with his own historical roots and disposition, he "adopts" the position of victim. Such "witnesses by adoption," as Hartman argues, "seek a new way to deal with a massively depressing event. They cannot testify with the same sense of historical participation, for it did not happen to *them*. This lack does not lessen, however, a moral and psychological burden. Despite missing memories . . . they look for a legacy, or a strong identification with what happened."[25] He identifies with an imagined character in order to, in Hartman's terms, borrow a "legacy" of identity.

In an attempt to construct this legacy by bridging the gap between fantasy and reality, Kubert authenticates his story in terms of both public, documented records and family archives: "Based on the stories I heard from my parents, the things I read and available historical data, I wrote and drew this book. I've incorporated information in letters my parents received from survivors and relatives during and after the war. I backtracked and reread authenticated references concerning dates, times and places. The experience was very personal. . . . It was something I felt I had to do."[26] Thus Kubert's parallel self is a boy not entirely unlike his own biography. Yossel and his family are from Yzeran, the shtetl in Poland from which Kubert's parents fled. Like Kubert, Yossel is a boy gifted in drawing comics. But here is where their fictional and actual paths diverge. While Kubert and his family set sail for a new life in America, the fictionalized Yossel and his family are ordered from their home, now designated "the property of the Reich," and are forcibly incarcerated in the Warsaw Ghetto. For Kubert, then, the events taking place in Europe, as they frame the fate of his imagined double, create a metaphorical shadow, a counterexistence with a clear, unitary antagonist within which he can mediate and judge the unraveling of events.

Kubert establishes both a direct and an indirect representation of the Shoah through a doubling of voices. While the events are narrated through an adolescent's traumatized eyes, such direct "witnessing" is doubled by the implied author's/illustrator's drawings that provide another perspective overlaid on that of the first-person narrator's account. While the author has no direct lines, his voice is created through the images that accompany the text related by his young, fractured protagonist. However, such a multidirectional perspective is complicated by the pairing of the young protagonist's own drawings with those of the graphic artist. Like his creator, the young protagonist

Yossel loves to draw comics. Early on in the story, Yossel, who narrates the unfolding chronicle of events, explains, "I have been drawing from the time I could hold a pencil. Since I was two or three years old. That's what my mother and father told me. And I always loved to draw. Especially cartoon strips. To see the things I imagined in my mind come to life on paper."[27] During one of the selections of victims, Yossel's parents and sister are deported to Auschwitz, while Yossel's life is provisionally spared because he can draw, "amusing the [guards] with . . . cartoons."[28] For Yossel, art is a provisional escape from deportation and death, a form of protest in which Yossel might temporarily, like the author, "create [his] own world" and "drive [his] fears into little corners and crevices."[29] Drawing provides the young Yossel with the invented means to take control of his life and thus create a fantasized rescue narrative. As he says, "Even in the ghetto, being able to draw gave me a feeling of salvation. A sense of security."[30] Drawing provisionally offers Yossel a sense of relief, taking him out of himself and his situation: "Often when I drew late into the night, I would fall asleep on my drawings. And then, I would dream that my characters came to life and I was with them. In the jungles, or on the spaceship, or in the big cities, or deep in the earth's core. And it was wonderful."[31] Ironically, while Yossel in fantasy escapes the ghetto, his creator inserts himself into the terror and barbarity within the ghetto walls. So too for Kubert, art is a form of protest, of resistance. *Yossel*, then, is a counterfactual narrative yet one in which the artist/writer places his imagined younger self in a narrative already set by the rearranged facts of history.

The story of the Warsaw Ghetto Uprising is narrated primarily by Yossel, Kubert's fictional counterpart, who relates the events of the uprising as they occur in the "real time" of the narrative. It is significant that Yossel is conceived as a boy in the Warsaw Ghetto rather than an adult figure who would mirror the more contemporaneous persona of the artist/writer at the time of the book's production. As Baskind argues, "Violence against children—against the most defenseless and confused—is especially difficult to tolerate. Verbal and visual representations of such constitute palpable evidence of SS depravity and callousness and are exceptionally painful."[32] To a certain extent then, in putting himself in Yossel's place, he also invites the reader to identify with his character; he puts us in Yossel's place as well, since as Baskind rightly acknowledges, "We have all been children; we have all experienced confusion, fear, and vulnerability. . . . Imagining those emotions through the eyes of a Jewish child in wartime Europe places a premium on Nazi monstrosities, augmenting and making more tangible the devastation and catastrophic impact of the Holocaust."[33] Imagining the fictionalized Yossel's participation in the resistance is not entirely beyond the realm of possibility since adults and youth were among the rebellion, minimally and insufficiently armed with weapons that had been smuggled into the ghetto.[34]

Although the controlling point of view is governed by Kubert's invented protagonist, the young voice in the midst of the experience is joined by another voice, the perspective of the distanced writer/illustrator, who draws the story that his protagonist narrates. While Kubert gives himself no actual lines in the text, the images he draws establish a lens through which we see the events unfold. Such a synchronization of narrating voices and perspectives is characteristic of Holocaust graphic narratives. For example, Katin's layered perspectives in *We Are on Our Own*—that of both her mother and herself as both a young child and adult narrator—create a widening lens through which we gain a foothold onto the events of their escape and hiding. So too Lemelman's second-generation account of his mother's life under Nazi occupation, *Mendel's Daughter*, attempts to re-create the immediacy of his mother's experiences and his own belated understanding of them by turning the narrative over to her "voice" and "authorship." In Kurzweil's third-generation graphic memoir, *Flying Couch*, three voices join in collaboration, zooming in and out as they navigate the interstices of differing narrating positions and degrees of distance. In Kubert's graphic novel, there is a doubling of voices, a self-referentiality complicated by the creation of the double, a conceit made especially emphatic in those images in which Kubert draws Yossel drawing.

Kubert illustrates his story by way of pencil sketches in large part to create the effect of "reportage."[35] The shadowing and black-and-white documentary-like images (burning buildings, crowds of people, uniformed Nazi guards, corpses splayed out on streets, frightened orphans huddled together) create a journalistic, reportorial effect, the "perfect confluence of form and function," as Baskind suggests, in which "the colorlessness evokes the immediacy of the moment and also the cold, emotional darkness of the time, in addition to the . . . severe, gloomy climate."[36] The pages of the graphic novel are dense, images without conventional panels that border on one another, interspersed with jagged, rectangularly framed text balloons. The effect is an assault of images that creates a breathless sense of urgency and immediacy. At the same time, the compounding of images, a cacophony of sound and sense, produces a claustrophobic effect, reproducing life within the shrinking, suffocating walls of the ghetto and also the experience of hiding underground, in the sewers, where the resistance fighters plan the revolt. Kubert's drawings are deeply disturbing: varying gradations of black and gray amid the colorless, leaden, deathly backdrop of the ghetto; faces made brittle by jagged lines of despair; hunched, smudged, broken figures; smokestacks bellowing dense, harsh, frenzied, black streaks. There is an ashen, somber quality to the images, suggestive of the devastating tenor of time running out, all the while creating a kind of timelessness. Kubert achieves an implied frenetic movement in these jagged cumulative images that contribute to the building of narrative tension and the heightening of an inevitable end.

The black-and-white images establish a stark austerity to the scenes, as if nothing is spared, creating a visual assault on the young protagonist as well as on the reader/viewer. The black-and-white drawings on the pages of the graphic novel are sharply contrasted to the book's cover, the only moment of color. The image on the cover is that of an incomplete, partially visible figure clad in prison garb. The left-hand side of the image bleeds off the margin of the book's cover, reaching beyond the confines of the page and, in doing so, creating the impression of timelessness, temporal as well as spatial distortions. Cut off at the left-hand shoulder, we see only an arm extended from the rolled-up sleeve of a tattered, worn, striped uniform. The prisoner's hand is upturned so that what is exposed is the tattoo on the underside of the prisoner's bared arm. The hand beckons to the viewer; its fingers are raised in entreaty, pointing to the right-hand edge of the cover, an invitation to open the pages of the book. The image of this anonymous figure—anonymous save for the number on his arm—is set against a backdrop of blue and pale-yellow stripes, the colors of the uniforms issued to concentration camp inmates. The vertically striped background also evokes bars or walled-in areas through which one cannot penetrate. In spite of the shock of color, our eyes are drawn, I would argue, to the numbers etched on the prisoner's arm, an identifying register that represents this singular individual but also all those victims of the Holocaust, those whose names were replaced by numbers.

Kubert's drawings are unrelenting images of horror: mounds of shoes, eyeglasses, hairbrushes, combs, and luggage, piled one on top of the other such that the individual items are rendered indistinct, suggestive synecdochically of the magnitude of those murdered; bodies being incinerated; enormous tanks that fill up the page; bodies hanging from lampposts; faces obliterated by death. The choice of pencil drawings rather than ink or paint is in part a gesture toward authentication, events drawn as they are recorded in the real time of the narrative. The impression of authenticity, however, is undercut throughout by its own artifice, an artifice that self-referentially creates the conditions of authenticity. The reportage and the dialogue that accompany the images, for the most part, are roughly framed in uneven rectangular and square boxes. Such sketchily windowed frames evoke billboards or newspaper entries and captions. Otherwise, text stands alone, commenting on the image and undelineated by borders or more conventional speech balloons. In a discussion of Kubert's distinctive style, Prager argues,

> The author has avoided using clearly defined lines or crisp blacks and whites. His stray pencil markings, distributed liberally across the image, some light and others dark, suggest that everything in Yossel's world transpires in . . . a gray zone. The gray that characterizes the pages is meant literally, in that it mirrors the washed-out world of the ghetto and the ash produced in the camps. . . .

> The regularity and precision of his text stands in stark contrast with the rough, imperfect images, and the juxtaposition of the two recalls an issue specific to the representation of such atrocities: Kubert's decision to represent the horrors of the Holocaust imperfectly constantly reminds readers that the images should not be taken to stand for authentic Holocaust experience. This is not a story as depicted by a witness.[37]

Prager here makes a valid distinction between "authentic" Holocaust experience and its accompanying bearing witness and the "imperfect" representation of that experience from a secondary witness, one who was not there. At the same time, however, the rough, blurred edges of the drawings, the pained faces of the victims, and the narrowing confines established through the heavy repetitiveness of unrelenting and escalating terror re-create the conditions of and foreshadow the inevitable outcome of the narrative. The visual/verbal tension established here emerges as both recognizable representations of events and a mediated interpretation of the act of bearing witness. In other words, "testimony" is expanded to include the possibility of alternate perspectives and images.

The varying shades and hues of black etchings—some only in outline—set against grayish, sepia-toned pages create an immediacy and urgency to the drawings, as if the sketches are hastily jotted down on paper while time is running out. Kubert explains, "When I finished the first page or two with pencil I felt that there was an immediacy in my drawings that I wanted to retain. . . . The effect I was looking for in the book was the feeling that the reader was looking over my shoulder while I drew what I saw happening in front of my eyes. So a lot of the drawings are incomplete. . . . I wanted the reader to feel he was right there as these events were happening."[38] The incompleteness of the drawings—their sense of unfinishedness—the absence of formal panels with distinct, separating borders, and the collage of images as they crowd onto the pages of the graphic novel all together create a kind of visual movement, a hurried momentum that captures the energy of the impending rebellion as well as the claustrophobic stagnation within the walls and in the sewers of the ghetto. Both the hurriedness and roughness of the drawings contribute to the effect of immediacy, as if they are drawn from within, as part of an interior monologue, "as if Yossel himself made them . . . as the events occurred," again conflating the artist with his young creation.[39] Kubert draws these images as if his protagonist is seeing them, images he sees before his eyes and those he conjures in the imagination.[40] The reader, "looking over the shoulder" of the graphic novelist, is invited into the immediacy, not only of the events being represented but also of the immediacy of authorial telling, a disturbingly intimate challenge to the reader.

Significantly, then, we see these images as if through the eyes of Yossel and the other victims of the ghetto and the death camp. Although the narrative takes place in the concentration camp only indirectly—as told by a witness to the horrified Yossel and others incarcerated in the Warsaw Ghetto—the perspective by which the reader views these drawings is that of an insider and outsider simultaneously. In other words, we are made privy to the horrors through the conventionally representative images but from a distance; we remain "outside" of the text, observers of the action taking place. At the same time, we are being asked to see the images from the complicated perspective of those who exist "inside" the experience of the text, a matter of being in two places simultaneously, as Alan Itkin suggests, creating the conditions in which to "imagine the scene, sensing it around them as if they were present."[41] Most often it is through Yossel's increasingly fractured and traumatized perspective by which we either "witness" or "hear" of the atrocities as he sees or learns of the events.

At one particularly horrific moment, we find ourselves looking into one of the ovens in the crematorium. The unnerving perspective we have is that of the Sonderkommandos—concentration camp prisoners forced to dispose of bodies—who have just placed a corpse into the furnace (fig. 5.1). This scene is narrated by an escapee of the death camps, the rabbi from Yossel's village, a former prisoner who, in order to survive, worked as a Sonderkommando in the gas chambers and the crematoria and whose gruesome task was to cart the dead from the gas chambers and pile them in the ovens, "three or four corpses at a time, maybe a total of seventy at once. About a thousand people a day."[42] The "I" of the text that hovers at the top right as we face the image unnervingly engages the reader in the moment of horror: "How many bodies did I carry to be incinerated? How many children? How many had I prodded into the furnace? . . . And how was it that I continued to live while so many others died?"[43] These questions are, only in part, rhetorical; we are placed in the position of silent witness but also of a bystander. The repetition of "I . . . I . . . I" pulls the reader in the position of both victim and the Sonderkommando. We see the Sonderkommandos gazing at the dead victim, and we see them from the victim's perspective, from behind his feet. Because there is no speech bubble for this utterance that emanates from the figure gazing into the oven, the text exists as a kind of disembodied aura that casts the reader, uncomfortably, in the role of the "I." The gaze of the Sonderkommando as he stands before the oven looking in is directly poised at the reader/viewer; thus the perspective from which we read the text and view the Sonderkommandos as they look in agony into the furnace is from within the oven.

Here, unsettlingly, we are in two places at once. We see the faces of the Sonderkommandos looking directly at us, yet they are looking into the incinerator. The viewer is outside looking in, yet we see the image—the feet as they extend outward—as if from inside the furnace—as if, in other words, we are the dead corpse. Disturbingly, as Baskind suggests, this grisly scene "situates the reader inside the oven, as if they were the reader's feet facing the rabbi,

"HOW MANY BODIES DID I CARRY TO BE INCINERATED? HOW MANY CHILDREN? HOW MANY HAD I PRODDED INTO THE FURNACE? I LOST COUNT. AND HOW WAS IT THAT I CONTINUED TO LIVE WHILE SO MANY OTHERS DIED?

FIGURE 5.1. The incinerator. Joe Kubert, *Yossel: April 19, 1943: A Story of the Warsaw Ghetto Uprising* (New York: iBooks, 2003), 62.

the reader thus a dead, soon-to-be-incinerated Jew. . . . Most of the drawings in Yossel sprawl into the reader's space pushing off the pages of the book, but only this one incident fully extends into that space."[44] The foreshortening of the body in the oven, which gives the illusion of depth, of the body receding into the incinerator, creates the impression of three-dimensional space as the body contracts inward. Such foreshortening and the crosshatching of the Sonderkommandos as they too recede into the shadows but from the other direction create considerable dramatic effect. Kubert thus bridges the gap between distance and proximity by creating the conditions in which we become direct witnesses through the angle of vision by which we view this image. Here the image attempts to bridge the distance between knowing and unknowability and thus creates the visual experience of witnessing *the other* from the tenuous position of *otherness*. Shoshana Felman, in a discussion of the limitations of witnessing, has suggested,

> It is . . . impossible to testify from inside otherness . . . in much the same way as it is impossible to testify, precisely, from inside death. It is impossible to testify from the inside because *the inside has no voice*. . . . In its absence to itself, the inside in *inconceivable* even to the ones who are already in. . . . And it is this threshold that now needs to be historically and philosophically recrossed. Inside the crematorium . . . there is loss: of voice, of life, of knowledge, of awareness, of truth, of the capacity to feel, of the capacity to speak. The truth of this loss constitutes precisely what it means to be inside the Holocaust. But the loss also defines an impossibility of testifying from inside to the truth of that inside. . . . The truth of the inside is even less accessible to an outsider. If it is indeed impossible to bear witness to the Holocaust from inside, it is even more impossible to testify to it from the outside. From without, the inside is entirely *ungraspable*.[45]

This image makes provisionally possible, I would like to argue, a visual crossing of the threshold of the "untransmittable" and the "inconceivable." It is in the image that Kubert attempts to place us, in Felman's terms, "neither simply inside nor simply outside, but paradoxically, *both inside and outside* . . . to set them both in motion and in dialogue with one another."[46] Thus the image speaks to the ability of the testimonial image to transcend the boundaries of otherness if only for the moment of visual rupture, all the while emphasizing the limits of such representation. Here inside and outside are "in motion and in dialogue with one another" as we move from outside the experience into the interiority of the crematorium. In witnessing this image, however, our field of vision recedes into a distance that we finally can't fathom. The interior perspective from which we view the Sonderkommandos looking into the oven all but collapses the distance between the viewer and the subject, and yet there is *all* the distance. For this image represents that which cannot finally be shown.

As David Patterson points out in his discussion of photographic images of Auschwitz, the image cannot distill the *experience* of the death camps; it cannot capture "what it was like." There is nothing of the "reassuring representable" in the image. Rather, as Patterson suggests, "Much more urgent than imagining what it was like is confronting how it implicates [the beholder of the image]."[47]

This is a truly gruesome, horrible scene, not in the least because of the complicated angle from which we experience this doubling of vision. In this simultaneity of direct and indirect narrative exposure, we are outside looking in, but we are also on the other side of the experience looking at the horrified, hopeless, and pained faces of those looking into the incinerator—that is, looking at us. Kubert thus calls into question the assumed limits of self-protective interiority by multiplying the places of the narrative gaze. The resulting depersonalization of the represented "subjects"—the dead bearer of the feet; the scowling, depleted Sonderkommandos; and the others outside the incinerators—provides an image of arresting horror that is less narrated than simply exposed.

On the pages that immediately precede this scene, we view crowds of people as they are ushered into the gas chamber and the opening of the locked doors to expose the piles of dead, gassed bodies. The perspective from which we view the body in the oven, a moment of ghastly intimacy, suddenly makes us the victim. This artistic conceit speaks to the position of the witness in terms of the limits of representation, as discussed by Jean-François Lyotard in his meditation on testimony and truth telling, "The Différend, the Referent, and the Proper Name."[48] If, Lyotard poses as a thought experiment, the only true witness is one who has seen an event with one's own eyes, then the only true witness in the case of the example of the gas chamber, "killing at the moment it was seen," or in this instance, the crematorium, is one who could not speak, since "if one is dead, one cannot testify that it is because of the gas chamber" or the crematorium. If only the dead are the true witnesses—that is, if only the dead can speak for the dead—then Holocaust memory is beyond representation, an unacceptable position to take and one that Lyotard debunks, since, as he concludes, "Auschwitz is the most real of realities."[49] As Eric Sundquist argues in response to claims of the impossibility of Holocaust representation, "There are many reasons to reject this mystification of the gas chamber, from which, like a black hole in existential space, nothing can emerge and about which no words can be ventured. There are numerous eyewitness descriptions of what transpired in the gassing procedure to which the words of someone miraculously returned from the dead would add very little."[50] In Kubert's image of the body as it extends from the oven, a body headed for incineration, we are witnesses from the position of watcher and watched, both victims of horror. The most "real of realities" is thus represented by Kubert by means of an aesthetic of horrific confirmation, with multiple perspectives authenticating the incontrovertibility of the horror. But Kubert's drawing is only that: an image. There is no pretense here that we are witnessing, as Michael Roth puts it, "the really-real—the past in its essence." Rather, such images can only make provisionally possible "flashes of understanding of the traumatic past."[51] Thus while we enter the past through the image, the artificiality and stasis of the image put us at a "fixed distance" from the past.[52] Kubert's drawn image of the Sonderkommandos looking into the incinerator as we, from our doubled-perspective, look both *from without* and *from within* is not a representation of reality, if by which we mean a reality that is perceptually present, but rather the image magnifies a representation of absence, of what once might have been, as Roth suggests.[53] We see the Sonderkommandos seeing into the incinerator; we can't see what they see. As Roland Barthes has suggested, history "is constituted only if we consider it, only if we look at it—and in order to look at it, we must be excluded from it."[54] Thus the image is, at best, a likeness of a reality from which we are absent.

Kubert develops these tensions between absence and presence in direct and indirect ways, both immediate and distant, narrated and imaged throughout the graphic novel. When, for example, we are introduced to the workings of the concentration camp, we come to such information with preestablished knowledge but also from the shocked and horrified position of Yossel and others in the ghetto who have not witnessed such events directly. We hear the witness's tales of horror as they do, as the story within the story interrupts and intervenes in the narrative. In this intersection, Kubert creates a juxtaposed "disturbance" in vision and thus in the projected interiority of the subject. It is at this juncture that we are introduced to the arrival of the messenger, "a stranger" who escaped the camps to tell the tale of horrors.[55] Starving and brutalized, "a man, or what was once a man . . . gaunt, filthy, bones pushing against translucent skin and shredded clothes, unable to stand upright. . . . such fear, such pain," the stranger reveals himself to be a landsman from Yzeran, the rebbe—not a stranger to Yossel—who was deported to the camps.[56] The narrating voices, the storytellers, are thus complicated here by the introduction of another narrator, the rabbi from the concentration camp. The tale he tells (the story within the story) is one of abject horror: people tattooed, "like animals"; shaved heads; men and women separated; "clothes . . . piled up, watches, money, eyeglasses, luggage, anything of value . . . taken"; inmates assigned to barracks, to hard labor, "no place to move . . . no place to breathe," beaten, starved, murdered, "fed into ovens."[57] It is here that the rebbe, before miraculously escaping, saw Yossel's mother, father, and sister, who during one of the selections in the camp "joined a long line heading toward a building . . . [with] a smokestack pouring a stinking black plume. . . . The last time anyone saw them."[58] The rebbe covers his eyes because he can't bear to see again what he has witnessed in the death camp as he recounts his experience.[59] In the retelling of events, however, he can no longer bring himself to see what he has already seen. The rebbe's instinctive reaction to his own tale of escalating horror—head buried deep in his hands—mirrors the reader's response to the event that we hear through eyewitness testimony and through the secondary, mediated witnessing of the images that animate the story. Such a layering of voices from different perspectives speaks to the communal efforts involved in testimony.

Kubert's indirect narrative voice is created by the images and icons of the experience that Yossel and the rebbe articulate in the text that follows alongside the images. In setting the text for the most part in jagged frames, separated from the images, Kubert creates two developing plotlines that intersect, if not visually, then thematically. When, for example, Yossel hears the rebbe's story of the destruction of the inhabitants of Yzeran, the young protagonist responds by saying, "His words formed vivid pictures in my mind. I could see the things he described, as if they were happening in front of my eyes."[60] The rebbe's words are transformed into pictures. In this moment, Kubert creates three interlocking directions of witnessing, of giving testimony: the rebbe's firsthand witnessing—"I have seen this with my own eyes"; Yossel's narrative response to the rebbe's words, a secondhand witnessing; and the graphic artist's drawing of representative images of the atrocities that the rebbe relates and that Yossel imagines.[61] Here author/illustrator and protagonist merge in Yossel's insistence that "I **had** to draw so the pictures would sink into my brain. So I could see the things he described."[62] Here witnessing is a matter of seeing both without and within (as illustrated in the scene of the oven).

Bearing witness, thus, is a collective enterprise, a chorused expression of lamentation and moral reckoning and the ongoing articulation and extension of memory. For it is Kubert who visualizes the rebbe's story that Yossel "hears."[63] Under the text box at the bottom of the page on which the rebbe begins his story is a frighteningly intense drawing of a collection of faces huddled together, faces distorted in pain and suffering against a backdrop of jagged, peaked lines representing the barbed enclosures of the cattle car in which they are imprisoned and the concentration camp that is their destination. The shapes of the heads are disproportionate to bodies we cannot see, for the figures are cut off below their faces, a collective expression of the magnitude of suffering Kubert wants to covey: faces imploring, mouths stretched open in soundless lamentation. Words here are unnecessary, to be sure, since the starkness of the image represents the enormity of the scene, but also the lack of intermediating text implies that their cries go unheard. These are images unconstrained by panels or frames, suggesting the uncontained disposition of the Nazi genocide, a willful departure from the norms of decency and humanity. Indeed, the two faces at the upper-left corner of the image look more animalistic than human.[64]

The degradation of all that is human is reflected in a later image of camp inmates, similarly dressed in prison garb, faceless, reduced to numbers. The rebbe, holding his anguished face in his hands, describes the sight of rows upon rows of prisoners: "Those inmates who passed before my eyes were no longer people. No longer human. Numbers. Tattooed animals. . . . They were only grey, slow moving ghosts."[65] The roughly sketched drawing below the text box evokes the familiar image of the assent of humans, the forward-looking evolution of humanity. In Kubert's image, we see the corruption of humanity. Walking in the same direction, the line of prisoners represents the descent of humankind (fig. 5.2). Such dissonant and arresting images represent the dislocation, upheaval, and eradication of lives, the very tenor of existence for those victims of the Shoah.

Through the synchronistic chorus of visual images and text, Kubert thus creates a mosaic of narrating perspectives, drawing upon a variety of stylistic and recurring Holocaust tropes and conceits that enact the fractured, catastrophic rupture of lives and history. At one particular juncture in the narrative, there is a disturbing mirror image of discordant icons, the visual doubling of a swastika on the upper-left side of one page and the Star of David on the bottom of the facing page. The one, the swastika—a symbol of destruction—is on the rise, and the other, the Star of David—a symbol of survival—is shown descending. We see these two images as a piece—what is and what once was.[66] Such iconic tensions and the characteristic jagged lines of the images reflect the escalating Nazi assault that forces the narrative into the moment of the rebellion.

Kubert also depicts life in the ghetto in heavy, ominous black tones, dark lines scribbled over shapes to represent the tense, chaotic uncertainty and confusion of the moment of the rebellion. The resistance fighters, gathered in the sewers of the ghetto, are further hidden in the shadows of Kubert's drawings (fig. 5.3). The frantic motion represented by the jagged dark lines suggests the urgency of the moment, the experience of hiding in the sewers and its claustrophobic fear created by the layering of scrawled, overlapping,

FIGURE 5.2. The descent of humankind. Joe Kubert, *Yossel: April 19, 1943: A Story of the Warsaw Ghetto Uprising* (New York: iBooks, 2003), 46.

FIGURE 5.3. Hiding in the sewers. Joe Kubert, *Yossel: April 19, 1943: A Story of the Warsaw Ghetto Uprising* (New York: iBooks, 2003), 116.

indistinct marks. Kubert creates a kind of heaviness in these images, the foreboding weight of the moment. The thick gradations of shades, shadows, and textures represent the gradations of traumatic memory but also the increasing movement and progression of the Germans as they advance in order "to purge the ghetto, to deport or kill the entire population, to eliminate all signs of an uprising, to destroy the ghetto, to raze it to the ground, to leave no one alive."[67] Kubert draws Yossel and the other resistance fighters waiting in the sewers for the onslaught, submerged under the weight of heavy crosshatching with severe black lines, their faces obscured. Kubert thus creates the desperate, tense moment of the impending arrival of the armed Germans: "They were coming. . . . In a moment they would be here. . . . They were here."[68] Each instant of the Nazis' menacing approach is isolated in a separate rectangular text box, the boxes functioning as footsteps as they march toward the impending confrontation and conflagration. Such a technique—gradations of black and white, crosshatching, and shadowing—throughout the narrative contributes to the tense, heavy, claustrophobic weight of terror and suffering.

There are no humorous interludes here as there are in Amy Kurzweil's third-generation narrative (the subject of the previous chapter); there are no moments that shift in temporality and location to a softer, colorful, more hopeful time such as those—albeit infrequent—in Miriam Katin's memoir (the subject of chapter 1). There are no retrospective moments in which the narrator self-parodically looks back at her own coming of age as the child of Holocaust survivors as we saw in Bernice Eisenstein's second-generation memoir (chapter 3). There is no continuing generational saga that establishes the conceit for Lemelman's drawings of hands as metonyms extending memory into the future (as discussed in chapter 2), for here, in Kubert's graphic novel, there is no future.

Tragically, of course, neither Kubert's nor Yossel's drawings can save the young protagonist from the barbarities of history, nor can drawing ultimately protect those brought to life for the performative moment of the graphic novel. Drawing here functions tropically much as speech does. That is, the images function prosopopeically; they reanimate the dead, a substitution for the absent voice of the speaker. In creating presence, as Susan Gubar suggests, the figure of prosopopoeia rhetorically "allows the authors who manipulate it to summon the posthumous voice, to conceive of subjectivity enduring beyond the concentration camp, and thereby to suggest that the anguish of the Shoah does not, and will not dissipate."[69] Prosopopoeia is thus a trope of substitution, of validating and commemorating the presence of the dead by reanimating their voices, but it is also a trope of memory. Those reimagined, re-enlivened—if only for the textual moment—stand in for the dead, voices of collective trauma. Drawing has been in Kubert's graphic novel a metonymy for the expression of life and voice, a trope of defense against the immediate reality of the uncontrollable situation in which his characters find themselves. As Yossel admits, "I hold my scraps of paper and pencil close to my chest. Protecting them. As if they were my mother. My father. My sister."[70] Yet the staccato punctuation of the lines anticipates and enacts the fragmentation of his world, shattered as it is spoken.

Yossel, after learning of his family's final moments, finds himself no longer able to imagine them onto the page. The rebbe's silence after disclosing the moment in which he saw Yossel's mother, father, and sister walking into the crematorium is a harbinger of the protagonist's inability to represent them through images as well as his own impending silence—that is, his death. Yossel can no longer draw them for they can no longer be imagined back into life, and visualizing their deaths is too painful for the young protagonist to imagine. Yossel thus mourns their absence through graphic silence: "I wanted to draw a picture of Papa, Mama, Chaiya. I could see them clearly in my mind. . . .

I could not draw them. I could not."[71] Paradoxically, the young artist for whom drawing enabled him to imagine, if momentarily, "a different world" cannot bear to draw their deaths into life.[72] Drawing thus ultimately fails him, an absence mirrored in the textual caesura, the silence of the moment: "No one said a word. Only silence. . . . Struck dumb with fear, pain, and sorrow."[73] The absence of creation is made emphatic by the single drawing that fills the entire page on which Yossel is shown holding a pencil up against a blank sheet of paper. His pencil poised on the page, he cannot draw (fig. 5.4).

The blank spaces on the page thus function tropically, visual representations of loss, an ellipsis of speech. As Susan Suleiman suggests, "The white spaces signal emptiness, a disruption or arrest of speech, but they can also be thought of as reinforcing the meanings of reduction and abandonment," figures of negation.[74] Yossel thus anticipates the outcome of the work of the resistance and thus prefigures his own death: "If I could not draw, I would not survive."[75] Like the image he draws of a superman descending in the narrow confines of the ghetto walls set aflame by the Germans, Yossel too, at the novel's end, will go down in flames. The golems of his cartoon drawings can no longer save the Jewish people from disaster. The superheroes of Yossel's revenge fantasy are only that: a fantastical, imaginary projection of his desire. Ironically, however, as Baskind points out, "those same superheroes keep Yossel alive longer than many other Warsaw Jews, including his parents and sister, who are deported and killed in the camps, because Nazis exploit the young artist's talent for their own enjoyment."[76] There are limits, however, even to the opportunistic, self-interested amusement of those who take even greater satisfaction in mass murder. And so the fantasy of rescue and retribution played out in Yossel's drawings collapse in the face of real catastrophe.[77]

Yossel's superheroes, endowed with superhuman capabilities—creations that could "tear the German soldiers apart . . . vanquish all evil doers . . . make mincemeat of the swastika murderers"—even in fantasy, can no longer save him,[78] for the "real monsters" are the Nazis, against whom Yossel's imaginary heroes are impotent, living only on paper and in his wishful fantasies—"if only our heroes were real."[79] The "real heroes," of course, were those like the fictionalized Yossel and Mordecai, the leader of the resistance who fought and died.[80] Thus Kubert will draw Yossel into life only to erase him. Indeed, we have anticipated the protagonist's death from the first line of the narrative in which Yossel, descending the rickety cellar steps above which he hears "the incessant bombing" of the Nazis as they storm the ghetto, portends, "I am going to die here." Ironically, the affirmation of self—"I am" (the opening words of the graphic novel)—in the very moment of articulation is reversed, inverted by its dissociative, deafening antagonist. Indeed, as Yossel warns us at the novel's opening, "there is no escape."[81] Thus at the story's end, Yossel will narrate his own death through silence.

FIGURE 5.4. The absence of creation. Joe Kubert, *Yossel: April 19, 1943: A Story of the Warsaw Ghetto Uprising* (New York: iBooks, 2003), 81.

Hiding in the sewers that stretch beneath the ghetto, the insurgency is insufficiently armed against the Nazis who hunt them down with flamethrowers. The repeated images of Yossel's face moments before his death show him to be aging instantaneously (fig. 5.5). Coming into focus from the initial faceless sketch at the far left, Yossel is no longer the young, innocent boy that he is shown to be in the second iteration of this quadrupled image. In the third depiction, he looks directly at the reader/viewer, only to look away in the fourth drawing. Looking up once again in the penultimate visage, his gaze is

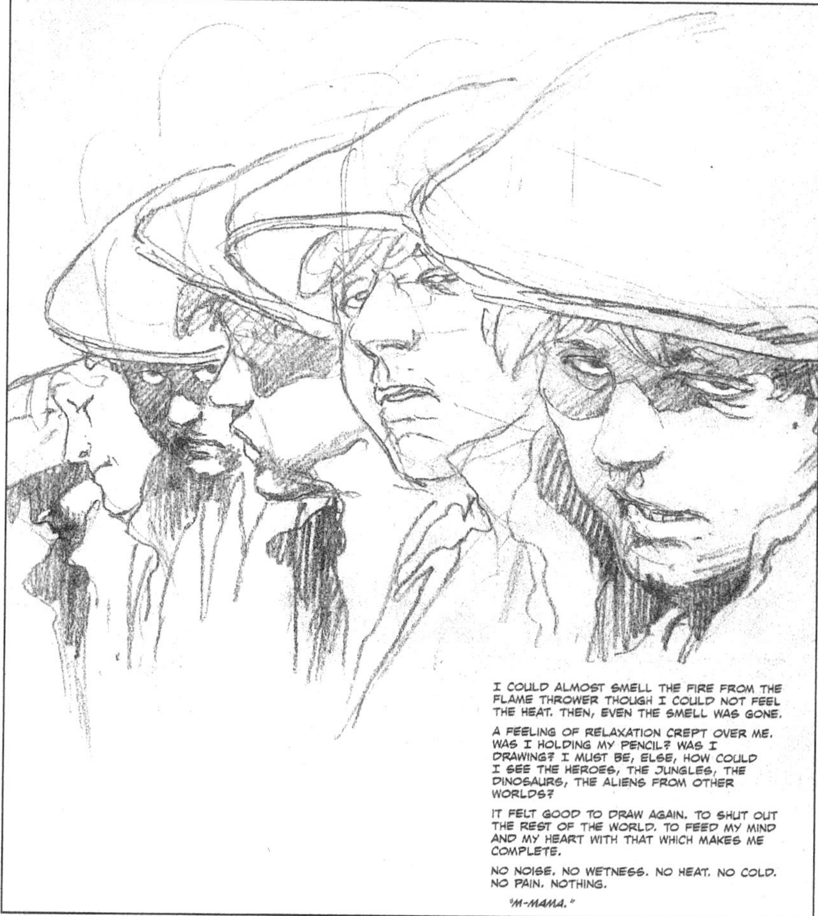

I COULD ALMOST SMELL THE FIRE FROM THE FLAME THROWER THOUGH I COULD NOT FEEL THE HEAT. THEN, EVEN THE SMELL WAS GONE.
A FEELING OF RELAXATION CREPT OVER ME. WAS I HOLDING MY PENCIL? WAS I DRAWING? I MUST BE, ELSE, HOW COULD I SEE THE HEROES, THE JUNGLES, THE DINOSAURS, THE ALIENS FROM OTHER WORLDS?
IT FELT GOOD TO DRAW AGAIN. TO SHUT OUT THE REST OF THE WORLD. TO FEED MY MIND AND MY HEART WITH THAT WHICH MAKES ME COMPLETE.
NO NOISE. NO WETNESS. NO HEAT. NO COLD. NO PAIN. NOTHING.
"M-MAMA."

FIGURE 5.5. The cry. Joe Kubert, *Yossel: April 19, 1943: A Story of the Warsaw Ghetto Uprising* (New York: iBooks, 2003), 119.

knowing, his eyes slanted, cast in recognition of his end. In the final image on the right-hand side bleeding off of the page, Yossel, Kubert's double, appears aged, dying: exhausted, defeated, face mottled, eyes heavy-lidded, sunken and darkened, receding into the depths. Yossel has indeed come to the end of the line. His final word—"M-mama"—is a universal cry, an expression of the most basic of human utterances in the face of inhuman suffering. As Eric Sundquist, in his analysis of recurring Holocaust tropes and patterns, writes, "The world of the Holocaust is pervaded by many such cries of despair—strangled, choking voices; shrieks and murmurs; stillness and muteness. No single manifestation of speech or silence is foundational, and yet the silencing of the human voice by murder surely has priority, and perhaps no human voice has greater priority than that of a child . . . calling to its mother."[82] Yossel's final cry is followed by a caesura, a break in utterance, a rupture, a rent in the narrative. On the facing page we see the armed Nazi soldiers standing over the dead body of Yossel and others of the now obliterated insurgence.

Yossel's death is followed by total silence, an *aposiopesis*, a trope signifying the deliberate suspension of speech but also the cessation of sound and voice, the complete and calculated silence signaled by the *praeciscio*, the omission and ellipsis of all words, a "simple silence."[83] This has been a narrative whose pages all along have been filled with noise, with the sounds and shapes of anguished suffering, with incomprehension, with startled awareness: the shouts of the Nazi guards; the rumbling of tanks as they plow through the uneven streets of the ghetto; the "constant flow of Jewish people that came into the ghetto . . . [carrying] all their worldly possessions on hand-carts . . . on horse and wagons"; the selections; the sputtering of the carts hauling dead bodies; the bombing; the explosions; even the whispering murmurs of the insurgence crouched in the sewers.[84] This has been a story filled with a clamor, a frenetic tenor and movement of sound—until it isn't. At the narrative's end, all sound, all text, radically stops. This sudden cessation of speech disrupts the narrative arc for the performance of silence, a rhetorical trope summoned at moments of inarticulable loss.

The final image on the last page of the book is that of a blank sheet of paper set against jagged black scribbling, a midrashic extension of the charred remains of the dead (fig. 5.6). The sheet of paper, upon which there are no words, is torn, crumpled, and partially scorched by the soot of the flames. As Baskind argues, the final page "is empty, devoid of imagery, just as Yossel is now devoid of breath."[85] Represented silence becomes the means by which Kubert reenacts annihilation, creating an afterimage of absence that remains long after the speaker is rendered speechless. This is, as Michel Kichka poses in his second-generation graphic memoir, an "eloquent" silence, eloquent because it is an expressive silence, fluid and persuasive.[86] In other words, this is a silence that speaks. From the Latin "eloqui," "speaking out," the eloquence of the silence in this final image speaks emphatically to the erasure of life that the trope of silence enacts. As Berel Lang has argued, such troping of the language in Holocaust literature "pushes certain features of writing to their limits," thus performing moments of disequilibrium, making possible the representation of the extreme and of traumatic extremity.[87] Silence is thus a trope of omission and erasure but also a figure of measurement, an expression of the depth and scope of individual and collective suffering. The understatement inherent in the final image of the blank page creates an extremity of impossible restitution in its utter silence and signals the threat to historical, collective, and personal memory. Thus the blank, charred, empty piece of paper at the novel's end is a synecdoche for voice interrupted but also an invitation to enter the space of memory, to respond to and extend the voice of the witness.

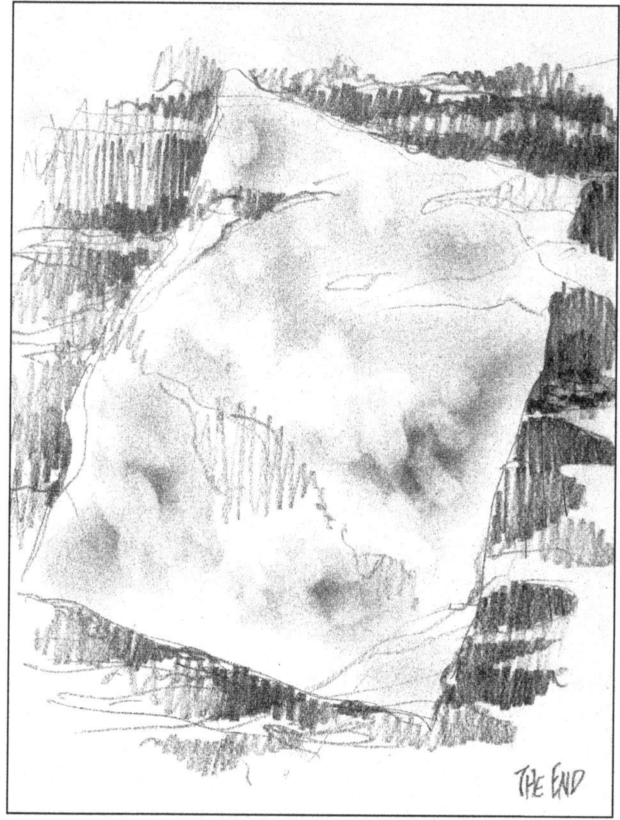

FIGURE 5.6. Annihilation. Joe Kubert, *Yossel: April 19, 1943: A Story of the Warsaw Ghetto Uprising* (New York: iBooks, 2003), 121.

Kubert thus draws his double and, by extension, himself in and out of history, fracturing the narrative, an interruption in the continuity of generations, the Holocaust—as Monica Osborne succinctly puts it, "The ultimate tear in the historical narrative."[88] Voice, after all, signifies remembrance. Thus at the narrative's close, the cessation of utterance represents the end of testimony. As Didi-Huberman suggests, "To bear witness is to tell in spite of all that which it is impossible to tell entirely. The impossible is doubled when the difficulty of telling is compounded by the difficulty of being heard."[89] The final midrashic moment, then, is a response to silence. While this final image represents silence, an absence of testimony, the blank sheet of scorched paper is itself evidence of what might have been. Throughout the graphic novel, Kubert's images have been distinguished by their incompleteness, often only outlines of unfilled-in sketches, drawings that show in their roughness the fragmentation and disintegration of a world. As Tal Bruttmann suggests, Kubert, through his variations of light and dark pencil shadings, "delivers an unfinished product."[90] The images are unfinished because bearing witness to the narrative of the past by necessity is incomplete. They remain in need of further moral reckoning. Thus Kubert's final image of a blank sheet of paper represents that on which something conditionally *might have been* or *might yet be* written.

The final image stands in place of Yossel's words, thus creating in that absence the "voice" of the graphic artist. Kubert here essentially takes over the telling by way of drawing the soundless, unnarrated image, a drawing that, paradoxically, through its emptiness, is a cautionary measure against erasure. The trope of the empty page is both an expression of absence and a substitution for text, for a language of bearing witness. Here silence is thus measured against its adversarial, insistent other—the blank piece of charred paper the material form of voice. The "silent" sheet of paper stands as sentry, witness to the events that occurred. For as the narrator of Anne Michaels's novel *Fugitive Pieces* insists, "There's no absence, if there remains even the memory of absence."[91] Kubert's final image is thus an invitation to continue testimony, a call to participatory witnessing, "to step into the presence of absence," as second-generation graphic artist Bernice Eisenstein proposes.[92] Thus as Osborne suggests, "Inherent in the practice of midrashic writing is a profound awareness of silences that cannot be filled, but to which we must respond—an understanding that our words bear an ethical responsibility to the subjects they claim to address or to reveal."[93] Yossel's silence then, as well as that of Kubert's authorial hand at the graphic novel's end, signals the eradication of voice, generations cut off, a lamentable interruption in generational continuity and the extension of memory, but one that calls for—that demands—a response.

6

Visual Landscapes of Memory

Fracturing Time and Space

> The past became present . . . Peopled with ghosts and murderers.
> —Eli Wiesel, *The Gates of the Forest*

> Can one die in Auschwitz after Auschwitz?
> —Eli Wiesel, "An Old Acquaintance"

I want to end with a return to the aftermath of war: with the liberation of the concentration camps, with the tallies of numbers dead, with the relocation and reinvention of the lives of those who survived, with the calculation of the scope and enormity of what transpired under Nazi rule, and with the articulation and extension of Holocaust memory. In this concluding chapter, I want to return, retrospectively, to 1955, to "Master Race," an early Holocaust graphic narrative, a work of comics immersed in both the felt resonances of war and its consequent responses. In many ways, as I hope to suggest, looking back provides a context for reading more contemporary Holocaust graphic narratives, setting the stage—if only in retrospect—for the ongoing dialogue that has taken place over time, an expansion of both memory and genre. Returning to an interpretive place of origin suggests a range and depth of perspective, a tunneling back in time that anticipates the extended intergenerational midrashic responses to the fractures of Holocaust history. Such a tunneling back in time opens up interpretive possibilities for situating the contemporary Holocaust graphic narrative within a range of possible directions and perspectives from which to approach and adjudicate the events of the past and their lasting imprint on post-Holocaust generations. In this regard then, I want to return to an early comics narrative from the end of the decade immediately following the war, to 1955 and the publication of Al Feldstein and Bernie Krigstein's remarkable—in both content and design—"Master Race," a short piece that is, in many ways, a precursor to the genre of Holocaust graphic narratives.

Initially published in the debut issue of EC Comics' *Impact* magazine, "Master Race," like so many works of Holocaust literary expression, defies clear generic classification. Neither a single comics panel nor an extended, unfolding narrative of the length and development that characterize the genre of Holocaust graphic narratives, "Master Race" consists of an eight-page short story arranged in a comic strip format. Its brevity and economical composition, however, are set in disquieting contrast to the depth and complexity of the seemingly innocuous backdrop for the story: an encounter between two men on a subway car. The understated economy of the composition, the anonymity of the surroundings—a subterranean passageway in an unnamed city in America (although we assume that it takes place in New York)—the matter-of-fact tone, and the largely dispassionate, implacable voice that persistently unspools, not unlike the subway train that propels ahead to its inevitable conclusion, make all the more emphatic the enormity of the situation that will unfold. Indeed, the understated backdrop that introduces the initial story line will dramatically fall into its motivational depths.

This is, as John Benson, David Kasakove, and Art Spiegelman have said, "a comic book rarity; a story with such density and breadth of technique . . . layers of meaning and detail both in its form and visual content."[1] Its brevity is deceptive; in a mere eight pages, Krigstein draws a portrait of a man derailed by memory as he plunges into the dark past. Understatement very quickly will give way to an amplification made all the more extreme by its juxtaposition. For the apparently chance encounter between two men who find themselves seated in the same subway car is not the innocent meeting of two passing strangers. These are men who have met before, and this is no chance encounter. As the anonymity and concealment of the two men give way, the one will be exposed as a victim of the Holocaust and the other man will be unmasked as perpetrator, as the commander of Belsen, the concentration camp where the other man was imprisoned. But the identity of each man is initially concealed and only slowly, ambiguously revealed. The pacing is something of a paradox: on the one hand, the ambiguity of the two men has the effect of being drawn out; on the other hand, the developing moment of identification takes place over the course of only two and a half pages, twenty fleeting panels. Such pacing establishes both stasis and motion, suggestive of the moment of trauma as the narrative movement projects its subjects into the past.

Here Krigstein and Feldstein create the conditions for a reckoning of history, a face-off between the legislated machinery of domination and annihilation and the targeted object of this tyranny. This is a story of extreme psychological depth, a revenge fantasy that captures the complex relation between victim and victimizer, persecutor and persecuted, tormenter and the condemned. It is, in large part, "the chilling, aloof, precise, clean rendering . . . this contrast between the apparently detached style and the extreme emotional content of the story" that pronounces its stark moral reckoning and unmollified judgment in response to the complex web of those responsible for the Holocaust.[2] For, while Krigstein's graphic narrative may turn on an initial ambiguity of victim and victimizer, such obscurity only exposes the inner core of malice and brutality. Its composition mirrors the chaos of the time and the motives of those responsible. The story's temporal and spatial setting—ten years since the end of the war in a place and time removed from the events of the Holocaust—establishes the conditions for the debilitating and destabilizing structures of memory and the unconscious, the ways in which the past becomes present in the extended moment of trauma. Significantly, "Master Race" re-creates the immediacy of the Holocaust in its prolonged aftermath, thus eclipsing the proximity of the "real" time in which the narrative is staged. Not entirely unlike Joe Kubert's *Yossel*, writer and illustrator have created a "what-if" historical narrative. Here narrative time gives way to psychic time, a highly charged, fraught condition in which, as the narrator of Elie Wiesel's "An Old Acquaintance" makes uncomfortably emphatic, "time changes pace, country." And "the present," that slippery, unstable place, "is in the grip of all the years black and buried."[3]

"Master Race," in outline, is the story of two men who meet, seemingly by chance, on a subway car as it travels to an undisclosed location. The story's opening scenario begins benignly and unexceptionally enough: a man descends the subway stairs, purchases a token from the clerk at the window of the kiosk, waits on the platform for the inbound train, and takes his seat on board the subway car, along with other entering passengers. But the seeming ordinariness of the action belies and ultimately exposes its grim, macabre underbelly. The juxtaposed patterns of dark and light, the claustrophobic perspective of the panels, and the peculiarly detached yet ominous narrative voice all set the tone for the extraordinary scene that follows. The descending passenger, a man we are introduced to as Carl Reissman by the disembodied, omniscient voice that speaks directly to Reissman as he enters the scene in panel 1, is cloaked in obscurity. In his initial appearance, as he descends from the light of day into the darkness of the subway, Reissman's eyes are blackened, shadowed by the brim of his hat. His face is shrouded in darkness as he purchases a subway token from the clerk seated behind a grated window. As he passes through the turnstile leading to the subway platform, he looks down, his faced masked in shadows. His back is to us as he looks toward the approaching train, and he is still partially obscured as he enters the subway car, his face only disclosed once he is seated. And even then, his eyes, unmasked, are hooded; he is a man in hiding, a man whose past at this point has yet to be unveiled, though, as we are told, a man haunted by "those bloody war years," visited by memories that "you can never forget . . . memories [that] will haunt you forever . . . as even now they haunt you while you descend the subway stairs into the quiet semi-darkness" of the station.[4] This introductory scene, again an ostensibly innocuous, ordinary occasion of a man entering a subway station—after all, the other passengers as they go through the turnstile and enter the train seem to go about their business routinely—resists the customary routinized motions of daily life. The tonal qualities of the scene, Reissman's posture and comportment as he descends the steps to the subway, the view we have of him behind the barred opening of the ticket station, and the insinuations of his past as disclosed parsimoniously by an omniscient, repetitive dark voice all create the uncanny conditions that will unfold. The familiar is defamiliarized, destabilized by patterns of concealment and ambiguity. The conditions that bring Reissman to the foreground and to the underground of the subway are, to be sure, anything but ordinary.

Indeed, this is no ordinary subway train. As it approaches the station, it too is enshrouded in the darkness of the compressed walls of the subterranean cavern. We view the train in a single panel rushing toward us, its implied motion established by the angle in which the train rounds the bend of the tracks. Significantly, this panel is introduced directly beneath the panel in which we first see Reissman. While Reissman descends from the sunlight of the street above into the underground darkness, the train emerges from the darkness of the tunnel into the semidarkness of the station. The placement of the panels and the parallel introduction of Reissman and the train, both solitary images as they advance forward in the panel, suggest the impending, inescapable relation between the two. Both the man and the train are central players in this narrative. Indeed, the following panel brings the two together, alone, as the train pulls into the station; here, as Benson, Kasakove, and Spiegelman suggest, "the viewpoint shifts to include the platform, so that Reissman and the train are now in confrontation," staged to enter the dark corridor together.[5] To be sure, the train will become Reissman's antagonist, the embodiment of and conveyance to the past darkness from which he hoped to escape. The movement of the train, as it presses forward, subsuming most of the panel, looms over the small figure of Reissman, who is minimized in the bottom-left corner of the panel's frame; only the back of his hat and shadowed upper part of his shoulders are visible. The image of the train dwarfs the figure of Reissman, and Krigstein creates the effect of the train getting ever larger as it approaches the contracting image of Reissman; the top of the train reaches all the way to the ceiling of the tunnel, and the walls on either side of the train are compressed, creating a claustrophobic, suffocating effect that seems to squeeze the waiting Reissman into the corner of the frame. As the train emerges from the darkness of the underground tunnel, its lights advancing toward the front of the panel, the "onrushing steel monster" aggressively "roars out of the black cavern, shattering the silence of the almost deserted station."[6] As the train enters the station to greet the oncoming passengers, it ominously "grinds to a hissing stop," and once the passengers are boarded, the train "lurches, thundering" as it leaves the station, entering once again "the black chasms tunneling beneath the city"—tunneling, that is, back into a memory that lies beneath the surface of the teeming life of the city but also that resides in the unconscious, that graveyard of repression.[7]

As the train "groans . . . and jerks to a stop" at the next station, another passenger will board, taking up center stage of a single, emphatic panel. The analogous introduction of this new figure, a solitary image alone in the panel, connects Reissman, the train, and the entering passenger in a triad; the parallel constructions anticipate the necessary relation of these three figures. Indeed, the subway car will be the container for the interaction between the two men, both container and prison. As the anonymous passenger settles into his seat across the aisle from Reissman, he is shown mirroring and doubling the other man's passive comportment. While he is drawn in profile and Reissman is shown from behind, both are positioned reading a newspaper. As the subway car "doors slam shut," however, Reissman's attempts to distract himself by reading the paper are thwarted by the felt presence of the other man; "the words are meaningless. Nothing has meaning any more. . . . Nothing but the sickening sensation" of the danger embodied by the other man.[8] The two men do not acknowledge one another, yet it is clear that Reissman has already, alarmingly recognized his silent companion, and in one of the few occasions in the narrative of an interior monologue, Reissman, hidden in the shadows behind the open paper and immobilized by fear, is shown with a speech balloon over his head in an expression of interior panic. As if he could will the inevitable from happening and defend himself against his escalating anxiety, Reissman ineffectually rails against conditions over which he has no control: "No! No! He can't hurt me now! He can't! He wouldn't!"[9] The move from the absolute "can't" to the conditional "wouldn't" suggests that Reissman is retreating into himself, trying to make himself invisible, a pretense of autonomy and anonymity, the delusion that the future is not mortgaged to the past.

There is, however, no defense against memory. For as the train once again departs the station and as it "screams around a curve in its subterranean route," the sound "shrill and sharp . . . setting your teeth on edge," Reissman and the anonymous passenger together are back in time, back in the reaches of memory reawakened in the darkness of a history from which there is no escape.[10] It is significant that the action that will unfurl takes place underground, for the memories that surface are encased in the unconscious, memories that, as the omniscient narrator presages, "will haunt" Reissman "forever."[11] The subway car emerges as the embodiment of Reissman's unconscious psychic state and the place to enact his deeply phobic apprehension.[12] As the train burrows deeper into the underground passageways, deeper into the labyrinth of memory, that which is hidden, concealed in memory, will emerge, memories reawakened. Memory is thus personified and the dark shape of the past anthropomorphizes itself in the figure of the man who joins Reissman on the train, a cadaverous figure who stands as guardian of the past, a black-garbed Charon who will ferry the train back in time to hell.

At this point in the narrative, however, Reissman's identity is still uncertain, as is that of the man dressed in black who appears unbidden in the doorway of the train. We are told at the story's opening that Reissman is an immigrant relocated "in America . . . ten years and thousands of miles away from [his] native Germany."[13] We know that he is haunted by memories of the war, "the horror . . . the hate . . . the suffering," despite the fact that the events took place "a long time ago."[14] But Reissman's identity during the war is shrouded in disguise. We are meant to assume by his initial hunched, defensive posture, his shadowy disposition, his frightened demeanor, and his immediate and unrestrained frightened response to the cadaverous black-clad man who enters the subway car that he is a victim, a survivor of the devastation of the Shoah. Indeed, the embarking passenger's posture, carriage, and bearing, when he boards the train in which Reissman is already encased, is ominous. The newly arrived passenger is projected onto the scene as a figure of death, one of the conductors of Paul Celan's death fugue, one whose orders condemn others to "a grave in the air."[15] Despite the fact that Reissman is incapacitated by fear, that he feels followed by some unseen menace from the past, and that he seems to recognize the black-clad figure as his tormentor, there is something off in this characterization, something disquietingly wrong in this seemingly simple equation of victim and victimizer. The repeated exhortation of "You can never forget. . . . You'll keep remembering . . . remembering," a refrain throughout the narrative that visually hangs over Reissman's head as he descends the subway stairs and huddles into the seat of the train, evokes the position of the survivor haunted by memories of the past, a characteristic archetypal pattern in Holocaust literature. Reissman thus represents here the posture of the victim in shattering fear. However, such representative signs of suffering are undercut by the ominous, forbidding tone of the narrative, the building sense of Reissman's paranoia, the extreme condition of his visual carriage, his watchful gaze, and his attempts at concealment. He looks less eroded by years of suffering than by an obsessive distrust of his surroundings. Reissman's attempts at concealment ironically suggest that he has something to hide; he does not want to be discovered.

Our attempts to identify these two men in relation to each other and to history are foiled by visual gestures of concealment and by the guiding narrative voice that follows Reissman throughout the opening panels. The story is told in second-person narration, a disconcerting and disembodied voice-over narration that introduces the story by directing the words of the text at Reissman. But the opening accusatory direct address "you"—"*You* can never forget, can you, Carl Reissman? *You* can never forget. . . . Those memories will haunt *you* forever . . . as even now they haunt *you* while *you* descent the subway stairs"—in its repetitive resonance, seems to include the reader as well as the story's protagonist in this assessment.[16] Thus the narrative voice establishes a direct address to Reissman, but it also indirectly addresses the reader, thus locating us in an uneasy relation to both Reissman and the past. The narrating voice is complicated by its position to the subject as well. While Krigstein establishes a distanced narrating voice, one "outside" the narrative, the speaker knows Reissman, recognizes him, and yet is outside the frame of the experience. Krigstein creates an omniscient authorial presence as a kind of offstage commentary, an undefined voice, not a character in its own right. Yet while this is an anonymous, distanced voice, one seemingly outside the action, it is not a disinterested presence. Rather, this is a prescient voice, a voice that will ultimately both follow and direct the narrative to its inescapable conclusion. This is a voice that both directs and warns, a cautionary voice that anticipates the story's outcome and pulls us in. It is the voice of the survivor, of one who knows, one who was *there*, a voice that threatens, not unlike that of Primo Levi's poetic speaker in "Shema," who points an admonishing finger at the poem's internal addressee, cautioning, "You who live secure / In your warm houses" to pay heed to the words of the speaking voice.[17] In both evocations of Holocaust testimony, the reader becomes that "you," an unwitting observer and participant cautioned to hear the wrathful, admonishing words of the prophet and messenger.

Our assumptions about victim and victimizer and the intentional ambiguities that shape the opening pages of the graphic narrative collapse with the sudden appearance of the anonymous passenger. The ominous, droning words of the offstage voice-over escalate, gaining both momentum and implied volume until they merge into the sounds of the train's screams as it swerves on its tracks, screams that, in turn, radically morph into "another shrill scream . . . the scream of a little man with wild eyes and black hair and a small black moustache . . . Sieg Heil . . . Sieg Heil . . . Sieg Heil!"[18] As the train plummets deeper into the traumatic past, into memory and history, in a rapid and progressive series of panels, Krigstein shows the escalating violence and intensity with which the execution of events were carried out: destruction of property, arrests, incarceration, crematories, medical experiments, mass graves. As the train descends into the past, the identities of the two men are exposed. Here, in a characteristic conceit of Holocaust narratives, the past becomes present; the past is evoked and reanimated through the language of trauma. And at that moment of return, in a series of flashbacks, Carl Reissman's identity is exposed in stages that rapidly advance over the course of the next four pages: initially, Reissman is shown to be one of a crowd of Nazi supporters, arms raised in rigid salute, possessed by a "hysterical mission of word conquest"; then he emerges as a uniformed member of the Gestapo, armed and advancing in a feverish swell of "hate that poured through the streets with clubs and guns"; he is a willing participant in pogroms, book burnings, in the "tidal wave of frenzied hate-fears and blood-letting and exploding violence . . . a wild uncontrolled wave that swept you and your kind along with it." At the final moment of exposure, Reissman is shown to rise to monstrous heights, filling a panel with blood dripping from his hands, transformed into the commander of Belsen concentration camp, overseer of "the gas chambers that hourly annihilated hundreds and hundreds of your countrymen . . . the unmerciful tortures . . . the screams in the night . . . the pitiful wailing of the doomed . . . the mad experiments with human guinea pigs . . . the wanton waste of human life."[19] As the rapid flashbacks gain momentum, Reissman's identity and that of the other man on the train move apart; their identities, at first ambiguous, separate and crystalize.

What is the effect of the initial ambiguity? Why confuse our frame of reference? The initial confusion is at least partially resolved by the subjective interiority of memory. That is, when Reissman descends the stairs into the darkness of memory, into the chasms of his unconscious fears, he is overcome by anxiety and dread, not because he feels guilt for his previous actions but because he fears retribution, the words of the survivor echoing in his head as he vows retaliatory vengeance: "Someday, I'll get you, Reissman! I'll get you . . . if it's the last thing I do!"[20] This is a deeply disturbing visual scene, not only for the fractured Reissman but for the reader. The survivor's face in this image is magnified and screaming in rage, and although he screams maniacally at Reissman, he looks directly out of the panel toward the reader. As Benson, Kasakove, and Spiegelman suggest, it is troubling that "the Man's vengeful stare is directed squarely, not only at Reissman, but at the reader as well. The reader is no longer a detached observer as he has been throughout the flashback; Reissman's guilt is now [the reader's] guilt."[21] In the recognition of the other man, whose death mask brings back his pledge of retaliation, Reissman finally becomes unhinged, a moment the narrative has anticipated all along. His already fraught condition is destabilized to the extent that his fear materializes affectively. And as we tunnel back in time, it's not entirely clear whether there is, indeed, another man who exists outside of Reissman's unconscious and debilitating psyche or if he imagines him into being.

Significantly, the nameless passenger, in his solitary, isolated appearance in the doorway of the train, is not shown boarding the subway car. Rather, suddenly, without prelude, the man abruptly appears as something of a specter on the threshold. His appearance, seemingly conjured, casts an uncanny uncertainty about his actual presence on the scene. Is this figure an actual passenger on the train? Reissman seems to be the only person aware of his presence. In fact, in a subsequent panel where Reissman and the man are shown on opposite sides of the car, there is one other seated passenger who seems unaware of them both. He is drawn with his back to both Reissman and the unidentified man. Such ambiguity would seem to suggest that the man in black, the survivor, exists solely in Reissman's unstable, fractured mind, the tangible embodiment of Reissman's already deranged condition. Indeed, the man in black seems oblivious to Reissman; as he sits intent on reading his paper, he is neither "looking at" nor "noticing" his fellow passenger. Yet Reissman, on the other hand, is sentiently aware of his antagonist. As the narrator insists in an unnerving voice that increasingly seems to exist only in Reissman's psyche, "But **you've** seen **him**, Carl! You've seen his **face**. . . . The one you **knew** someday you'd see again"[22]

Thus the function of the ambiguity in "Master Race," as well as the choice of second-person narration, is now apparent. This is, we are meant to believe, an entirely subjective experience despite the minimal interior monologue and the fact that we too see the man in black. Nonetheless, we view Reissman coming unhinged by fear, paranoia, and phobic dread. Reissman is motivated by an inherent distrust of the *other*, and thus, in a complex web of transference, he projects the object of his distrust onto himself. In his fractured, paranoid state, he transforms the other, the survivor, into the embodiment of his own monstrous character. He projects onto the other, the man in black, his own base and lethal impulses. It is rhetorically crucial that the voice that guides the narration is not the voice of Reissman's guilty conscience. We know this, in part, because of the lack of an internal monologue; we do not "hear" Reissman thinking about his past actions with anything like regret. The controlling narrative voice is one of indictment, one that targets and casts judgment on Reissman and those like him—"you and your kind."[23] The unidentified voice-over speaker accuses Reissman not only of heinous, unconscionable acts but also of cowardice, one who fled at the close of the war, "running pell-mell across Europe, hiding your clothes, losing yourself in among the streams of refugees that choked the roads and highways before the advancing allied armies."[24] His fear is that his crimes will be uncovered and that he will be held accountable; his flight and disguise after the war were designed to avoid accountability. Reissman is shown to be motivated by self-interest alone rather than any sense of guilt, shame, or acknowledged culpability. And for his unconscionable crimes, he will be punished.

Ironically, Reissman's transportation back to the darkness from which he fled is by means of the subway train, evoking the cattle cars that transported millions of concentration camp victims to their deaths. In fact, in something of a cinematic moment, the scene shifts to a panel in which we see, through a window, the faces of other passengers crowded together, eyes staring vacantly, "alone in their own little worlds of fear."[25] On the one hand, Reissman is not alone in this subway-turned-cattle-car; on the other hand, he is very much alone, encased in his fear. In this particular image, he sits on the other side of the window, separated from the other passengers; he averts his eyes from their stares. He is not one of them. A disturbingly recognizable icon of deportation and death, the train will take Reissman back to the site of his complicity in the suffering of others, to the concentration camp under his command, and ultimately to his death by railway. Krigstein has, in many ways, constructed a surreal set of images as an architecture for suggesting the interiority of the situation on the train. In an uncanny, eerie twist, it is Reissman, a Nazi commander responsible for countless deaths, who will be taken by rail to his death, for the two men stand as embodied figures of historical wreckage and reckoning: Reissman, the Nazi war criminal, and the other, nameless man on the train, a survivor who rises in his wrath to cast judgment on the other man and fulfill his pledge of revenge, to avenge the destruction and suffering that he and millions of others endured.[26] Indeed, we are meant to imagine that the survivor has been biding his time, lying in wait for the deeply apprehensive Reissman who, above all else, fears being caught.

The implicit sense that their meeting was inevitable, that, in fact, the other man, the avenging survivor, was waiting for the right moment to confront Reissman, is suggested by Krigstein's introduction of the man in black who boards the train. While Reissman senses many people exiting the train, there only seems to be one lone passenger who boards. He is introduced in his anonymity—"Someone getting on"—yet he is given his own panel; understatement and anonymity give way to magnification and specificity. The figure of the entering passenger takes up almost the entire panel; we see no one else around him. He is situated in the threshold of the train, a cadaverous figure dressed entirely in black with the exception of four blue buttons on his jacket front. His hands are held rigidly at his sides, and he is looking down and slightly to his left, we assume, at Reissman, who in the adjacent panel senses someone looking at him and experiences a "chill . . . the cold chill . . . the chill of death."[27] The successive iteration of "chill," the progression from "chill" to "cold chill" and at last to "the chill of death," has the effect, again, of both momentary stasis and movement. Interestingly, the syntax creates the impression of movement. The repeated term holds Reissman in place; he is stationary, immobilized by anxiety, but at the same time, the syntactic building, the gradation of modifiers, suggests stages of awareness and advances the movement of the narrative to its inevitable conclusion. Memory here is shown to be punitive, inescapable, and Reissman is terrified at the presence of what he has yet to see (fig. 6.1).

The entering man's stance in the doorway of the train is that of a sentry, his watchful gaze directed at the other man. He wears a death mask, "framed in a Mondrian-like abstraction of Perfect Order, the certitude of retribution that is soon to fall upon Reissman."[28] The man in black, who has yet to be identified, is clearly Reissman's antagonist, as his erect, austere bearing would suggest. He is introduced by the omniscient narrative voice simply as ". . . someone getting on . . ." The ellipses that precede and follow the abbreviated line isolate the occasion of utterance, and thus the understatement heightens the tension and signals a shift in the narrative. His arrival is a prelude to the action that will set in motion both the train and the narrative arc. The passenger may not be known to us, but he is clearly recognizable to Reissman, who, "afraid to see what you know is there," imagines his presence before he sees him.[29] The survivor is the transferential embodiment of Reissman's fear, the image a

FIGURE 6.1. The man in black. Neal Adams, Rafael Medoff, and Craig Yoe, eds., *We Spoke Out: Comic Books and the Holocaust* (San Diego, Calif.: Yoe Books / IDW, 2018), 26.

projection of the past but also of Reissman's own propensity for violence. The survivor thus might be thought of as Reissman's criminal imaginary, and curiously, even though Reissman cringes in fear of the other man, his reaction is, in part, deeply narcissistic, self-focused; he imagines himself to be still powerful, important enough to be chased over the miles, continents, and years that have separated him from his actions. The survivor is crucial to Reissman's sense of self, to his identity, to the formation and stability of his ego. Ironically, of course, it is that very impulse that destabilizes his ego and focalizes his condemnation in the narrative.

It is significant that Reissman is named right from the start but the other man is not. The opening panel of the narrative introduces Reissman by name as he descends the subway stairs; the narrator in second-person address—"you, Carl Reissman"—singles him out: an indictment. The man in black, however, remains nameless. He is a symbolic figure, representative of the millions of survivors and victims of the Shoah. Giving Reissman a name rather than allowing him to be some anonymous perpetrator targets him and holds him accountable for his crimes; he has a name and a face, a madman motivated by grandiose notions of superiority and power, for which he will be punished. He is on trial. The controlling narrative voice is itself a punitive figure, a harbinger of doom that, early on, anticipates the outcome of the confrontation between the two men. Reissman is a marked man—"the concentration camp has left its mark upon you."[30] Like Cain, driven by the basest of motives, Reissman is responsible for the murder of his "brother," his fellow neighbors, countrymen, other human beings, "people you once knew and talked to and drank beer with."[31] Like Cain, his "brother's blood cries out . . . from the ground."[32] Thus he will be called to account, "cursed" and even "more cursed."[33] Like Cain, Reissman, shunned by all, is sentenced to become "a restless wanderer on earth," bereft of hearth, home, land, and the company of others.[34] In something of an ironic turn, Reissman, willingly inured to the suffering of others by committing such violent actions on other human beings, ultimately condemns himself. For as Hannah Arendt put it in another context of second-person accusation, "Just as you supported and carried out a policy of not wanting to share the world with the Jewish people and the people of a number of other nations—as though you and your superiors had any right to determine who should and who should not inhabit the world . . . no one, that is, no member of the human race, can be expected to want to share the earth with you."[35] Thus unlike Cain, Carl Reissman's unhappy wandering will come to an end, and he will die.

There is a striking and somewhat uncanny similarity between the narrative conceit in "Master Race" and another haunting narrative that responds to the psychological aftereffects of the war. Eli Wiesel's short narrative "An Old Acquaintance"—collected in the volume of prose pieces *Legends of Our*

Time and published in 1968, over a decade after the initial publication of Feldstein and Krigstein's graphic narrative—stages a curiously similar set of circumstances in the performance of trauma.[36] "An Old Acquaintance" creates the analogous conditions of ambiguity that initially frame the 1955 comics story, conditions that ultimately cast doubt on the objectivity of events as they unravel in the interior reaches of both central characters' fraught psyches. Wiesel's "An Old Acquaintance" tells the deceptively simple story of a man riding a bus on a busy thoroughfare in Tel Aviv on a hot summer evening not long after the war. The narrative, like that of "Master Race," begins with an ordinary, unremarkable event that radically will reverse itself. The seemingly ordinary occasion of Wiesel's story is rapidly undercut by the conditions in which it is set and the lens through which we view the opening scene. Told in first-person narration by an unidentified passenger riding the bus to an undisclosed location, the seeming objectivity of the narrative perspective very quickly gives way to the narrator's debilitating anxiety. The experience of being on the bus becomes increasingly oppressive, a feeling of claustrophobia brought on by the "heavy stagnant heat which . . . weighs on every gesture and breath, blurs every image," the suffocating air that makes it difficult for Wiesel's narrator to breathe.[37] As the heat closes in on him, the narrator can barely contain his anxiety, an exaggerated response to what otherwise would be an unexceptional, if uncomfortable, summer evening on a crowded bus. In an attempt to quell his rising anxiety, the narrator focuses on another passenger, an anonymous middle-age man sitting across the aisle from him. As he does so, his anxiety only escalates. In a moment of extreme distress and with chilling conviction, he believes himself to recognize this otherwise anonymous and unexceptional fellow traveler as the Jewish barracks chief in Monovitz-Buna, one of the forced labor subcamps in Auschwitz, the concentration camp where the narrator was imprisoned. At the moment of recognition, we move into the interiority of the narrator's terribly phobic, unrestrained dread, and the bus quickly descends into the past, a descent over which he has no control.

Like the subway car in which Reissman finds himself trapped in "Master Race," the bus in Wiesel's story becomes the means of transport back in time and place, "somewhere in the universe of hate," the container for the central characters' incapacitating fear and memories of the past.[38] But it is also the restricted, constricting space of the interiority of both characters' unconscious fears. The reality of the worlds outside dissolves; nothing exists beyond the confined, claustrophobic space of both the bus and the subway car, creating the illusion of spatial immediacy. As they descend into the traumatic past, the conveyances become the compressed spaces of the unconscious, and both characters come undone by their memories. It is significant that, in both instances, the other passengers that they believe themselves to recognize only materialize inside the space of the psyche. Both antagonists are brought about by the claustrophobic conditions of the means of conveyance, and it is increasingly unclear in both narratives whether the fellow passengers, once identified, exist outside of the central characters' subjective interiority. In fact, in both instances, we come to suspect that they do not exist outside of the central characters' chaotic psychological disorientation but rather that they emerge as extreme responses to trauma, thus functioning as projections of the characters' unconscious and not entirely irrational fears.

There is an interesting turn, however, in the comparison of the two narratives, and it is in the final confrontation between the two pairs of travelers that the corresponding conditions give way. While both construct initial ambiguities concerning identity, in Feldstein and Krigstein's comics story, the ambiguity is resolved: Reissman is the Nazi war criminal; the arriving passenger, in another time and place, his victim. In Wiesel's story, however, the ambiguities are never entirely resolved. The identity of the passenger on the bus, even once seemingly recognized by the narrator, remains uneasily ambiguous. At first identified as a Jewish kapo in Monovitz-Buna, in a shape-shifting sleight of hand, he suddenly transforms into a Nazi, shouting in German. It is in the confusion of perspective that the two men, in Wiesel's narrative, become doubles, a transfer of identities, and the identities of the two men keep shifting back and forth. For Wiesel, there is no stable shape to memory. All familiar landmarks and moorings disappear; there is no mediating distance between trauma and identity. Both men, at the story's close, disembark the bus together, and while they finally part, the doubling will not, for the narrator "will carry [the other man's] secret with [him]."[39] Characteristic of Wiesel's Holocaust writing, uneasy questions of judgment and self-adjudication persist long after liberation; the perpetration of evil does not dissipate but remains forever in the survivor's sense of self, no matter how reinvented.[40]

The essential difference between the two narratives stems from their distinct authorizing perspectives. Wiesel writes from the position of survivor as one who directly experienced the events that he describes in the immediacy, urgency, and authority of the moment. Feldstein and Krigstein, American-born, write from a more distanced position of belated knowledge and indirect testimony and thus stand outside and project their vicariously imagined emotional responses onto the survivor as well as, in fantasy, enact their judgment onto the figure of the perpetrator. This essential distinction in large part accounts for the different turns that the narratives take. The response to the traumatic imprint of the relation between victim and victimizer is externalized in the comics story, but it is internalized from the point of view of the survivor in Wiesel's narrative. In the one, the impact is approximated, and in the other the psychological depth is further complicated. Thus the focus of Feldstein and Krigstein's graphic narrative is on the perpetrator as central character (even if the survivor has the final word) and Wiesel's on the survivor.

For, finally, the focus of Wiesel's Holocaust meditations is on the survivor's capacity for responsible living in the extended aftermath of the Nazi genocide rather than on revenge. Thus at the close of "An Old Acquaintance," the narrator is running from the other man, who is still "shouting obscenities and threats" to his retreating form, and the survivor is left with the certainty that he will continue "to try to understand him, to divine his evil; even at the risk of being contaminated" by such knowledge. In the final confrontation between the two men at the story's end, Wiesel's narrator, "suddenly aware of [his] impotence, of [his] defeat," will release his former tormentor; he will "let him go free."[41] Feldstein and Krigstein, conversely, will eke out judgment and ultimate retribution on the perpetrator of evil. Both narratives, then, respond to the disquieting question summoned by Wiesel's narrator: "Can one die in Auschwitz, after Auschwitz?"[42] For Wiesel, the answer is yes, again and again and again in the extended interior trauma of the Holocaust. In "Master Race," the punitive resolution is literally rather than figuratively enacted, a distinction that is made imperative in Reissman's death at the end.

The final scene of the comics narrative shows Reissman running from his persecutor, the avenging figure of the survivor who has returned to make good on his promise of vengeance. In an analogous moment to that in which Reissman first identified his antagonist, the survivor recognizes his previous tormentor. As the "spark of far-away, long-ago recognition ignites his face," the man in black menacingly rises from his seat, "his mouth set in a grim taught line," his face a skull-like mask of death, "his eyes cloud with hate, his fists clench" as he advances toward the cowering Reissman.[43] The moment of recognition brings about a shift in the power dynamic between the two men. The survivor is pictured at this moment as a crouched animal ready to spring upon his prey. The train comes to a stop and, as the doors open, Reissman, ominously encouraged by the narrative voice-over to flee, bolts from the subway car, his own face now a skeletal mask, anticipating the resolution of the impending confrontation. There is, of course, nowhere to run except in the path of the oncoming train, since he carries the fear in him. In an ironic reversal, persecutor will become persecuted, predator prey, and the man in black is shown in pursuit of Reissman, at first stalking him and then chasing him along the long corridor of the subway platform, his arms raised in castigating, final judgment. Not surprisingly, the platform is deserted save for these two men alone, together running, the one in pursuit of the other. Where are the other passengers, those disembarking or entering the subway car? The scene as the two men run along the long, seemingly endless passageway has a surreal, nightmarish quality; in one particular image, they are shown running under a pile of emaciated, distorted bodies of the dead. In this nightmare, they are frozen, alone, together alone; it is their isolated, private trauma being played out despite the fact that the black-clad pursuer is a representative figure, a "personification of the millions . . . caught" in the chaos and malignancy of the times.[44] Once again, it is not clear whether his antagonist aggressively pursues Reissman outside the confines of his distorted psyche.

Notably, in the final scene of "Master Race," on the last page, the consistently ever-present voice-over is no longer present. The panels in which Reissman falls to his death are silent. As the subway approaches, the man in black halts, his hands now at his sides as he watches the receding Reissman run, arms outstretched toward the oncoming train. The nine consecutive narrow panels in which Reissman falls from the platform slow time; he is shown falling in slow motion as his foot slips from the platform and in a last-ditch effort seems to grasp onto the side of the platform. We see him lose his grip of the rail, and slowly, in nine deliberate, progressive panels, we see him fall to his death. As Art Spiegelman suggests, "The cumulative effect carries an impact—simultaneously visceral and intellectual."[45] But Reissman's death as he falls onto the rails of an approaching subway train is cloaked in initial ambiguity. Does he fall or does he jump? In the final analysis, we are meant to believe that his death was unintentional, at least on his part. The silence of the scene is shattered by his death, followed by a panel in which both sound and motion are achieved in the depiction of the series of repeated images of the faces of the passengers on board the train as it crushes Reissman. As Benson and others suggest, the last image of the train as it pounds ahead toward the front of the panel "reflects back to the nearly identical panel on page 1. There is a return to the every day reality that existed before the drama began."[46] The final four panels show the man in black as he is viewed not only by the reader but, for the first time, by other passengers as they disembark, disturbed and confused by what has just occurred, a man who fell onto the rails. No one on the train was witness to the chase since we have been meant to believe that his pursuer was a figment of Reissman's fantasy. However, in a disconcerting turn of events, it now seems that there is indeed another figure who exists outside of Reissman's imagination. The man in black, now visible to others, responds to the passengers' queries by affirming the intentionality of Reissman's death: "He ran up the platform and then jumped under the wheels of the train coming in the other way."[47] Despite the fact that, from our vantage point outside the story, we have seen Reissman grasp onto the rails in a futile attempt to stave off his fall, the man in black, the survivor and sole witness to this event, spins it to shift the onus of responsibility onto Reissman. It is the survivor who will now orchestrate the events. There is a kind of elegance to the final moment of reckoning. The survivor, in perfect simplicity, describes the physical action of Reissman's punishment to close a narrative developed to this point primarily in the psychic terrain of paranoia.

But the story concludes ambiguously. Having been asked by one of the passengers in the penultimate panel whether he had ever seen the dead man before, the man in black denies any familiarity, any previous association with the other man. Yet his negative reply is arrested in midsentence; the man in black starts to say more but stops: "No! He . . ."[48] In the final panel, the man in black is shown alone, as he was in his first iteration. We see him from behind, walking away into the darkness—into the dark corridor of the panel, the darkness of the past and the interior darkness of that which remains concealed in memory. He is no longer needed, at least not on this occasion, since he has fulfilled his obligation to avenge. As he departs the scene, he completes the utterance begun in the previous panel, yet there is no one present in the final panel to hear the completion of his thought. The final words of the narrative, spoken by the survivor who, either speaking aloud or to himself, denies any connection between the two men: "He was a perfect stranger . . ."[49] Significantly, the story ends with an ellipsis, a trailing off, suggestive of that which is still unsaid and what may still become. The open-ended nature of the closing panel makes emphatic the imperative for ongoing Holocaust testimony and accountability.

Epilogue

An Inheritance of Memory

> There are moments when the filament of time bends, loops, blurs. The present becomes permeable. The past leaps forward and insists itself upon us without warning.
> —Julie Orringer, *Flight Portfolio*

> Another history, not his, not one he'd ever know, sifted its weight over him like ash.
> —Ehud Havazelet, *Bearing the Body*

As I hope to have shown throughout this book, Holocaust graphic narratives provide a unique space for the exploration and expression of traumatic rupture. Through the intersection of text and image and the wide range of modes of visualizing trauma, graphic narratives contribute to the project of the midrashic extension of memory. The visual elements of the medium create a doubling of experience in creating simultaneously a multiplicity of narrative and visual points of view. As Jane L. Chapman, Dan Ellin, and Adam Sherif suggest, "As cultural record, the comics form can serve as a prompt and space for negotiations on the common ground between history, trauma, memory and testimony."[1] The medium lends itself to a personal and personalizing mode of expression that, in the instances of the graphic narratives I have examined here, explores the contours of mediated and inherited memory. Through the blending and blurring of both genre and narrative perspective, made emphatic by visual as well as textual cues, the graphic narrative focuses simultaneously on the teller and the story that is being told. In doing so, layers of stories and storytellers intersect in mediating the experience of understanding historical circumstances larger than oneself, a history that defines and gives shape to individual consciousness. The intersection and disjunction in temporality and location—both a moving back and forth and a simultaneity in time and place—as established through the arrangement and juxtaposition of image and text create the destabilizing conditions for the continuing and unresolved aftereffects of the traumatic imprint of the Holocaust, aftereffects that invite further description, interpretation, and the response of ethical testimony.

As I've suggested in my introductory remarks, there is a long history of response by comics artists to the Nazi era, and a substantial body of literature bears witness to the extension of Holocaust memory and its traumatic imprint. The graphic narrative, as a hybrid form that draws on the complex relations between text and image, creates the discursive conditions for a disruption of temporal linearity and spatial boundaries. The disruption makes emphatic the extended legacy of the Holocaust and its accompanying moral and ethical register. The graphic narratives that I have discussed in this book are largely contemporary gestures of history and testimony as these expressions unfold intergenerationally. Further, the genre of the Holocaust graphic narrative, as it has developed over the decades since the end of the Second World War, emerges from the convergence of these two discursive forms: graphic narrative and Holocaust testimony. These two forms together perform a midrashic extension of memory, bracketing history as it comments on it.

While all the narratives discussed here attempt to get at the generational extension of memory and trauma as mediated by the intersection of words and images, they display an elastic and fluid range of possibilities in the ways in which text and image are mediated and orchestrated. All pay tribute to memory as Holocaust graphic narratives navigate and negotiate their way through the past. All share characteristics drawn from the twinned genres of Holocaust literature and the medium of comics: the enactment of traumatic rupture; the blurring of genres; the bending, blending, and bleeding of past and present; the layering of narrative voices; the intersection of history and the imagination; the establishment of distance and proximity; the self-referential interplay of narrating voices; the temporal and spatial transitions as we move through time and place and memory; the creation of immediacy and urgency; the attempts at authenticity in the telling of stories that have no end.

In Holocaust graphic narratives, the speech act itself is materialized as performative, especially so because of the inherently performative character of the drawn image set against the stage of history. Simply put, the pictures speak. Further, the creation of text bubbles, as I suggest at the beginning, makes narrative voice a visual artifact of memory, a living expression of historical reckoning and accountability. Such a materializing of voice takes a variety of expressive, interpretive forms: the rectangular speech boxes and panels suggestive of the ways in which memory is contained and hidden in Miriam Katin's *We Are on Our Own* and whose soft edges blur memory; the way that speech is contained within the panels or is left hanging, unbracketed, in Martin Lemelman's *Mendel's Daughter*, as a way of insisting on the literalization of the speaking voice; the way that text is inscribed directly on the drawings in Bernice Eisenstein's *I Was a Child of Holocaust Survivors* so that the image "speaks"; the circular speech balloons of the present juxtaposed to the antiquated, worn text of the past that demonstrates the intergenerational extension of memory and trauma in Amy Kurzweil's *Flying Couch*; the sharp, staccato, penciled irregularities of the text boxes in Joe Kubert's *Yossel*, suggestive of the tenuousness of breath remaining; and the looming text that hangs over the Nazi war criminal in Al Feldstein and Bernie Krigstein's "Master Race," following him to his retributive end. Finally, where there is no text, where there is, instead, a deafening absence of voice, the silence materializes as a caution against the erosion of testimony and the erasure of history.

Through the elastic shapes of intersecting and overlapping text and image, Holocaust graphic narratives create new ways of envisioning memory and testimony, new ways of entering the text of history. As Hillary Chute suggests, through such visual-verbal structures, the genre "can offer an absorptive intimacy with their narratives while defamiliarizing received images of history."[2] Such a defamiliarizing of the image reshapes our perception of the events of history by juxtaposing the uncanny with the familiar, the seen with the unseen, *in the image*. The image defamiliarizes, disfigures, in order to make familiar—that is, the recognizable shape of the limitations of representability, the limits of knowing. In other words, the image shapes memory by what is visualized but also what is elided; that is, the image suggests absence, its uncanny other. Paradoxically the image both draws us into the past and, at the same time, reflects back to us what we cannot perceive. There is value in knowing what we do not—cannot—know: a blueprint for the continuation of testimony that is interactive, performative, and responsive. The genre of comics storytelling distills an immediacy and urgency that places both reader and narrator / graphic artist in the midst of the experience of what it means to be a collaborative and participatory witness to traumatic memory.

Thus as I hope to have shown, Holocaust graphic narratives constitute a genre of *difference*, a prism of contrasts, tensions, antitheses, and juxtaposed perspectives. Such a hybridity of voices and structures magnifies a refracting lens, a bending of the light through which we view the traumatic past. It amplifies its subjects by penetrating, by making visible, moments of traumatic experience. Graphic narratives, as Chute proposes, "intervene against a culture of invisibility by taking . . . the risk of representation. . . . Trauma does not always have to be disappearance; it can be plentitude, an excess of signification."[3] These richly figured works of art and narration make the past present in the immediacy and proximity of the visual, material recall of memory. Such visual-textual encounters thus conflate primary and secondary modes of witnessing, bridging the gap amplified by the erosions of time and distance. As a genre of witnessing then, Holocaust graphic narratives, in retracing the traumatic tracks of memory, inscribe the weight of history on generations that follow in its wake.

Acknowledgments

Comics and Holocaust graphic narratives were a decidedly new and unexpected turn in my scholarship, and I am indebted to many people for their assistance and encouragement as I began thinking about verbal-visual performances of memory and trauma. My engagement with the genre began when several students enrolled in my Holocaust literature seminar, after having read Art Spiegelman's *Maus*, asked me if I would consider offering a course on the Jewish graphic novel. Preparing for that course constituted my first venture into the history of Jewish comics and the rich and growing field of Jewish graphic narratives.

Not only my students but my colleagues at Trinity University and elsewhere have been enormously encouraging and helpful. I would like to thank, in particular, my colleagues in the Department of Communication, Aaron Delwiche and Jennifer Henderson. I would like to thank them both for their gracious and good-natured help with the language of comics and their tolerance for yet one more question. I would also like to thank Jackson Pollock scholar Michael Schreyach, in the Department of Art and Art History, for his generous tutorial on foreshortening and other art-related matters.

I am, as always, grateful to have such generous and supportive colleagues and friends outside of my own institution. I would like to thank Alan L. Berger, Raddock Family Eminent Scholar Chair in Holocaust Studies at Florida Atlantic University, in particular, for pointing me in the direction of commentary on the black-and-white fire of the Torah. I very much appreciate the thoughtful guidance of David Patterson, Hillel A. Feinberg Chair in Holocaust Studies at the University of Texas at Dallas, and I would like to recognize his invaluable work on the ethics of the image in *The Holocaust and the Nonrepresentable: Literary and Photographic Transcendence* (SUNY Press, 2018), which came to inform my thinking for part of chapter 5. I also am indebted to my friend and colleague Debra Shostak, professor emerita of English at the College of Wooster, for pointing out the similarity in Miriam Katin's drawings and German expressionism, and, in particular, the work of the German expressionist Käthe Kollwitz. I would also like to express my appreciation to Samantha Baskind, Ranen Omer-Sherman, and Sarah Lightman for their advice and encouragement when I first began the project. In addition to those mentioned already, I would like to thank Hilene Flanzbaum, Sandor Goodhart, Holli Levitsky, Sharon Oster, and my friends and colleagues who meet annually at the Jewish American and Holocaust Literature Symposium, an open and accommodating forum for freewheeling and good-humored dialogue and for introducing new directions in the related fields of Jewish American and Holocaust studies.

As always, I am grateful for the funding for this project that I have received from Trinity University and for the enthusiastic support of Claudia Stokes, chair of the English Department. I would like to recognize the excellent work of my two Mellon Summer Undergraduate Research Fellows, Julia Poage and Ariel Del Vecchio, who assisted me in exploring the complex forms of memorial art. I would also like to thank our department secretary, Stephanie Velasquez, for her help with securing permissions, formatting, and scanning images for the book. I am most appreciative of the support and assistance of Elisabeth Maselli at Rutgers University Press, who was enthusiastic about the project from the start and with whom it has been a genuine pleasure to work. So too I greatly appreciate the valuable and thoughtful comments made by the two anonymous reviewers of my manuscript in its early stages. And I want to thank Willis Salomon, now as always, for cogent and sound advice on editing and revision.

To my family, for their patience and considerable forbearance in listening to me talk endlessly about Holocaust graphic narratives, for this, as in all things, I am lovingly and boundlessly grateful.

Notes

Introduction

1 Paul Gravett, interview, "Miriam Katin: Coming to Terms," December 17, 2015, http://www.paulgravett.com/articles/article/miriam_katin.
2 Leonard Rifas, "War Comics," in *The Routledge Companion to Comics*, ed. Frank Bramlett, Roy T. Cook, and Aaron Meskin (New York: Routledge, 2017), 190.
3 Hillary L. Chute, *Disaster Drawn: Visual Witness, Comics, and Documentary Form* (Cambridge, Mass.: Belknap Press / Harvard University Press, 2016), 152. Chute's book is an excellent and groundbreaking study of documentary graphic narratives and has been very influential in my own thinking about the genre, as has much of Chute's important work on comics narratives in general.
4 Ariela Freedman, "Introduction," Forum: Comics and the Canon, guest ed. Ariela Freedman, *Partial Answers: Journal of Literature and The History of Ideas* 13, no. 2 (June 2015): 251.
5 Scott McCloud, *Understanding Comics: The Invisible Art* (New York: William Morrow / HarperCollins, 1993), 63.
6 Will Eisner, *Comics and Sequential Art* (Tamarac, Fla.: Poorhouse Press, 1985).
7 See, for example, Ari Folman's graphic narrative of the Lebanon War, *Waltz with Bashir* (New York: Metropolitan, 2009); and Josh Neufeld's *A.D.: New Orleans after the Deluge*, the graphic depiction of Hurricane Katrina (New York: Pantheon, 2009). Both these authors might be considered graphic journalists rather than graphic novelists.
8 Martha J. Cutter and Cathy J. Schlund-Vials, *Redrawing the Historical Past: History, Memory, and Multiethnic Graphic Novels* (Athens: University of Georgia Press, 2018), 16.
9 McCloud, *Understanding Comics*, 66, 71.
10 Chute, *Disaster Drawn*, 1.
11 In *Understanding Comics*, 3, Scott McCloud draws his cartoon-self bemoaning the way in which comics, albeit for good reason, have been misregarded.
12 Joshua Lambert, "How Comics Help Us Combat Holocaust Fatigue," *Forward*, February 9, 2017, forward.com/culture/361784/how-comics-help-us-combat-holocaust-fatigue.

13 See Gillian Whitlock, "Autographics: The Seeing 'I' of the Comics," *Modern Fiction Studies* 52, no. 4 (2006): 967.
14 The recent fracas over Larry David's monologue on *Saturday Night Live* (November 4, 2017) as well as the "survivor" episode of *Curb Your Enthusiasm* (aired on March 7, 2004) speaks to the anxiety over the issue of Holocaust humor. For an interesting study of the history of Jewish humor in general, see Jeremy Dauber, *Jewish Comedy: A Serious History* (New York: W. W. Norton, 2017).
15 Philip Roth, "The Conversion of the Jews," in *Goodbye, Columbus and Five Short Stories* (New York: Modern Library, 1966), 150.
16 Freedman, "Introduction," 252.
17 Jan Baetens and Charlotte Pylyser, "Comics and Time," in *The Routledge Companion to Comics*, 308.
18 I am, of course, referring to Orwell's well-known essay on totalitarianism and the misuse of language, originally published in 1946, "Politics and the English Language," in *A Collection of Essays* (New York: Harvest, 1981), 170.
19 Lambert, "How Comics Help Us."
20 David Grossman, *Writing in the Dark*, trans. Jessica Cohen (New York: Farrar, Straus and Giroux, 2008), 64.
21 Saul Bellow, *The Bellarosa Connection* (New York: Penguin, 1989), 2. For a discussion of Bellow's novella in relation to *The Victim* and *Mr. Sammler's Planet*, see my chapter on "Bellow and the Holocaust" in *The Cambridge Companion to Saul Bellow*, ed. Victoria Aarons (Cambridge University Press, 2017), 55–67. Here I suggest the ways in which Bellow's three novels reflect the shifting attitudes in America toward the Holocaust.
22 Edmund de Waal, *The Hare with Amber Eyes* (New York: Farrar, Straus and Giroux, 2010), 279.
23 Jeffrey Clapp, "Nicotine Cosmopolitanism: From Italo Svevo's Trieste to Art Spiegelman's New York," Forum: Comics and the Canon, guest ed. Ariela Freedman, *Partial Answers: Journal of Literature and the History of Ideas* 13, no. 2 (June 2015): 311.
24 Chute, *Disaster Drawn*, 4.
25 Chute, 27.
26 Georges Didi-Huberman, *Images in Spite of All: Four Photographs from Auschwitz*, trans. Shane B. Lillis (Chicago: University of Chicago Press, 2008), 163.
27 Hillary L. Chute, *Graphic Women: Life Narrative and Contemporary Comics* (New York: Columbia University Press, 2010), 2.
28 Andrea Simon, *Bashert: A Granddaughter's Holocaust Quest* (Jackson: University Press of Mississippi, 2002), 38.
29 Lawrence L. Langer, *Holocaust Testimonies: The Ruins of Memory* (New Haven: Yale University Press, 1991), xv.
30 Langer, xv.
31 See, in particular, Aaron Meskin, "Defining Comics," in *The Routledge Companion to Comics*, 221–229; Hillary Chute, "Comics as Literature? Reading Graphic Narrative," *PMLA* 123, no. 2 (March 2008): 453–455; and Stephen E. Tabachnick, "Introduction," in *The Cambridge Companion to the Graphic Novel*, ed. Stephen E. Tabachnick (Cambridge, U.K.: Cambridge University Press, 2017), 1–7.
32 Chute, "Comics as Literature?," 453.
33 Chute, 459.
34 Victoria Aarons, "A Genre of Rupture: The Literary Language of the Holocaust," in *The Bloomsbury Companion to Holocaust Literature*, ed. Jenni Adams (London: Bloomsbury, 2014), 27–45.

35 Aarons, 29.
36 Berel Lang, *Holocaust Representation: Art within the Limits of History and Ethics* (Baltimore, Md.: Johns Hopkins University Press, 2000), 10.
37 Lang, 35.
38 Aarons, "A Genre of Rupture," 33.
39 See Daniel Mendelsohn's memoir *The Lost: A Search for Six of Six Million* (New York: HarperCollins, 2006), 88.
40 Amy Kurzweil, *Flying Couch: A Graphic Memoir* (New York: Catapult / Black Balloon, 2016), 47, 49.
41 I have borrowed this phrase from Howard Nemerov's poem "Life Cycle of Common Man," in *The Collected Poems of Howard Nemerov* (Chicago: University of Chicago Press, 1977).
42 Neal Adams, Rafael Medoff, and Craig Yoe, eds., *We Spoke Out: Comic Books and the Holocaust* (San Diego, Calif.: Yoe Books / IDW, 2018).
43 For readers interested in *Maus*, in particular, I would point out only a few of the substantive scholarly analyses that take on Spiegelman's work from a variety of perspectives and approaches: Hillary L. Chute's extensive work on *Maus*, including "*Maus's* Archival Images and the Postwar Comics Field," in Hillary L. Chute, *Disaster Drawn*, 153–196; Lisa Naomi Mulman, "A Tale of Two Mice: Graphic Representations of the Jew in Holocaust Narrative," in *The Jewish Graphic Novel: Critical Approaches*, ed. Samantha Baskind and Ranen Omer-Sherman (New Brunswick, N.J.: Rutgers University Press, 2010); and Jennifer Glaser, "Art Spiegelman and the Caricature Archive," in *Redrawing the Historical Past: History, Memory, and Multiethnic Graphic Novels*, ed. Martha J. Cutter and Cathy J. Schlund-Vials (Athens: University of Georgia Press, 2018). Let me reiterate that this abbreviated list only minimally reflects the extent and substance of the scholarship on this important work.
44 Samantha Baskind, "A Conversation with Miriam Katin," in *The Jewish Graphic Novel*, 240.
45 Wendy Stallard Flory, "The Search: A Graphic Narrative for Beginning to Teach about the Holocaust," in *Visualizing Jewish Narrative: Jewish Comics and Graphic Novels*, ed. Derek Parker Royal (London: Bloomsbury, 2016), 158.
46 Lemelman, *Mendel's Daughter: A Memoir* (New York: Free Press, 2006), 4.

Chapter 1

1 Paul Gravett, interview, "Miriam Katin: Coming to Terms," December 17, 2015, http://www.paulgravell.com/articles/article/miriam_katin (originally appeared in *ArtReview Magazine*, October 2015).
2 In an interview with Samantha Baskind, Katin comments on the early influence of Kollwitz's paintings: "The impression her drawings made on me must have been lasting and important"; "A Conversation with Miriam Katin," in *The Jewish Graphic Novel*, ed. Samantha Baskind and Ranen Omer-Sherman (New Brunswick, N.J.: 2008), 241. We can see this influence primarily in the soft strokes of Kollwitz's etchings and the close-ups of the faces of her female subjects.
3 Diederik Oostdijk points out in "'Draw Yourself Out of It': Miriam Katin's Graphic Metamorphosis of Trauma" that Katin "cannot only speak and write about her trauma, but that she also needs to visualize it to herself," in large part because of the inability to remember the events she describes; *Journal of Modern Jewish Studies* 17, no. 1 (2018): 86.

4 For an interesting study of child survivors and the ways in which "the threads of their past histories . . . are inextricably woven into their present lives and constitute a much longer, more complicated story," see Beth B. Cohen's *Child Survivors of the Holocaust: The Youngest Remnant and the American Experience* (New Brunswick, N.J.: Rutgers University Press, 2018), 151.
5 Miriam Katin, *We Are on Our Own: A Memoir* (Montreal: Drawn & Quarterly, 2006), 7.
6 Katin, 18.
7 Katin, 188.
8 Katin, 69.
9 Tal Bruttmann, "The Holocaust through Comics," in *Re-examining the Holocaust through Literature*, ed. Aukje Kluge and Benn E. Williams (Newcastle upon Tyne, U.K.: Cambridge Scholars, 2009), 193.
10 Katin, *We Are on Our Own*, 3.
11 Katin, 4.
12 Katin, 4.
13 Katin, 5.
14 Melvin Jules Bukiet, *Nothing Makes You Free: Writings by Descendants of Jewish Holocaust Survivors* (New York: W. W. Norton, 2003), 13.
15 Susan Rubin Suleiman, "The 1.5 Generation: Thinking about Child Survivors and the Holocaust," *American Imago* 59, no. 3 (2002): 277.
16 Suleiman, 277.
17 Samantha Baskind, "A Conversation with Miriam Katin," in *The Jewish Graphic Novel*, 237.
18 Suleiman, "The 1.5 Generation," 286.
19 Irena Klepfisz, "Poland, 1944: My Mother Is Walking down the Road," in *Truth and Lamentation: Stories and Poems on the Holocaust*, ed. Milton Teichman and Sharon Leder (Urbana: University of Illinois Press, 1994), 264.
20 Cathy Caruth, *Literature in the Ashes of History* (Baltimore, Md.: Johns Hopkins University Press, 2013), xi.
21 Caruth, 9.
22 Caruth, 6 (emphasis mine).
23 Katin, *We Are on Our Own*, 8.
24 For an interesting study of child survivors and the effects of the instability of reliable memories on identity, see Robert Krell's *Messages and Memories: Reflections on Child Survivors of the Holocaust*, 2nd ed. (Vancouver, British Columbia: Memory Press, 2001). See also Phyllis Lassner's chapter, "The American Voices of Hidden Child Survivors: Coming of Age Out of Time and Place," in *New Directions in Jewish American and Holocaust Literatures: Reading and Teaching*, ed. Victoria Aarons and Holli Levitsky (Albany: State University of New York Press, 2019), 47–68.
25 The New York Comics & Picture-Story Symposium, "The New York Comics Symposium: Miriam Katin," *Rumpus*, October 4, 2013, http://therumpus.net/2013/10/the-new-york-comics-symposium-miriam-katin/.
26 Paul Valent, *Child Survivors of the Holocaust* (New York: Brunner-Routledge, 2002), 1–2.
27 Katya Bloom, *The Embodied Self: Movement and Psychoanalysis* (New York: Routledge, 2006).
28 Bloom, 17.
29 Bloom, 204.

30 Valent, *Child Survivors*, 4–5.
31 Shoshana Felman and Dori Laub, *Testimony: Crises of Witnessing in Literature, Psychoanalysis, and History* (New York: Routledge, 1992), 75–76. See also the account written by child survivor Dori Katz, *Looking for Strangers: The True Story of My Hidden Wartime Childhood* (Chicago: University of Chicago Press, 2013).
32 Felman and Laub, *Testimony*, 76.
33 Valent, *Child Survivors*, 51.
34 Katin, *We Are on Our Own*, 126.
35 Valent, *Child Survivors*, 286.
36 Valent, 47.
37 Valent, 249.
38 Valent, 47.
39 Valent, 275.
40 Katin, *We Are on Our Own*, 3.
41 Katin, 120–121.
42 Katin, 122.
43 Katin, 120–121.
44 Katin, 118.
45 For a theoretical study of psychoanalytic play therapy and the value of play for children, see, among others, the work of Anna Freud, "*The Methods of Child Analysis*," in *The Writings of Anna Freud* (New York: International Universities Press, 1974), 1–19; and Melanie Klein, *The Psychoanalysis of Children* (London: Hogarth, 1932).
46 Valent, *Child Survivors*, 271.
47 Valent, 271.
48 Valent, 281.
49 Edmund de Waal, *The Hare with Amber Eyes* (New York: Farrar, Straus and Giroux, 2010), 15–16.
50 De Waal, 13.
51 Gravett, "Miriam Katin."
52 De Waal, *Hare with Amber Eyes*, 348 (emphasis mine).
53 Jean-Philippe Marcoux, "'To Night the Ensilenced Word': Intervocality and Postmemorial Representation in the Graphic Novel about the Holocaust," in *Visualizing Jewish Narrative: Jewish Comics and Graphic Novels*, ed. Derek Parker Royal (London: Bloomsbury, 2016), 204.
54 Katin, *We Are on Our Own*, 6.
55 Charles Hatfield, *Alternative Comics: An Emerging Literature* (Jackson: University Press of Mississippi, 2005), 57.
56 Hillary L. Chute, *Disaster Drawn: Visual Witness, Comics, and Documentary Form* (Cambridge, Mass.: Belknap / Harvard University Press, 2016), 4.
57 Julie Orringer, *Flight Portfolio* (New York: Knopf, 2019), 16.
58 Chute, *Disaster Drawn*, 4.
59 Hatfield, *Alternative Comics*, 127.
60 Harriet E. H. Earle, *Comics, Trauma, and the New Art of War* (Jackson: University Press of Mississippi, 2017), 46.
61 Katin, *We Are on Our Own*, 128.
62 Katin, 128.
63 Susan Sontag, *Regarding the Pain of Others* (New York: Farrar, Straus and Giroux, 2003), 47.
64 Susan Sontag, *On Photography* (New York: Farrar, Straus and Giroux, 1973), 4.

65 Sontag, 4.
66 Sontag, 24.
67 Sontag, 22.
68 Katin, *We Are on Our Own*, 125.
69 Berel Lang, *Holocaust Representation: Art within the Limits of History and Ethics* (Baltimore, Md.: Johns Hopkins University Press, 2000), 10, 35.
70 Lang, 9–10.
71 Lang, 36.
72 Ava Kadishson Schieber, *Present Past* (Evanston, Ill.: Northwestern University Press, 2016).
73 Chute, *Disaster Drawn*, 157.
74 Grace Paley, "The Immigrant Story," in *Enormous Changes at the Last Minute* (1974; repr., New York: Farrar, Straus, and Giroux, 1983), 171.
75 Katin, *We Are on Our Own*, 63.
76 Gravett, "Miriam Katin."
77 Samantha Baskind and Ranen Omer-Sherman, eds., *The Jewish Graphic Novel: Critical Approaches* (New Brunswick, N.J.: Rutgers University Press, 2008), 240.
78 I am drawing here upon the teaching of my professors and mentors during my PhD studies in the Rhetoric Department at the University of California, Berkeley, the poet Leonard Nathan and William J. Brandt, author of, among other works, *The Rhetoric of Argumentation* (Indianapolis, Ind.: Bobbs-Merrill, 1970), for whom I am forever grateful and whose work has long since come to inform my own.
79 See Wayne C. Booth, *The Company We Keep: An Ethics of Fiction* (Berkeley: University of California Press, 1988).
80 Katin, *We Are on Our Own*, 37.
81 Katin, 43.
82 Katin, 39.
83 Chute, *Disaster Drawn*, 206.
84 Booth, *Company We Keep*, 9, 450.
85 Cathy Caruth, *Unclaimed Experience: Trauma, Narrative, and History* (Baltimore, Md.: Johns Hopkins University Press, 1996), 7.
86 Jane L. Chapman, Dan Ellin, and Adam Sherif, *Comics, the Holocaust and Hiroshima* (London: Palgrave Macmillan, 2015), 59.
87 Scott McCloud, *Understanding Comics: The Invisible Art* (New York: William Morrow / HarperCollins, 1993), 94.
88 McCloud, 102.
89 McCloud, 67.
90 McCloud, 66.
91 Chute, *Disaster Drawn*, 35.
92 Bernard Malamud, "Idiots First," in *The Complete Stories*, ed. Robert Giroux (New York: Noonday / Farrar, Straus and Giroux, 1997), 280.
93 McCloud, *Understanding Comics*, 62.
94 McCloud, 63.
95 Harriet Earle, "Panel Transitions in Trauma Comics," *Alluvium* 2, no. 1 (2013), http://dx.doi.org/10.7766/alluvium.v2.1.02.
96 Walter Benjamin, "Theses on the Philosophy of History," in *Illuminations: Essays and Reflections*, ed. Hannah Arendt, trans. Harry Zohn (New York: Schocken, 2007), 255. I am most appreciative of one of the anonymous readers of an early version of this manuscript for reminding me of the appropriateness of Benjamin's remarks.

97 Chapman, Ellin, and Sherif, *Comics, the Holocaust and Hiroshima*, 74.
98 Earle, "Panel Transitions."
99 McCloud, *Understanding Comics*, 102.
100 For a more extended discussion of time and the intersection of temporalities and memories, see Victoria Aarons and Alan L. Berger, *Third-Generation Holocaust Representation: Trauma, History, and Memory* (Evanston, Ill.: Northwestern University Press, 2017), especially 106.
101 Chute, *Disaster Drawn*, 77.
102 Chapman, Ellin, and Sherif, *Comics, the Holocaust and Hiroshima*, 38.
103 McCloud, *Understanding Comics*, 30.
104 Rocco Versaci, *This Book Contains Graphic Language: Comics as Literature* (New York: Continuum, 2007), 98.
105 Benjamin, "Theses on the Philosophy of History," 255.
106 Chute, *Disaster Drawn*, 27.
107 Hatfield, *Alternative Comics*, 73.
108 Katin, *We Are on Our Own*, 71.
109 Katin, 72.
110 Katin, 70.
111 Arlene Stein, *Reluctant Witnesses: Survivors, Their Children, and the Rise of Holocaust Consciousness* (New York: Oxford University Press, 2014), 6.
112 Miriam Katin, *Letting It Go* (Montreal, Quebec: Drawn & Quarterly, 2013), 9.
113 Elisabeth El Refaie, *Autobiographical Comics: Life Writing in Pictures* (Jackson: University Press of Mississippi, 2012), 163.
114 Earle, *Comics, Trauma*, 17.
115 Sontag, *Regarding the Pain of Others*, 86.
116 Miriam Katin's second graphic narrative, *Letting It Go*, is something of a sequel to *We Are on Our Own*. It picks up as Katin's grown son announces to his mother his decision to move to Berlin. *Letting It Go* is a three-generational portrait of the ongoing complexities in navigating the legacy of the Holocaust.

Chapter 2

1 Eva Hoffman, *After Such Knowledge: Memory, History and the Legacy of the Holocaust* (New York: PublicAffairs, 2004), xv.
2 Hoffman, 187.
3 Martin Lemelman, *Mendel's Daughter: A Memoir* (New York: Free Press, 2006).
4 Lemelman, 147.
5 Lemelman, 5.
6 Art Spiegelman, *Maus I: A Survivor's Tale: My Father Bleeds History* (New York: Pantheon, 1986), 73.
7 Spiegelman, 40.
8 Charles Hatfield, *Alternative Comics: An Emerging Literature* (Jackson: University Press of Mississippi, 2005), 144.
9 Lemelman, *Mendel's Daughter*, 5.
10 Lemelman, 5. It is interesting to read this self-conscious guarantee of authenticity from a second-generation writer against, say, survivor Primo Levi's need to write, at the close of the author's preface that introduces his firsthand account of his deportation and experience as an inmate in Auschwitz, that "it seems to me unnecessary to add that none of the facts are invented"; *Survival in Auschwitz* (New York:

Touchstone / Simon & Schuster, 1996), 10. Of course, in articulating that which is "unnecessary" to include, Levi ironically underscores exactly the opposite and thus paraliptically calls attention to the need to punctuate the veracity of his eyewitness account.

11 Jessica Lang, *Textual Silences: Unreadability and the Holocaust* (New Brunswick, N.J.: Rutgers University Press, 2017), 66.

12 Marianne Hirsch. *Family Frames: Photography, Narrative and Postmemory* (Cambridge, Mass.: Harvard University Press, 1997), 22.

13 Lang, *Textual Silences*, 67.

14 Lemelman, *Mendel's Daughter*, 1.

15 Lemelman, 120–121.

16 Lemelman, 121.

17 Marianne Hirsch, *The Generation of Postmemory: Writing and Visual Culture after the Holocaust* (New York: Columbia University Press, 2012), 36.

18 Hirsch, 5.

19 Hirsch, 206.

20 Lemelman, *Mendel's Daughter*, 225.

21 Hillary L. Chute, "Comics as Literature? Reading Graphic Narrative," *PMLA* 123, no. 2 (March 2008): 457.

22 Leon Cohen, "Artist Sought Realism in Graphic Memoir of His Shoah-Survivor Mother," *Wisconsin Jewish Chronicle*, March 31, 2008, http://www.jewishchronicle.org/2008/03/31/artist-sought-realism-in-graphic-memoir-of-his-shoah-survivor-mother/.

23 Lemelman, *Mendel's Daughter*, 219.

24 Lemelman, 3.

25 Lemelman, 3.

26 Jean-Philippe Marcoux, "'To Night the Ensilenced Word': Intervocality and Postmemorial Representation in the Graphic Novel about the Holocaust," in *Visualizing Jewish Narrative: Jewish Comics and Graphic Novels*, ed. Derek Parker Royal (London: Bloomsbury, 2016), 206.

27 Lemelman, *Mendel's Daughter*, 4.

28 Melvin Jules Bukiet, *Nothing Makes You Free: Writings by Descendants of Jewish Holocaust Survivors* (New York: W. W. Norton, 2002), 17–18.

29 Lemelman, *Mendel's Daughter*, 211–213.

30 Lemelman, 226.

31 S. Lillian Kremer, *Witness through the Imagination: Jewish American Holocaust Literature* (Detroit, Mich.: Wayne State University Press, 1989).

32 Jane L. Chapman, Dan Ellin, and Adam Sherif, *Comics, the Holocaust and Hiroshima* (London: Palgrave Macmillan, 2015), 70.

33 Deuteronomy 11:18–19, *Tanakh: A New Translation of the Holy Scriptures According to the Traditional Hebrew Text* (Philadelphia: Jewish Publication Society, 1985), 293.

34 Art Spiegelman, *Breakdowns: Portrait of the Artist as a Young %@&*!* (New York: Pantheon, 2008).

35 Karl A. Plank, "Decentering the Holocaust: What Bezmozgis and Englander Are Talking About," *Religion & Literature* 48, no. 2 (Summer 2016): 134.

36 Heidi Schlipphacke, "The Future of Melancholia: Freud, Fassbinder, and Anxiety after War," *Pacific Coast Philology* 52, no. 1 (2017): 11–12.

37 Lemelman, *Mendel's Daughter*, 5.

38 Lemelman, 97.

39 Chute, "Comics as Literature?," 457.
40 Lemelman, *Mendel's Daughter*, 117.
41 Ruth Kluger, *Still Alive: A Holocaust Girlhood Remembered* (New York: Feminist Press, 2001), 83.
42 My Jewish Learning, accessed May, 25, 2017, http://www.myjewishlearning.com/article/ask-the-expert-covering-your-eyes-for-shema/.
43 I am indebted to one of the anonymous readers of an early version of my manuscript for drawing my attention to the Hebrew word for "hand," which adds greatly to the richness of Lemelman's drawing and thus to my analysis of it.
44 Scott McCloud, *Understanding Comics: The Invisible Art* (New York: William Morrow / HarperCollins, 1993), 63.
45 McCloud, 66.
46 I am grateful to my colleague, Holocaust scholar Alan L. Berger, for pointing out the metaphor of the black and white "fires" of the Torah. The black fire refers to the explicit meaning of the text, while the white fire—the spaces between the lines, the words, and the letters—represents the hidden, more concealed, and thus deeper meaning of the black ink on parchment. Both the black and white fires contribute to the meaning of the text.
47 Hillary L. Chute, *Disaster Drawn: Visual Witness, Comics, and Documentary Form* (Cambridge: Mass.: Belknap / Harvard University Press, 2016), 35.
48 Lemelman, *Mendel's Daughter*, 215.
49 Lemelman, 113.
50 We find this impulse to locate and articulate the stories of individual family members in contemporary Holocaust literature. Daniel Mendelsohn's third-generation memoir *The Lost: A Search for Six of Six Million*, for example, both suggests the magnitude of the devastation and focuses in on the personal, the individual. Unlike the vast and nameless scale of six million murdered—a referent routinely issued to articulate the annihilation of Jews during the Shoah and a number that in its abstraction runs the risk of effacement or of becoming a placeholder for individual lives lost—locating specific family members gives a name and a "face" to the dead, the particulars of experience.
51 Lemelman, *Mendel's Daughter*, 217.
52 Lemelman, 217.
53 Susan Gubar, "Prosopopoeia and Holocaust Poetry in English: Sylvia Plath and Her Contemporaries," *Yale Journal of Criticism* 14, no. 1 (2001): 191.
54 Nadine Fresco, "Remembering the Unknown," *International Review of Psycho-Analysis* 11 (1984): 419.
55 In Lemelman's "rewriting" of the Shema, we are reminded of Primo Levi's midrashic poem "Shema" that stands as an epigraph to his 1947 memoir, *If This Is a Man (Survival in Auschwitz): The Nazi Assault on Humanity*, trans. Stuart Woolf (New York: Touchstone / Simon & Schuster, 1996).
56 Laurike in 't Veld, "Introducing the Rwandan Genocide from a Distance: American Noir and the Animal Metaphor in 99 Days," *Journal of Graphic Novels and Comics* 6, no. 2 (2015): 140.
57 Thierry Groensteen, *Comics and Narration*, trans. Ann Miller (Jackson: University Press of Mississippi, 2013; originally published in 2011 by Presses Universitaires de France), 87.
58 Lemelman, *Mendel's Daughter*, 186.
59 Chute, *Disaster Drawn*, 21.

60 McCloud, *Understanding Comics*, 85.
61 McCloud, 69, 92.
62 Lemelman, *Mendel's Daughter*, 187.
63 Philip Roth, *Why Write? Collected Nonfiction 1960–2003* (New York: Library of America, 2017), 393.
64 Lemelman, *Mendel's Daughter*, 147.
65 Lemelman, 115.
66 Lemelman, 144.
67 Lemelman, 169.
68 Lemelman, 215.
69 Primo Levi, *The Drowned and the Saved*, trans. Raymond Rosenthal (New York: Vintage, 1989), 83–84. For an important discussion of Levi's remarks on the "true witness," see Giorgio Agamben, *Remnants of Auschwitz: The Witness and the Archive*, trans. Daniel Heller-Roazen (New York: Zone Books, 2002), esp. 33–35.
70 Eli Wiesel, "Nobel Acceptance Speech," Nobelprize.org, Nobel Media AB (2014), June 4, 2018, http://www.nobelprize.org/nobel_prizes/peace/laureates/1986/wiesel-acceptance_en.html.
71 Lemelman, *Mendel's Daughter*, 217.
72 Lemelman, 5.
73 Lemelman, "Author Interview," in *Mendel's Daughter*, 226.
74 Samantha Baskind, "A Conversation with Miriam Katin," in *The Jewish Graphic Novel: Critical Approaches*, ed. Samantha Baskind and Ranen Omer-Sherman (New Brunswick, N.J.: Rutgers University Press, 2010), 241.
75 Katin in Baskind, 237.
76 Martin Lemelman, *Two Cents Plain: My Brooklyn Boyhood* (New York: Bloomsbury, 2010), 14, 27. This line is attributed to both parents on separate but corresponding occasions.
77 Lemelman, 13.
78 Lemelman, 27.
79 Lemelman, 10.

Chapter 3

1 Bernice Eisenstein, *I Was a Child of Holocaust Survivors* (New York: Riverhead Books, 2006), 167. The phrase "the unbearable lightness of being" calls to mind Milan Kundera's 1984 novel *The Unbearable Lightness of Being* as well as Friedrich Nietzsche's notion of "eternal return," the recurrence of all things over eternity. The latter speaks to the return of memory, a characteristic preoccupation among second-generation Holocaust novelists.
2 Eva Hoffman, *After Such Knowledge: Memory, History and the Legacy of the Holocaust* (New York: PublicAffairs, 2004), 25.
3 Hoffman, 28.
4 Eisenstein, *I Was a Child*, 29.
5 Eisenstein, 178.
6 Eisenstein, 178.
7 GroupLit, "Interview with Bernice Eisenstein, Author of *I Was a Child of Holocaust Survivors*," 2011, accessed August 25, 2017, http://grouplit2011.blogspot.com/2011/11/interview-with-bernice-eisenstein-on.html.
8 Eisenstein, *I Was a Child*, 16.

9 Hillary L. Chute, *Disaster Drawn: Visual Witness, Comics, and Documentary Form* (Cambridge, Mass.: Belknap / Harvard University Press, 2016), 4.
10 Miriam Harris, "Releasing the Grip of the Ghostly: Bernice Eisenstein's *I Was a Child of Holocaust Survivors*," in *The Jewish Graphic Novel: Critical Approaches*, ed. Samantha Baskind and Ranen Omer-Sherman (New Brunswick, N.J.: Rutgers University Press, 2008), 130.
11 Jean-Philippe Marcoux, "'To Night the Ensilenced Word': Intervocality and Post-memorial Representation in the Graphic Novel about the Holocaust," in *Visualizing Jewish Narrative: Jewish Comics and Graphic Novels*, ed. Derek Parker Royal (London: Bloomsbury, 2016), 208.
12 Ehud Havazelet, "To Live in Tiflis in the Springtime," in *Like Never Before* (New York: Farrar, Straus and Giroux, 1998), 239.
13 Eisenstein, *I Was a Child*, 10.
14 Hoffman, *After Such Knowledge*, 14–15.
15 Jill Bennett, *Empathic Vision: Affect, Trauma, and Contemporary Art* (Stanford, Calif.: Stanford University Press, 2005), 2.
16 Bennett, 2.
17 Eisenstein, *I Was a Child*, 6.
18 Eisenstein, 84.
19 GroupLit, "Interview with Bernice Eisenstein."
20 Eisenstein, *I Was a Child*, 27.
21 Eisenstein, 167.
22 Eisenstein, 27. The metaphor of the protective covering of new "skin" evokes Charlotte Delbo's account in *Days and Memory*. Delbo likens the change she went through in Auschwitz to "a snake shedding its old skin"; see Charlotte Delbo, *Days and Memory*, trans. Rosette Lamont (Evanston, Ill.: Marlboro / Northwestern University Press, 2001; originally published in French as *La memoire et les jours*, 1985), 1.
23 Eisenstein, *I Was a Child*, 24.
24 Eisenstein, 20.
25 Hoffman, *After Such Knowledge*, ix.
26 GroupLit, "Interview with Bernice Eisenstein."
27 Eisenstein, *I Was a Child*, 36.
28 Eisenstein, 11.
29 Daniel Mendelsohn, *The Lost: A Search for Six of Six Million* (New York: Harper-Collins, 2006), 15.
30 Eisenstein, *I Was a Child*, 16.
31 Arlene Stein, *Reluctant Witnesses: Survivors, Their Children, and the Rise of Holocaust Consciousness* (New York: Oxford University Press, 2014), 133.
32 Susan Sontag, *Regarding the Pain of Others* (New York: Farrar, Straus and Giroux, 2003), 81.
33 Michel Kichka, *Second Generation: The Things I Didn't Tell My Father* (France: Dargaud, 2012; English trans., January 27, 2016, Amazon Digital Services), 6.
34 Kichka, 5.
35 Art Spiegelman, *Maus II: A Survivor's Tale: And Here My Troubles Began* (New York: Pantheon, 1991), 16.
36 Sidra DeKoven Ezrahi, "Representing Auschwitz," *History and Memory* 7, no. 2 (Fall–Winter 1995): 145.
37 Kichka, *Second Generation*, 6.

38 Georges Didi-Huberman, *Images in Spite of All: Four Photographs from Auschwitz*, trans. Shane B. Lillis (Chicago: University of Chicago Press, 2008), 19.
39 Kichka, *Second Generation*, 7.
40 Marianne Hirsch, *The Generation of Postmemory: Writing and Visual Culture after the Holocaust* (New York: Columbia University Press, 2012), 34.
41 Eisenstein, *I Was a Child*, 167.
42 Berel Lang, *Holocaust Representation: Art within the Limits of History and Ethics* (Baltimore, Md.: Johns Hopkins University Press, 2000), 18.
43 GroupLit, "Interview with Bernice Eisenstein."
44 Harris, "Releasing the Grip of the Ghostly," 137.
45 Harris, 130.
46 Harris, 130.
47 Samantha Baskind, "Picturing 'The Holiest Thing': Joe Kubert's Children of the Warsaw Ghetto," in *Visualizing Jewish Narrative: Jewish Comics and Graphic Novels*, ed. Derek Parker Royal (London: Bloomsbury, 2016), 177.
48 Eisenstein, *I Was a Child*, 17.
49 Eisenstein, 175.
50 Thane Rosenbaum, "An Act of Defiance," in *Elijah Visible: Stories* (New York: St. Martin's Griffin, 1996), 63.
51 Hoffman, *After Such Knowledge*, 14.
52 Thane Rosenbaum, "Cattle Car Complex," in *Elijah Visible*, 5.
53 Hoffman, *After Such Knowledge*, 28.
54 Melvin Jules Bukiet, *Nothing Makes You Free: Writings by Descendants of Jewish Holocaust Survivors* (New York: W. W. Norton, 2002), 13.
55 Hoffman, *After Such Knowledge*, 13.
56 Eisenstein, *I Was a Child*, 38.
57 Hoffman, *After Such Knowledge*, x–xi.
58 Bukiet, *Nothing Makes You Free*, 14.
59 Kichka, *Second Generation*, 18.
60 Bukiet, *Nothing Makes You Free*, 14.
61 Charles Hatfield, *Alternative Comics: An Emerging Literature* (Jackson: University Press of Mississippi, 2005), 114.
62 Eisenstein, *I Was a Child*, 25.
63 Eisenstein, 20.
64 Hatfield, *Alternative Comics*, 114–115.
65 Eisenstein, *I Was a Child*, 22.
66 Eisenstein, 53.
67 Hoffman, *After Such Knowledge*, 187.
68 Eisenstein, *I Was a Child*, 24.
69 Eisenstein, 36.
70 Hoffman, *After Such Knowledge*, 188.
71 Europe Comics, "Interview with Michel Kichka," February 4, 2016, http://www.europecomics.com/interview-with-michel-kichka/.
72 Kichka, *Second Generation*, 78.
73 Europe Comics, "Interview with Michel Kichka."
74 Marcoux, "'To Night the Ensilenced Word,'" 209.
75 Chute, *Disaster Drawn*, 223.
76 Harris, "Releasing the Grip of the Ghostly," 130.
77 Hatfield, *Alternative Comics*, 114.

78 Eisenstein, *I Was a Child*, 10.
79 Eisenstein, 61.
80 Eisenstein, 65.
81 Eisenstein, 65.
82 Scott McCloud illustratively discusses this relation between what is depicted and what is, by extension, perceived in relation to time in *Understanding Comics: The Invisible Art* (New York: HarperCollins, 1993), 99.
83 Spiegelman, *Maus II*, 41.
84 Spiegelman, 42.
85 See Sigmund Freud, "Mourning and Melancholia," in *The Standard Edition of the Complete Psychological Works of Sigmund Freud*, vol. 14 (1914–1916), trans. James Strachey (London: Hogarth, 1957).
86 Spiegelman, *Maus II*, 43.
87 Hillary L. Chute, *Graphic Women: Life Narrative & Contemporary Comics* (New York: Columbia University Press, 2010), 2.
88 Eisenstein, *I Was a Child*, 88.
89 Marcoux, "'To Night the Ensilenced Word,'" 209.
90 In GroupLit, "Interview with Bernice Eisenstein, Author of *I Was a Child of Holocaust Survivors*," 2011, accessed August 25, 2017, http://grouplit2011.blogspot.com/2011/11/interview-with-bernice-eisenstein-on.html. Eisenstein speaks to the ways in which these artists influenced her approach to the graphic novel.
91 Michael Kaminer, "Bernice Eisenstein and the Persistence of Memory," in *Graphic Details: Jewish Women's Confessional Comics in Essays and Interviews*, ed. Sarah Lightman (Jefferson, N.C.: McFarland, 2014), 166.
92 Martha Kuhlman, "The Autobiographical and Biographical Graphic Novel," in *The Cambridge Companion to the Graphic Novel*, ed. Stephen E. Tabachnick (Cambridge, U.K.: Cambridge University Press, 2017), 113.
93 Kaminer, "Bernice Eisenstein," 162.
94 Malcolm Lester, "Bernice Eisenstein," in *Graphic Details*, 220.
95 Eisenstein, *I Was a Child*, 55–56.
96 Eisenstein, 113.
97 Chute, *Disaster Drawn*, 233.
98 McCloud, *Understanding Comics*, 103.
99 Chute, *Disaster Drawn*, 233.
100 Eisenstein, *I Was a Child*, 113. Interestingly, second-generation graphic novelist Michel Kichka draws upon the metaphor of "lightness" in finally being freed from debilitating anxiety to illustrate the narrative of the past and his father's concentration camp experience. Here lightness refers not to innocence but the freedom to move within the constraints of the past. See Kichka, *Second Generation*, 104.
101 Chute, *Disaster Drawn*, 254.
102 Eisenstein, *I Was a Child*, 18.
103 Lang, *Holocaust Representation*, 18.
104 Chute, *Graphic Women*, 3.
105 Eisenstein, *I Was a Child*, 174.
106 Bukiet, *Nothing Makes You Free*, 14.
107 Eisenstein, *I Was a Child*, 91.
108 Hoffman, *After Such Knowledge*, 14.
109 Eisenstein, *I Was a Child*, 158.
110 Eisenstein, 166–167.

111 Eisenstein, 169.
112 Eisenstein, 167.
113 Eisenstein, 100.
114 GroupLit, "Interview with Bernice Eisenstein."
115 Eisenstein, *I Was a Child*, 101.
116 Eisenstein, 111.
117 Eisenstein, 101.
118 Eisenstein, 178.
119 Lang, *Holocaust Representation*, 16.
120 Eisenstein, *I Was a Child*, 179.
121 Eisenstein, 187.
122 Eisenstein, 36.
123 Eisenstein, 189.
124 Eisenstein, 14.
125 Eisenstein, 16.
126 Objects are a common trope for memory and story in the genre of Holocaust literature in general, but particularly so in second- and third-generation narratives of loss and recovery. See especially chapter 3 in Victoria Aarons and Alan L. Berger, *Third-Generation Holocaust Representation: Trauma, History, and Memory* (Evanston, Ill.: Northwestern University Press, 2017); and Paule Lévy, "Storytelling, Photography, and Mourning in Daniel Mendelsohn's *The Lost*," in *Third-Generation Holocaust Narratives: Memory in Memoir and Fiction*, ed. Victoria Aarons (Lanham, Md.: Lexington Books / Rowman & Littlefield, 2016), 57–72.
127 Eisenstein, *I Was a Child*, 24.
128 Martin Lemelman, *Mendel's Daughter: A Memoir* (New York: Free Press, 2006), 5.
129 Eisenstein, *I Was a Child*, 151–152.
130 Ariela Freedman, "Charlotte Salomon, Graphic Artist," in *Graphic Details*, 38.
131 Eisenstein, *I Was a Child*, 7.
132 Harris, "Releasing the Grip of the Ghostly," 132.
133 Anne Michaels, *Fugitive Pieces* (New York: Vintage International, 1998), 30.
134 Anne Michaels and Bernice Eisenstein, *Correspondences* (New York: Alfred A. Knopf, 2013).
135 Michaels and Eisenstein, *Correspondences*.
136 Michaels and Eisenstein.
137 Bernice Eisenstein, "Coda from Memory Unearthed," Lodz Ghetto Photographs of Henryk Ross: A Collection of Holocaust Photographs, accessed July 24, 2018, http://agolodzghetto.com/essaydetails/5?t:state:flow=19610a49-16af-4542-93f4-ff51486a3761. These words also appear in the opening line of the lyrics of "Tsu Eyens, Tsvey, Dray" ("It's One, Two, Three"), a song composed by Hans Eisler and adapted by Leyb Rozental, written in the Vilna Ghetto. See "The Songs They Sang: A Musical Narrative of the Vilna Ghetto," accessed July 24, 2018, http://www.thesongstheysang.com/images/TSTS_CD_Booklet.pdf.
138 Michaels and Eisenstein, *Correspondences*.
139 Eisenstein, *I Was a Child*, 154.
140 Eisenstein, 186.

Chapter 4

1 Amy Kurzweil, *Flying Couch: A Graphic Memoir* (New York: Catapult / Black Balloon, 2016), 51.

2 Kurzweil, 1.
3 Eva Hoffman, *After Such Knowledge: Memory, History and the Legacy of the Holocaust* (New York: PublicAffairs, 2004), 185.
4 Lisa Appignanesi, *Losing the Dead: A Family Memoir* (London: Vintage, 2000), 8.
5 Kurzweil, *Flying Couch*, 50.
6 For a very interesting discussion of a French third-generation graphic narrative, see Alan L. Berger, "Life after Death: A Third-Generation Journey in Jérémie Dres's *We Won't See Auschwitz*," in *Third-Generation Holocaust Narratives: Memory in Memoir and Fiction*, ed. Victoria Aarons (Lanham, Md.: Lexington Books, 2016), 73.
7 Kurzweil, *Flying Couch*, 51.
8 Charles Hatfield, *Alternative Comics: An Emerging Literature* (Jackson: University Press of Mississippi, 2005), 109.
9 Philip Roth, *The Counterlife* (New York: Farrar Straus Giroux, 1988), 124, 370.
10 Adam Phillips, *Missing Out: In Praise of the Unlived Life* (New York: Farrar, Straus and Giroux, 2012), 35.
11 Rocco Versaci, *This Book Contains Graphic Language: Comics as Literature* (New York: Continuum, 2007), 94.
12 Creative Writing at the New School, "Q&A with MFA Alum Amy Kurzweil," November 9, 2016, https://newschoolwriting.org/qa-with-mfa-alum-amy-kurzweil/.
13 Kurzweil, *Flying Couch*, 95.
14 The metaphor of a bridge to memory, linking generations, is a characteristic trope in third-generation Holocaust narratives. See, for example, Julie Orringer's third-generation novel of her grandparents' experience in Hungary during the Nazi genocide, *The Invisible Bridge* (New York: Knopf, 2010).
15 Kurzweil, *Flying Couch*, 159.
16 Kurzweil, 219, 222.
17 Kurzweil, 30.
18 Kurzweil, 216.
19 Kurzweil, 222.
20 Kurzweil, 11.
21 Andrés Romero-Jódar, *The Trauma Graphic Novel* (New York: Routledge, 2017), 171.
22 Versaci, *This Book Contains Graphic Language*, 58.
23 Kurzweil, *Flying Couch*, 1.
24 Hatfield, *Alternative Comics*, 64.
25 Dana Mihăilescu, "Mapping Transgenerational Memory of the Shoah in Third Generation Graphic Narratives: On Amy Kurzweil's Flying Couch (2016)," *Journal of Modern Jewish Studies* 17, no. 1 (2018): 98.
26 Kurzweil, *Flying Couch*, 69.
27 Kurzweil, 285.
28 Mihăilescu, "Mapping Transgenerational Memory," 107.
29 Kurzweil, *Flying Couch*, 20.
30 Kurzweil, 21.
31 Kelly Kautz, "An Interview with Amy Kurzweil of *Flying Couch*," accessed August 8, 2018, http://www.theskeletonclub.com/blog/amy-kurzweil-interview.
32 Kurzweil, *Flying Couch*, 77.
33 Kurzweil, 58.
34 Kurzweil, 243.
35 Versaci, *This Book Contains Graphic Language*, 39.

36 Kurzweil, *Flying Couch*, 183.
37 Kurzweil, 66.
38 Kurzweil, 89.
39 Such self-conscious self-reflection is characteristic of third-generation Holocaust literary representation, a matter of calling attention to the limitations of any artistic representation of the Holocaust. As third-generation graphic artist Leela Corman's autobiographical narrator, in the brief comics sketch "The Book of the Dead," wonders, "My grandparents survived the Holocaust. . . . How can I, as an artist living a relatively pampered life, honor their memories?" There is, as she and others suggest, no resolution to the search for knowledge and adequate expression. As she explains, "War is a hole I sit on top of. I sit here, distant from it, in my place of privilege, because a few of my family members managed to survive the Holocaust, barely, and lately I've been wondering if I'm doing their memories any favors by being an artist." Thus at the narrative's close, Corman self-reflexively draws herself drawing, with the caption "So this is it, this is all I can offer, to the living and to the dead"; *Tablet Magazine*, May 4, 2016, http://www.tabletmag.com/jewish-life-and-relition/201031/the-book-of-the-dead.
40 Kurzweil, *Flying Couch*, 47.
41 Versaci, *This Book Contains Graphic Language*, 58.
42 Kurzweil, *Flying Couch*, 118.
43 Kurzweil, 112–115.
44 Versaci, *This Book Contains Graphic Language*, 49.
45 Kurzweil, *Flying Couch*, 183.
46 Kurzweil, 236.
47 Kurzweil, 177.
48 Kurzweil, 162.
49 Jérémie Dres, *We Won't See Auschwitz*, trans. Edward Gauvin (London: SelfMadeHero, 2012), 5.
50 Dres, 12.
51 Marianne Hirsch, "Objects of Return," in *After Testimony: the Ethics and Aesthetics of Holocaust Narrative for the Future*, ed. Jakob Lothe, Susan Rubin Suleiman, and James Phelan (Columbus: Ohio State University Press, 2012), 200.
52 Kurzweil, *Flying Couch*, 187.
53 Dres, *We Won't See Auschwitz*, 190.
54 Dres, 173.
55 Dres, 117.
56 Dres, 11.
57 Marc Sobel, "The Rutu Modan Interview," *Comics Journal*, May 29, 2013, http://www.tcj.com/rutu-modan/2/.
58 Kurzweil, *Flying Couch*, 32.
59 Kurzweil, 88.
60 Kurzweil, 44–45.
61 Kurzweil, 268.
62 See Hoffman's meditation on the aftermath of the Shoah, *After Such Knowledge*.
63 Kurzweil, *Flying Couch*, 229–230.
64 Kurzweil, 230.
65 Leela Corman, "The Book of the Dead," in *We All Wish for Deadly Force* (Philadelphia: Retrofit Comics, 2016).
66 Mihăilescu, "Mapping Transgenerational Memory," 99.

67 Jessica Lang, *Textual Silence: Unreadability and the Holocaust* (New Brunswick, N.J.: Rutgers University Press, 2017), 87–88.
68 Corman, "Drawing Strength from My Grandfather."
69 Corman.
70 Leela Corman, "Bearing Witness at Buchenwald," *Tablet Magazine*, April 20, 2017, http://www.tabletmag.com/jewish-life-and-religion/230037/bearing-witness-at-buchenwald.
71 This image is reminiscent of the second of two epigraphs that introduces Saul Bellow's second novel, *The Victim*, published in 1947, a work that might be understood as Bellow's first literary approach to the Holocaust. The epigraph, taken from De Quincey's *The Pains of Opium*, describes a hellish scene of the waters of the sea that, as they churn, reveal the drowning faces of human beings, "imploring, wrathful, despairing, faces that surged upward by thousands, by myriads, by generations," faces representative of the millions murdered in the Shoah and that come to haunt the protagonist of Bellow's novel in the singular figure of one man, the antisemite who follows the protagonist, Asa Leventhal, throughout Manhattan; Saul Bellow, *The Victim* (New York: Vanguard, 1947). While in Corman's graphic narrative, the millions dead are represented by imploring, grasping hands, both hands and faces function as metonyms for those murdered in the Shoah. Both Corman and Bellow seem to be suggesting that we are responsible for the fate of others; "Look at us," the dead implore Corman's deeply unnerved protagonist ("Bearing Witness at Buchenwald"). To pretend otherwise, both Corman and Bellow caution, is a pathological act of cowardice. Thus Corman introduces her narrative with the citizens of Germany, bystanders to the atrocities conducted in their towns, forced to view the bodies of the dead before they are buried. For a more thorough discussion of Bellow's *The Victim*, see Victoria Aarons, "Faces in a Sea of Suffering: The Human Predicament in Saul Bellow's *The Victim*," *Partial Answers: Journal of Literature and History of Ideas* 14, no. 1 (2016): 63–81.
72 Corman, "Bearing Witness at Buchenwald."
73 Emily Steinberg, "Berlin Story: Time, Memory, Place," *Cleaver Magazine*, December 15, 2017, https://www.cleavermagazine.com/berlin-story-time-memory-place-by-emily-steinberg.
74 Kurzweil, *Flying Couch*, 245.
75 Kurzweil, 249.
76 Kurzweil, 272–273.
77 Kurzweil, 51.
78 Kurzweil, 275.
79 Kurzweil, 290–294.
80 I am, of course, liberally borrowing this phrase from Delmore Schwartz's short story "In Dreams Begin Responsibilities," whose protagonist, the American-born child of immigrants, must come to terms with his father's character in order to fashion his own. The story was first published in 1937 in the debut issue of *Partisan Review* and later anthologized in the collection *In Dreams Begin Responsibilities and Other Stories* (New York: New Directions, 1978). The title is a reference to Yeats's 1914 collection of poems "Responsibilities" (1914).
81 Kurzweil, *Flying Couch*, 283.
82 Leela Corman, "The Blood Road," *Tablet Magazine*, April 11, 2018, http://www.tabletmag.com/jewish-life-and-religion/259635/the-blood-road.
83 Amir Eshel, *Futurity: Contemporary Literature and the Quest for the Past* (Chicago: University of Chicago Press, 2013), 4.

84 Kurzweil, *Flying Couch*, 209.
85 Kurzweil, 207.
86 Berger, "Life after Death," 73.

Chapter 5

1 An earlier, much abbreviated discussion of this graphic novel appears in Victoria Aarons, "Reimagining History: Joe Kubert's Graphic Novel of the Warsaw Ghetto Uprising," in *New Directions in Jewish American and Holocaust Literatures: Reading and Teaching*, ed. Victoria Aarons and Holli Levitsky (Albany: State University of New York Press, 2019), 69–84.
2 Sandor Goodhart, "'A Land that Devours Its Inhabitants': Midrashic Reading, Emmanuel Levinas, and Prophetic Exegesis," special issue, "Emmanuel Levinas and Jewish Thought: Translating Hebrew into Greek," *Shofar* 26, no. 4 (Summer 2008): 18.
3 Goodhart, 20.
4 Sara R. Horowitz, "Auto/Biography and Fiction after Auschwitz: Probing the Boundaries of Second-Generation Aesthetics," in *Breaking Crystal: Writing and Memory after Auschwitz*, ed. Efraim Sicher (Urbana: University of Illinois Press, 1998), 290.
5 Horowitz, 290.
6 Brad Prager, "The Holocaust without Ink: Absent Memory and Atrocity in Joe Kubert's Graphic Novel *Yossel: April 19, 1943*," in *The Jewish Graphic Novel: Critical Approaches*, ed. Samantha Baskind and Ranen Omer-Sherman (New Brunswick, N.J.: Rutgers University Press, 2008), 117.
7 Joe Kubert, *Yossel: April 19, 1943: A Story of the Warsaw Ghetto Uprising* (New York: iBooks, 2003), iii.
8 Philip Roth, "My Uchronia," in *Why Write? Collected Nonfiction 1960–2013* (New York: Library of America, 2017), 338.
9 Alison Landsberg, "America, the Holocaust, and the Mass Culture of Memory: Toward a Radical Politics of Empathy," *New German Critique* 71 (Spring–Summer 1997): 66.
10 Kubert, *Yossel*, ii.
11 Andrew M. Gordon, "Alternate Jewish History: Philip Roth's *The Plot against America* and Michael Chabon's *The Yiddish Policemen's Union*," in *New Directions in Jewish American and Holocaust Literature*, 86.
12 Kubert, *Yossel*, ii. This sense of being among the "lucky" harkens back to Saul Bellow's fraught American Jewish protagonist Asa Leventhal in Bellow's second novel, *The Victim*, published in 1947. Feeling the weight of antisemitism and his own "survivor guilt," Leventhal too considers himself one of the lucky ones, lucky, as he anxiously puts it, to have "gotten away with it"; Saul Bellow, *The Victim* (New York: Vanguard, 1947), 33. Leventhal, throughout Bellow's ominously charged novel, believes himself to have narrowly escaped what might have been his fate. Leventhal remains haunted by "that part of humanity of which he was frequently mindful . . . the part that did not get away with it—the lost, the outcast, the overcome, the effaced, the ruined" (16). A similar apprehension and unease are articulated in Kubert's sense that he might have been, were it not for the fortunes of circumstance and luck, "caught in that maelstrom, sucked in and pulled down with the millions of others who were lost" (*Yossel*, ii).
13 Kubert, *Yossel*, i.

14 Philip Roth, *The Counterlife* (New York: Farrar, Straus and Giroux, 1986), 77, 156.
15 Michael Leal, "An Interview with Joe Kubert," Comics Cube, August 14, 2012, http://www.comicscube.com/2012/08/an-interview-with-joe-kubert-by-michael.html.
16 Curiously, in one of the early tales of the legendary figure formed from clay and brought to life by Rabbi Lowe in order to protect the Jews, the golem is named Josef, referred to as Yossele.
17 Kubert, *Yossel*, 7.
18 Kubert, iii.
19 Prager, "Holocaust without Ink," 115.
20 Prager, 126.
21 Samantha Baskind, "Picturing 'The Holiest Thing': Joe Kubert's Children of the Warsaw Ghetto," in *Visualizing Jewish Narrative: Jewish Comics and Graphic Novels*, ed. Derek Parker Royal (London: Bloomsbury, 2016), 181.
22 Cathy Caruth, *Literature in the Ashes of History* (Baltimore, Md.: Johns Hopkins University Press, 2013), 3.
23 Caruth, 3.
24 Geoffrey H. Hartman, *The Longest Shadow: In the Aftermath of the Holocaust* (Bloomington: Indiana University Press, 1996), 8.
25 Hartman, 8.
26 Kubert, *Yossel*, iii.
27 Kubert, 7.
28 Kubert, 29.
29 Kubert, 7, 13.
30 Kubert, 23.
31 Kubert, 13.
32 Samantha Baskind, *The Warsaw Ghetto in American Art and Culture* (University Park: Pennsylvania State University Press, 2018), 156.
33 Baskind, 156.
34 For a very interesting discussion of youth activists and children smugglers in the Warsaw Ghetto, see Rachel L. Einwohner, "Opportunity, Honor, and Action in the Warsaw Ghetto Uprising of 1943," *AJS* 109, no. 3 (November 2003): 650–675.
35 Robert Faires, "A Different Kind of World: Comics Artist Joe Kubert Talks about His Life as It Was and as It Might Have Been," *Austin Chronicle*, November 5, 2004, http://www.austinchronicle.com/books/2004-11-05/236000/.
36 Baskind, *Warsaw Ghetto*, 217.
37 Prager, "Holocaust without Ink," 118.
38 Leal, "Interview with Joe Kubert."
39 Baskind, *Warsaw Ghetto*, 217.
40 Baskind, 217.
41 Alan Itkin, "Bring Up the Bodies: The Classical Concept of Poetic Vividness and Its Reevaluation in Holocaust Literature," *PMLA* 133, no. 1 (2018): 109.
42 Kubert, *Yossel*, 61.
43 Kubert, 62.
44 Baskind, *Warsaw Ghetto*, 227.
45 Shoshana Felman, "The Return of the Voice: Claude Lanzmann's *Shoah*," in *Testimony: Crises of Witnessing in Literature, Psychoanalysis, and History*, Shoshana Felman and Dori Laub (New York: Routledge, 1992), 231–232.
46 Felman, 232.

47 David Patterson, *The Holocaust and the Nonrepresentable: Literary and Photographic Transcendence* (New York: State University of New York Press, 2018), 265.

48 Jean-François Lyotard, "The Différend, the Referent, and the Proper Name," *Diacritics* 14, no. 3 (Fall 1984): 4. Alison Landsberg offers a discussion of this passage in terms of historical revisionism and the speciousness of such arguments in her interesting essay on Holocaust testimony and memory, "America, the Holocaust, and the Mass Culture of Memory: Toward a Radical Politics of Empathy," *New German Critique* 71 (Spring–Summer 1997): 63–86.

49 Lyotard, "Différend, the Referent, and the Proper Name," 14.

50 Eric J. Sundquist, "Black Milk: A Holocaust Metaphor," in *New Directions in Jewish American and Holocaust Literature*, 26.

51 Michael S. Roth, "Why Photography Matters to the Theory of History: *Images in Spite of All: Four Photographs from Auschwitz* by Georges Didi-Huberman and Shane B. Lillis, and *Why Photography Matters as Art as Never Before* by Michael Fried," *History and Theory* 49, no. 1 (February 2010): 102.

52 See Stanley Cavell's discussion of the cinematic image in *The World Viewed: Reflections on the Ontology of Film* (Cambridge, Mass.: Harvard University Press, 1979), esp. 40–41.

53 Roth, "Why Photography Matters," 102.

54 Roland Barthes, *Camera Lucida: Reflections on Photography*, trans. Richard Howard (New York: Hill and Wang, 1982), 65.

55 Kubert, *Yossel*, 37. The figure of the messenger is a recurring trope in Holocaust literature, the appearance of a seeming stranger who returns to tell the tale of what he has witnessed. More often than not, the herald initially is not believed, his account the stuff of horrific and grotesque fantasy, as we see here when the rebbe who appears unbidden and whose account of "death camps" is initially seen by those not there as "another fairy tale," beyond the capacity of a human mind to envision (38). We find such a conceit too in Elie Wiesel's *Night*, when, early on the narrator, a messenger, Moishe the Beadle, will miraculously return to tell the tale of mass murder of Jews in the forest in Poland. But he is not to be believed: "Day after day, night after night, he went from one Jewish house to the next, telling his story. . . . He spoke only of what he had seen. But people not only refused to believe his tales, they refused to listen. . . . 'They think I'm mad,' he whispered"; Elie Wiesel, *Night*, trans. Marion Wiesel (New York: Hill and Wang / Farrar, Straus and Giroux, 2006), 7. Henry Gonshak, in a comparative analysis of three Holocaust graphic novels as they contrast to Spiegelman's *Maus*, takes issue with some of Kubert's "historical inaccuracies—or, more precisely, historical omissions" in *Yossel* that result in "a sentimental tale of heroic martyrdom" (70, 77). One of the issues Gonshak points to in support of his argument is the unbelievability of the return of the camp inmate, whose "eloquence and verbosity" belie his weakened, infirm condition (69). Such quibbling, I think, is probably more appropriate for a historical account than it is for a work of fiction. While Kubert says in his introductory remarks to the graphic novel that he drew upon archival documents and histories in designing the book, he also makes it clear that he takes considerable literary license in imagining his "what-if" narrative. See Henry Gonshak, "Beyond *Maus*: Other Holocaust Graphic Novels," *Shofar* 28, no. 1 (Fall 2009): 55–79.

56 Kubert, *Yossel*, 37.

57 Kubert, 41, 42, 66.

58 Kubert, 80.

59 Kubert, 77.
60 Kubert, 39.
61 Kubert, 50.
62 Kubert, 43.
63 Kubert, 39.
64 We are reminded once again of the chilling word of Primo Levi's poem "Shema," which stands as an epigraph to his memoir, *Survival in Auschwitz*: "Consider if this is a man . . . / Who dies because of a yes or a no. / Consider if this is a woman / Without hair and without name / With no more strength to remember / Her eyes empty . . ."; Primo Levi, *Survival in Auschwitz: The Nazi Assault on Humanity*, trans. Stuart Woolf (Touchstone / Simon & Schuster, 1996), 11.
65 Kubert, *Yossel*, 46.
66 Kubert, 83–84.
67 Kubert, 113.
68 Kubert, 116.
69 Susan Gubar, "Prosopopoeia and Holocaust Poetry in English: Sylvia Plath and Her Contemporaries," *Yale Journal of Criticism* 14, no. 1 (2001): 192.
70 Kubert, *Yossel*, 5.
71 Kubert, 81.
72 Kubert, 115.
73 Kubert, 82.
74 Susan Rubin Suleiman, "The Edge of Memory: Literary Innovation and Childhood Trauma," in *The Future of Memory*, ed. Richard Crownshaw, Jane Kilby, and Antony Rowland (New York: Berghahn, 2010), 101.
75 Kubert, *Yossel*, 104.
76 Baskind, *Warsaw Ghetto*, 219.
77 We find an elaborate fantasy of revenge ironically played out in Daniel Torday's third-generation novel *The Last Flight of Poxl West*, narrated by a young Jewish boy who, like his peers, is drawn to stories of Jewish heroism, imagined tales, as he puts it, "not of survival, but of action" (New York: St. Martin's, 2015), 6. Kubert, in killing off his double, his alter ego Yossel, fantasizes his own death but from the safe distance of the pencil as he draws Yossel going down in flames as he attempts to fight off the Nazis. There is something seductive about fantasizing one's own death, especially a heroic death in which one dies a martyr. Interestingly, while for Yossel, drawing is largely an unconscious defense mechanism, for Kubert as a graphic novelist, drawing would seem to be a conscious enactment, a form of control when the historical reality is insufficient.
78 Kubert, *Yossel*, 114.
79 Kubert, 100, 115.
80 Kubert's character Mordecai, the leader of the resistance, is based on the historical figure of Mordechai Anielewicz, leader of the Jewish Fighting Organization.
81 Kubert, *Yossel*, 2.
82 Sundquist, "Black Milk," 22.
83 See Arthur Quinn, *Figures of Speech: 60 Ways to Turn a Phrase* (Salt Lake City, Utah: Gibbs M. Smith, 1982), 34, 36. Tropes that enact silence, loss, and absence, such as *aposiopesis*, *praecisco*, and *ellipsis*, are characteristic of all genres of Holocaust literature. A paradigmatic expression of the enactment of silence and annihilation is Dan Pagis's poem "Written in Pencil in the Sealed Railway-Car."
84 Kubert, *Yossel*, 35.

85 Baskind, "Picturing 'The Holiest Thing,'" 179.
86 Michel Kichka, *Second Generation: The Things I Didn't Tell My Father* (France: Dargaud, 2012; English trans., January 27, 2016, Amazon Digital Services), 90.
87 Berel Lang, *Holocaust Representation: Art within the Limits of History and Ethics* (Baltimore, Md.: Johns Hopkins University Press, 2000), 36.
88 Monica Osborne, "The Midrashic Impulse: Reading Cynthia Ozick's *Heir to the Glimmering World* against Representation," *Studies in American Jewish Literature* 26 (2007): 23.
89 Georges Didi-Huberman, *Images in Spite of All: Four Photographs from Auschwitz*, trans. Shane B. Lillis (Chicago: University of Chicago Press, 2008), 105.
90 Tal Bruttmann, "The Holocaust through Comics," in *Re-examining the Holocaust through Literature*, ed. Aukje Kluge and Benn E. Williams (Newcastle upon Tyne, U.K.: Cambridge Scholars, 2009), 196.
91 Anne Michaels, *Fugitive Pieces* (New York: Vintage International, 1998), 193.
92 Bernice Eisenstein, *I Was a Child of Holocaust Survivors* (New York: Riverhead Books, 2006), 167.
93 Osborne, "Midrashic Impulse," 22.

Chapter 6

1 John Benson, David Kasakove, and Art Spiegelman, "An Examination of 'Master Race,'" in *A Comics Studies Reader*, ed. Jeet Heer and Kent Worcester (Jackson: University Press of Mississippi, 2009), 288.
2 Benson, Kasakove, and Spiegelman, 288.
3 Elie Wiesel, "An Old Acquaintance," in *Legends of Our Time* (New York: Holt, Rinehart and Winston, 1968), 40–41.
4 Al Feldstein and Bernie Krigstein, "Master Race," in *We Spoke Out: Comic Books and the Holocaust*, ed. Neal Adams, Rafael Medoff, and Craig Yoe (San Diego, Calif.: Yoe Books / IDW, 2018), 25.
5 Benson, Kasakove, and Spiegelman, "Examination of 'Master Race,'" 289.
6 Feldstein and Krigstein, "Master Race," 25.
7 Feldstein and Krigstein, 26.
8 Feldstein and Krigstein, 27.
9 Feldstein and Krigstein, 27.
10 Feldstein and Krigstein, 27.
11 Feldstein and Krigstein, 25.
12 It is interesting to consider Freud's discussion of the symbolism of trains in relation to Reissman's escalating anxiety as the motion of the train becomes a measure of his fear of losing control. Freud makes the case that the movement of travel by rail is linked to sexual pleasure, but as always with Freud, sexual pleasure is linked to anxiety and the desire to reinstate equilibrium and thus death. As Freud suggests, "In the event of repression," the movement of the train can bring about "a feeling of nausea . . . attacks of anxiety . . . a repetition of the painful experience," a traumatic response to the fear of losing control. See Sigmund Freud, "Infantile Sexuality," in *The Standard Edition of the Complete Psychological Works of Sigmund Freud*, vol. 7 (1901–1905), trans. James Strachey (London: Hogarth, 1953), 202. This subject is taken up provocatively by Wolfgang Schivelbusch as the "fear of derailment . . . a feeling of impotence due to one's being confined in a fast moving piece of machinery without being able to influence it in the least"; *The Railway Journey: The*

Industrialization of Time and Space in the Nineteenth Century (Berkeley: University of California Press, 1986), 78. In Feldstein's "Master Race," of course, the derailment Reissman suffers is psychic.

13 Feldstein and Krigstein, "Master Race," 25.
14 Feldstein and Krigstein, 26.
15 Paul Celan, "Death Fugue," in *Truth and Lamentation: Stories and Poems on the Holocaust*, ed. Milton Teichman and Sharon Leder (Urbana: University of Illinois Press, 1994), 223.
16 Feldstein and Krigstein, "Master Race," 25 (emphasis mine).
17 Primo Levi, "Shema," in *Truth and Lamentation*, 488.
18 Feldstein and Krigstein, "Master Race," 25, 27.
19 Feldstein and Krigstein, 27–29.
20 Feldstein and Krigstein, 30.
21 Benson, Kasakove, and Spiegelman, "Examination of 'Master Race,'" 298–299.
22 Feldstein and Krigstein, "Master Race," 27 (emphasis in source).
23 Feldstein and Krigstein, 28.
24 Feldstein and Krigstein, 30.
25 Feldstein and Krigstein, 26.
26 We are reminded here of the punishing father in Kafka's "The Judgment," who rises in his wrath to sentence his son to death, an act that robs the son of any agency or autonomy and propels him to his death.
27 Feldstein and Krigstein, "Master Race," 26.
28 Benson, Kasakove, and Spiegelman, "Examination of 'Master Race,'" 292.
29 Feldstein and Krigstein, "Master Race," 26.
30 Feldstein and Krigstein, 26.
31 Feldstein and Krigstein, 28.
32 Genesis 4:10, *Tanakh: A New Translation of the Holy Scriptures According to the Traditional Hebrew Text* (Philadelphia: Jewish Publication Society, 1985), 8.
33 Genesis 4:11, *Tanakh*, 8.
34 Genesis 4:14, *Tanakh*, 8.
35 Hannah Arendt, *Eichmann in Jerusalem: A Report on the Banality of Evil* (New York: Penguin, 2006), 279.
36 In a conversation I had with Eli Wiesel on the occasion of the symposium held at Boston University in celebration of his eightieth birthday (October 26–28, 2008), the author and Nobel laureate told me that the events of this narrative, while reimagined for the purposes of storytelling, were based on an actual experience that happened to him on a bus in Israel not long after the war. I have not been able to find evidence that Wiesel was familiar with "Master Race," and thus the similarities between the two pieces are all the more notable.
37 Wiesel, "Old Acquaintance," 39.
38 Wiesel, 52.
39 Wiesel, 52.
40 For an extended analysis of Wiesel's narrative, see Victoria Aarons, "Memory as Accomplice to History: Trauma and Narrative in Elie Wiesel's 'An Old Acquaintance,'" in *The Call of Memory: Learning about the Holocaust Through Narrative*, ed. Karen Shawn and Keren Goldfrad (Ben Yehuda Press, 2008), 425–433.
41 Wiesel, "Old Acquaintance," 52.
42 Wiesel, 52.
43 Feldstein and Krigstein, "Master Race," 30.

44 Feldstein and Krigstein, 31.
45 Art Spiegelman, "Ballbuster: Bernard Krigstein's Life between the Panels," *New Yorker*, https://www.newyorker.com/magazine/2002/07/22/ballbuster.
46 Benson, Kasakove, and Spiegelman, "Examination of 'Master Race,'" 304.
47 Feldstein and Krigstein, "Master Race," 31.
48 Feldstein and Krigstein, 31.
49 Feldstein and Krigstein, 32.

Epilogue

1 Jane L. Chapman, Dan Ellin, and Adam Sherif, *Comics, the Holocaust and Hiroshima* (London: Palgrave Macmillan, 2015), 76.
2 Hillary L. Chute, *Disaster Drawn: Visual Witness, Comics, and Documentary Form* (Cambridge, Mass.: Belknap / Harvard University Press, 2016), 141–142.
3 Chute, 5.

Bibliography

Aarons, Victoria. "Bellow and the Holocaust." In *The Cambridge Companion to Saul Bellow*, edited by Victoria Aarons, 55–67. New York: Cambridge University Press, 2017.

———. "Faces in a Sea of Suffering: The Human Predicament in Saul Bellow's *The Victim*." *Partial Answers: Journal of Literature and History of Ideas* 14, no. 1 (2016): 63–81.

———. "A Genre of Rupture: The Literary Language of the Holocaust." In *The Bloomsbury Companion to Holocaust Literature*, edited by Jenni Adams, 27–45. London: Bloomsbury, 2014.

———. "Memory as Accomplice to History: Trauma and Narrative in Elie Wiesel's 'An Old Acquaintance.'" In *The Call of Memory: Learning about the Holocaust through Narrative*, edited by Karen Shawn and Keren Goldfrad, 425–433. Teaneck, N.J.: Ben Yehuda Press, 2008.

———. "Reimagining History: Joe Kubert's Graphic Novel of the Warsaw Ghetto Uprising." In *New Directions in Jewish American and Holocaust Literatures: Reading and Teaching*, edited by Victoria Aarons and Holli Levitsky, 69–84. Albany: State University of New York Press, 2019.

Aarons, Victoria, and Alan L. Berger. *Third-Generation Holocaust Representation: Trauma, History, and Memory*. Evanston, Ill.: Northwestern University Press, 2017.

Adams, Neal, Rafael Medoff, and Craig Yoe, eds. *We Spoke Out: Comic Books and the Holocaust*. San Diego, Calif.: Yoe Books / IDW, 2018.

Agamben, Giorgio. *Remnants of Auschwitz: The Witness and the Archive*. Translated by Daniel Heller-Roazen. New York: Zone Books, 2002.

Appignanesi, Lisa. *Losing the Dead: A Family Memoir*. London: Vintage, 2000.

Arendt, Hannah. *Eichmann in Jerusalem: A Report on the Banality of Evil*. New York: Viking, 1963. Reprint, New York: Penguin, 2006.

Baetens, Jan, and Charlotte Pylyser. "Comics and Time." In *The Routledge Companion to Comics*, edited by Frank Bramlett, Roy T. Cook, and Aaron Meskin, 303–310. New York: Routledge, 2017.

Baraitser, Marion, and Anna Evans. *Home Number One*. London: Loki Books, 2006.

Bar-On, Dan. *Fear and Hope: Three Generations of the Holocaust*. Cambridge, Mass.: Harvard University Press, 1995.

Barthes, Roland. *Camera Lucida: Reflections on Photography*. Translated by Richard Howard. New York: Hill and Wang, 1982.

Baskind, Samantha. "A Conversation with Miriam Katin." In *The Jewish Graphic Novel: Critical Approaches*, edited by Samantha Baskind and Ranen Omer-Sherman, 237–243. New Brunswick, N.J.: Rutgers University Press, 2010.

———. "Picturing 'The Holiest Thing': Joe Kubert's Children of the Warsaw Ghetto." In *Visualizing Jewish Narrative: Jewish Comics and Graphic Novels*, edited by Derek Parker Royal, 172–184. London: Bloomsbury, 2016.

———. *The Warsaw Ghetto in American Art and Culture*. University Park: Pennsylvania State University Press, 2018.

Baskind, Samantha, and Ranen Omer-Sherman, eds. *The Jewish Graphic Novel: Critical Approaches*. New Brunswick, N.J.: Rutgers University Press, 2008.

Bellow, Saul. *The Bellarosa Connection*. New York: Penguin, 1989.

———. *The Victim*. New York: Vanguard, 1947. Reprint, New York: Penguin, 1988.

Benjamin, Walter. "Theses on the Philosophy of History." In *Illuminations: Essays and Reflections*, edited by Hannah Arendt and translated by Harry Zohn, 253–264. New York: Schocken, 2007.

Bennett, Jill. *Empathic Vision: Affect, Trauma, and Contemporary Art*. Palo Alto, Calif.: Stanford University Press, 2005.

Benson, John, David Kasakove, and Art Spiegelman. "An Examination of 'Master Race.'" In *A Comics Studies Reader*, edited by Jeet Heer and Kent Worceser, 288–305. Jackson: University Press of Mississippi, 2009.

Berger, Alan L. "Life after Death: A Third-Generation Journey in Jérémie Dres's *We Won't See Auschwitz*." In *Third-Generation Holocaust Narratives: Memory in Memoir and Fiction*, edited by Victoria Aarons, 73–87. Lanham, Md.: Lexington Books / Rowman & Littlefield, 2016.

Bloom, Katya. *The Embodied Self: Movement and Psychoanalysis*. New York: Routledge, 2006.

Booth, Wayne C. *The Company We Keep: An Ethics of Fiction*. Berkeley: University of California Press, 1988.

Brandt, William J. *The Rhetoric of Argumentation*. Indianapolis, Ind.: Bobbs-Merrill, 1970.

Bruttmann, Tal. "The Holocaust through Comics." In *Re-examining the Holocaust through Literature*, edited by Aukje Kluge and Benn E. Williams, 173–200. Newcastle upon Tyne, U.K.: Cambridge Scholars, 2009.

Bukiet, Melvin Jules. *Nothing Makes You Free: Writings by Descendants of Jewish Holocaust Survivors*. New York: W. W. Norton, 2002.

Caruth, Cathy. *Literature in the Ashes of History*. Baltimore, Md.: Johns Hopkins University Press, 2013.

———. *Unclaimed Experience: Trauma, Narrative, and History*. Baltimore, Md.: Johns Hopkins University Press, 1996.

Cavell, Stanley. *The World Viewed: Reflections on the Ontology of Film*. Cambridge, Mass.: Harvard University Press, 1979.

Celan, Paul. "Death Fugue." In *Truth and Lamentation: Stories and Poems on the Holocaust*, edited by Milton Teichman and Sharon Leder, 222–223. Urbana: University of Illinois Press, 1994.

Chapman, Jane L., Dan Ellin, and Adam Sherif. *Comics, the Holocaust and Hiroshima*. London: Palgrave Macmillan, 2015.

Chute, Hillary L. "Comics as Literature? Reading Graphic Narrative." *PMLA* 123, no. 2 (March 2008): 453–455.

———. *Disaster Drawn: Visual Witness, Comics, and Documentary Form*. Cambridge, Mass.: Belknap / Harvard University Press, 2016.

———. *Graphic Women: Life Narrative and Contemporary Comics*. New York: Columbia University Press, 2010.

Clapp, Jeffrey. "Nicotine Cosmopolitanism: From Italo Svevo's Trieste to Art Spiegelman's New York." Forum: Comics and the Canon. Guest ed. Ariela Freedman. *Partial Answers: Journal of Literature and the History of Ideas* 13, no. 2 (June 2015): 311–336.

Cohen, Beth B. *Child Survivors of the Holocaust: The Youngest Remnant and the American Experience*. New Brunswick, N.J.: Rutgers University Press, 2018.

Cohen, Leon. "Artist Sought Realism in Graphic Memoir of His Shoah-Survivor Mother." *Wisconsin Jewish Chronicle*, March 31, 2008. http://www.jewishchronicle.org/2008/03/31/artist-sought-realism-in-graphic-memoir-of-his-shoah-survivor-mother/.

Corman, Leela. "Bearing Witness at Buchenwald." *Tablet Magazine*, April 20, 2017. http://www.tabletmag.com/jewish-life-and-religion/230037/bearing-witness-at-buchenwald.

———. "The Blood Road." *Tablet Magazine*, April 11, 2018. http://www.tabletmag.com/jewish-life-and-religion/259635/the-blood-road.

———. "The Book of the Dead." *Tablet Magazine*, May 4, 2016. http://www.tabletmag.com/jewish-life-and-relition/201031/the-bood-of-the-dead.

———. "Drawing Strength from My Grandfather, Who Carried His Losses from the Holocaust." *Tablet Magazine*, December 30, 2013. http://www.tabletmag.com/jewish-life-and-relligion/156602/grandfather-carried-losses/?print=1.

———. *We All Wish for Deadly Force*. Philadelphia: Retrofit Comics, 2016.

Creative Writing at the New School. "Q&A with MFA Alum Amy Kurzweil." November 9, 2016. https://newschoolwriting.org/qa-with-mfa-alum-amy-kurzweil/.

Croci, Pascal. *Auschwitz*. New York: Harry N. Abrams, 2004.

Cutter, Martha J., and Cathy J. Schlund-Vials. *Redrawing the Historical Past: History, Memory, and Multiethnic Graphic Novels*. Athens: University of Georgia Press, 2018.

Dauber, Jeremy. *Jewish Comedy: A Serious History*. New York: W. W. Norton, 2017.

Dauvillier, Loic, Greg Salsedo, and Marc Lizano. *Hidden*. New York: First Second, 2012.

Delbo, Charlotte. *Days and Memory*. Translated by Rosette Lamont. Evanston, Ill.: Marlboro / Northwestern University Press, 2001. Originally published in French as *La memoire et les jours*, 1985.

de Waal, Edmund. *The Hare with Amber Eyes*. New York: Farrar, Straus and Giroux, 2010.

Didi-Huberman, Georges. *Images in Spite of All: Four Photographs from Auschwitz*. Translated by Shane B. Lillis. Chicago: University of Chicago Press, 2008.

Dres, Jérémie. *We Won't See Auschwitz*. Translated by Edward Gauvin. London: SelfMadeHero, 2012.

Earle, Harriet E. H. *Comics, Trauma, and the New Art of War*. Jackson: University Press of Mississippi, 2017.

———. "Panel Transitions in Trauma Comics." *Alluvium* 2, no. 1 (January 11, 2013). http://dx.doi.org/10.7766/alluvium.v2.1.02.

Einwohner, Rachel L. "Opportunity, Honor, and Action in the Warsaw Ghetto Uprising of 1943." *American Journal of Sociology* 109, no. 3 (November 2003): 650–675.

Eisenstein, Bernice. "Coda from Memory Unearthed." Lodz Ghetto Photographs of Henryk Ross: A Collection of Holocaust Photographs. Accessed July 24, 2018. http://agolodzghetto.com/essaydetails/5?t:state:flow=19610a49-16af-4542-93f4-ff51486a3761.

———. *I Was a Child of Holocaust Survivors*. New York: Riverhead Books, 2006.

Eisner, Will. *Comics and Sequential Art*. Tamarac, Fla.: Poorhouse, 1985.

El Refaie, Elisabeth. *Autobiographical Comics: Life Writing in Pictures*. Jackson: University Press of Mississippi, 2012.

Eshel, Amir. *Futurity: Contemporary Literature and the Quest for the Past*. Chicago: University of Chicago Press, 2013.

Europe Comics. "Interview with Michel Kichka." February 4, 2016. Accessed August 12, 2018. http://www.europecomics.com/interview-with-michel-kichka/.

Ezrahi, Sidra DeKoven. "Representing Auschwitz." *History and Memory* 7, no. 2 (Fall–Winter 1995): 121–154.

Faires, Robert. "A Different Kind of World: Comics Artist Joe Kubert Talks about His Life as It Was and as It Might Have Been." *Austin Chronicle*, November 5, 2004. https://www.austinchronicle.com/books/2004-11-05/236000/.

Farris, Emil. *My Favorite Thing Is Monsters*. Seattle: Fantagraphics, 2017.

Feldstein, Al, and Bernie Krigstein. "Master Race." In *We Spoke Out: Comic Books and the Holocaust*, edited by Neal Adams, Rafael Medoff, and Craig Yoe, 21–32. San Diego, Calif.: Yoe Books / IDW, 2018.

Felman, Shoshana, and Dori Laub. *Testimony: Crises of Witnessing in Literature, Psychoanalysis, and History*. New York: Routledge, 1992.

Flory, Wendy Stallard. "The Search: A Graphic Narrative for Beginning to Teach about the Holocaust." In *Visualizing Jewish Narrative: Jewish Comics and Graphic Novels*, edited by Derek Parker Royal, 157–170. London: Bloomsbury, 2016.

Folman, Ari. *Waltz with Bashir*. New York: Metropolitan, 2009.

Freedman, Ariela. "Charlotte Salomon, Graphic Artist." In *Graphic Details: Jewish Women's Confessional Comics in Essays and Interviews*, edited by Sarah Lightman, 38–50. Jefferson, N.C.: McFarland, 2014.

———. "Introduction." Forum: Comics and the Canon. Guest ed. Ariela Freedman. *Partial Answers: Journal of Literature and the History of Ideas* 13, no. 2 (June 2015): 251–254.

Fresco, Nadine. "Remembering the Unknown." *International Review of Psycho-Analysis* 11 (1984): 417–427.

Freud, Anna. "The Methods of Child Analysis." In *Introduction to Psychoanalysis*, 19–35. Vol. 1 of *The Writings of Anna Freud*. New York: International Universities Press, 1974.

Freud, Sigmund. "Infantile Sexuality." In *The Standard Edition of the Complete Psychological Works of Sigmund Freud*, vol. 7 (1901–1905), translated by James Strachey, 173–206. London: Hogarth, 1953.

———. "Mourning and Melancholia." In *The Standard Edition of the Complete Psychological Works of Sigmund Freud*, vol. 14 (1914–1916), translated by James Strachey, 237–258. London: Hogarth, 1957.

Galek, Michael, and Marcin Nowakowski. *Episodes from Auschwitz*. St. Joseph, Mo.: K&L, 2009.

Glaser, Jennifer. "Art Spiegelman and the Caricature Archive." In *Redrawing the Historical Past: History, Memory, and Multiethnic Graphic Novels*, edited by Martha J. Cutter and Cathy J. Schlund-Vials, 294–320. Athens: University of Georgia Press, 2018.

Gonshak, Henry. "Beyond *Maus*: Other Holocaust Graphic Novels." *Shofar* 28, no. 1 (Fall 2009): 55–79.

Goodhart, Sandor. "'A Land That Devours Its Inhabitants': Midrashic Reading, Emmanuel Levinas, and Prophetic Exegesis." Special issue, "Emmanuel Levinas and Jewish Thought: Translating Hebrew into Greek," *Shofar* 26, no. 4 (Summer 2008): 13–35.

Gordon, Andrew M. "Alternate Jewish History: Philip Roth's *The Plot against America* and Michael Chabon's *The Yiddish Policemen's Union*." In *New Directions in Jewish American and Holocaust Literature: Reading and Teaching*, edited by Victoria Aarons and Holli Levitsky, 85–101. Albany: State University of New York Press, 2019.

Gravett, Paul. Interview, "Miriam Katin: Coming to Terms." December 17, 2015. http://www.paulgravett.com/articles/article/miriam_katin.

Groensteen, Thierry. *Comics and Narration*. Translated by Ann Miller. Jackson: University Press of Mississippi, 2013.

Grossman, David. *Writing in the Dark*. Translated by Jessica Cohen. New York: Farrar, Straus and Giroux, 2008.

GroupLit. "Interview with Bernice Eisenstein, Author of *I Was a Child of Holocaust Survivors*." 2011. Accessed August 25, 2017. http://grouplit2011.blogspot.com/2011/11/interview-with-bernice-eisenstein-on.html.

Gubar, Susan. "Prosopopoeia and Holocaust Poetry in English: Sylvia Plath and Her Contemporaries." *Yale Journal of Criticism* 14, no. 1 (2001): 191–215.

Harris, Miriam. "Releasing the Grip of the Ghostly: Bernice Eisenstein's *I Was a Child of Holocaust Survivors*." In *The Jewish Graphic Novel: Critical Approaches*, edited by Samantha Baskind and Ranen Omer-Sherman, 129–143. New Brunswick, N.J.: Rutgers University Press, 2008.

Hartman, Geoffrey H. *The Longest Shadow: In the Aftermath of the Holocaust*. Bloomington: Indiana University Press, 1996.

Hatfield, Charles. *Alternative Comics: An Emerging Literature*. Jackson: University Press of Mississippi, 2005.

Havazelet, Ehud. "To Live in Tiflis in the Springtime." In *Like Never Before*, 231–250. New York: Farrar, Straus and Giroux, 1998.

Heuvel, Eric. *A Family Secret*. New York: Farrar, Straus and Giroux, 2009.

Heuvel, Eric, Ruud van der Rol, and Lies Schippers. *The Search*. New York: Farrar, Straus and Giroux, 2009.

Hirsch, Marianne. *Family Frames: Photography, Narrative and Postmemory*. Cambridge, Mass.: Harvard University Press, 1997.

———. *The Generation of Postmemory: Writing and Visual Culture after the Holocaust*. New York: Columbia University Press, 2012.

———. "Objects of Return." In *After Testimony: The Ethics and Aesthetics of Holocaust Narrative for the Future*, edited by Jakob Lothe, Susan Rubin Suleiman, and James Phelan, 198–220. Columbus: Ohio State University Press, 2012.

Hoffman, Eva. *After Such Knowledge: Memory, History and the Legacy of the Holocaust*. New York: PublicAffairs, 2004.

Horowitz, Sara R. "Auto/Biography and Fiction after Auschwitz: Probing the Boundaries of Second-Generation Aesthetics." In *Breaking Crystal: Writing and Memory after Auschwitz*, edited by Efraim Sicher, 276–294. Urbana: University of Illinois Press, 1998.

in 't Veld, Laurike. "Introducing the Rwandan Genocide from a Distance: American Noir and the Animal Metaphor in 99 Days." *Journal of Graphic Novels and Comics* 6, no. 2 (2015): 138–153.

Itkin, Alan. "Bring Up the Bodies: The Classical Concept of Poetic Vividness and Its Reevaluation in Holocaust Literature." *PMLA* 133, no. 1 (2018): 107–123.

Jablonski, Carla, and Leland Purvis. *Resistance*. New York: First Second, 2010.

Kaminer, Michael. "Bernice Eisenstein and the Persistence of Memory." In *Graphic Details: Jewish Women's Confessional Comics in Essays and Interviews*, edited by Sarah Lightman, 162–166. Jefferson, N.C.: McFarland, 2014.

Katin, Miriam. *Letting It Go*. Montreal, Quebec: Drawn & Quarterly, 2013.

———. *We Are on Our Own: A Memoir*. Montreal, Quebec: Drawn & Quarterly, 2006.

Katz, Dori. *Looking for Strangers: The True Story of My Hidden Wartime Childhood*. Chicago: University of Chicago Press, 2013.

Kautz, Kelly. "An Interview with Amy Kurzweil of 'Flying Couch.'" Accessed August 8, 2018. http://www.theskeletonclub.com/blog/amy-kurzweil-interview.

Kichka, Michel. *Second Generation: The Things I Didn't Tell My Father*. France: Dargaud, 2012. English translation, Amazon Digital Services, January 27, 2016.

Klein, Melanie. *The Psychoanalysis of Children*. London: Hogarth, 1932.

Kleist, Reinhard. *The Boxer: The True Story of Holocaust Survivor Harry Haft*. London: SelfMadeHero, 2014.

Klepfisz, Irena. "Poland, 1944: My Mother Is Walking down the Road." In *Truth and Lamentation: Stories and Poems on the Holocaust*, edited by Milton Teichman and Sharon Leder, 264. Urbana: University of Illinois Press, 1994.

Kluger, Ruth. *Still Alive: A Holocaust Girlhood Remembered*. New York: Feminist Press, 2001.

Krell, Robert. *Messages and Memories: Reflections on Child Survivors of the Holocaust*. 2nd ed. Vancouver, British Columbia: Memory Press, 2001.

Kremer, S. Lillian. *Witness through the Imagination: Jewish American Holocaust Literature*. Detroit, Mich.: Wayne State University Press, 1989.

Kubert, Joe. *Yossel: April 19, 1943: A Story of the Warsaw Ghetto Uprising*. New York: iBooks, 2003.

Kuhlman, Martha. "The Autobiographical and Biographical Graphic Novel." In *The Cambridge Companion to the Graphic Novel*, edited by Stephen E. Tabachnick, 113–129. Cambridge, U.K.: Cambridge University Press, 2017.

Kundera, Milan. *The Unbearable Lightness of Being*. New York: Harper & Row, 1984.

Kurzweil, Amy. *Flying Couch: A Graphic Memoir*. New York: Catapult / Black Balloon, 2016.

Lambert, Joshua. "How Comics Help Us Combat Holocaust Fatigue." *Forward*, February 9, 2017. http://www.forward.com/culture/361784/how-comics-help-us-combat-holocaust-fatigue.

Landsberg, Alison. "America, the Holocaust, and the Mass Culture of Memory: Toward a Radical Politics of Empathy." *New German Critique* 71 (Spring–Summer 1997): 68–86.

Lang, Berel. *Holocaust Representation: Art within the Limits of History and Ethics*. Baltimore, Md.: Johns Hopkins University Press, 2000.

Lang, Jessica. *Textual Silences: Unreadability and the Holocaust*. New Brunswick, N.J.: Rutgers University Press, 2017.

Langer, Lawrence L. *Holocaust Testimonies: The Ruins of Memory*. New Haven: Yale University Press, 1991.

Lassner, Phyllis. "The American Voices of Hidden Child Survivors: Coming of Age Out of Time and Place." In *New Directions in Jewish American and Holocaust Literatures: Reading and Teaching*, edited by Victoria Aarons and Holli Levitsky, 47–68. Albany: State University of New York Press, 2019.

Leal, Michael. "An Interview with Joe Kubert." *Comics Cube*, August 14, 2012. http://www.comicscube.com/2012/08/an-interview-with-joe-kubert-by-michael.html.

Lemelman, Martin. *Mendel's Daughter: A Memoir*. New York: Free Press, 2006.

———. *Two Cents Plain: My Brooklyn Boyhood*. New York: Bloomsbury, 2010.

Lester, Malcolm. "Bernice Eisenstein." In *Graphic Details: Jewish Women's Confessional Comics in Essays and Interviews*, edited by Sarah Lightman, 219–221. Jefferson, N.C.: McFarland, 2014.

———. *The Drowned and the Saved*. Translated by Raymond Rosenthal. New York: Vintage, 1989.

———. *Survival in Auschwitz: The Nazi Assault on Humanity*. Translated by Stuart Woolf. New York: Touchstone / Simon & Schuster, 1996.

Lévy, Paule. "Storytelling, Photography, and Mourning in Daniel Mendelsohn's *The Lost*." In *Third-Generation Holocaust Narratives: Memory in Memoir and Fiction*, edited by Victoria Aarons, 57–72. Lanham, Md.: Lexington Books / Rowman & Littlefield, 2016.

Lutes, Jason. *Berlin*. Montreal, Quebec: Drawn & Quarterly, 2018.
Lyotard, Jean-François. "The Différend, the Referent, and the Proper Name." *Diacritics* 14, no. 3 (Fall 1984): 4–14.
Malamud, Bernard. "Idiots First." In *The Complete Stories*, edited by Robert Giroux, 273–281. New York: Noonday / Farrar, Straus and Giroux, 1997.
Marcoux, Jean-Philippe. "'To Night the Ensilenced Word': Intervocality and Postmemorial Representation in the Graphic Novel about the Holocaust." In *Visualizing Jewish Narrative: Jewish Comics and Graphic Novels*, edited by Derek Parker Royal, 199–212. London: Bloomsbury, 2016.
McCloud, Scott. *Understanding Comics: The Invisible Art*. New York: William Morrow / HarperCollins, 1993.
Mendelsohn, Daniel. *The Lost: A Search for Six of Six Million*. New York: HarperCollins, 2006.
Meskin, Aaron. "Defining Comics." In *The Routledge Companion to Comics*, edited by Frank Bramlett, Roy T. Cook, and Aaron Meskin, 221–229. New York: Routledge, 2017.
Michaels, Anne. *Fugitive Pieces*. New York: Vintage International, 1998.
Michaels, Anne, and Bernice Eisenstein. *Correspondences*. New York: Alfred A. Knopf, 2013.
Mihăilescu, Dana. "Mapping Transgenerational Memory of the Shoah in Third Generation Graphic Narratives: On Amy Kurzweil's *Flying Couch* (2016)." *Journal of Modern Jewish Studies* 17, no. 1 (2018): 93–110.
Modan, Rutu. *The Property*. Translated by Jessica Cohen. New York: Drawn & Quarterly, 2013.
Mulman, Lisa Naomi. "A Tale of Two Mice: Graphic Representations of the Jew in Holocaust Narrative." In *The Jewish Graphic Novel: Critical Approaches*, edited by Samantha Baskind and Ranen Omer-Sherman, 85–93. New Brunswick, N.J.: Rutgers University Press, 2008.
Nemerov, Howard. "Life Cycle of Common Man." In *The Collected Poems of Howard Nemerov*, 221. Chicago: University of Chicago Press, 1977.
Neufeld, Josh. *A.D.: New Orleans after the Deluge*. New York: Pantheon, 2009.
New York Comics & Picture-Story Symposium. "The New York Comics Symposium: Miriam Katin." *Rumpus*, October 4, 2013. http://therumpus.net/2013/10/the-new-york-comics-symposium-miriam-katin/.
Oksman, Tahneer. *"How Come Boys Get to Keep Their Noses?": Women and Jewish American Identity in Contemporary Graphic Memoirs*. New York: Columbia University Press, 2016.
Oostdijk, Diederik. "'Draw Yourself Out of It': Miriam Katin's Graphic Metamorphosis of Trauma." *Journal of Modern Jewish Studies* 17, no. 1 (2018): 79–92.
Orringer, Julie. *Flight Portfolio*. New York: Knopf, 2019.
———. *The Invisible Bridge*. New York: Knopf, 2010.
Orwell, George. "Politics and the English Language." In *A Collection of Essays*, 156–170. New York: Harvest, 1981.
Osborne, Monica. "The Midrashic Impulse: Reading Cynthia Ozick's *Heir to the Glimmering World* against Representation." *Studies in American Jewish Literature* 26 (2007): 21–34.
Pagis, Dan. "Written in Pencil in the Sealed Railway-Car." In *Truth and Lamentation: Stories and Poems on the Holocaust*, edited by Milton Teichman and Sharon Leder, 491. Urbana: University of Illinois Press, 1994.
Pak, Greg, and Carmine Di Giandomenico. *X-Men: Magneto Testament*. New York: Marvel, 2008.
Paley, Grace. "The Immigrant Story." In *Enormous Changes at the Last Minute*, 169–174. 1974. Reprint, New York: Farrar, Straus and Giroux, 1983.

Parker Royal, Derek, ed. *Visualizing Jewish Narrative: Jewish Comics and Graphic Novels.* London: Bloomsbury, 2016.

Patterson, David. *The Holocaust and the Nonrepresentable: Literary and Photographic Transcendence.* New York: State University of New York Press, 2018.

Phillips, Adam. *Missing Out: In Praise of the Unlived Life.* New York: Farrar, Straus and Giroux, 2012.

Plank, Karl A. "Decentering the Holocaust: What Bezmozgis and Englander Are Talking About." *Religion & Literature* 48, no. 2 (Summer 2016): 133–153.

Prager, Brad. "The Holocaust without Ink: Absent Memory and Atrocity in Joe Kubert's Graphic Novel *Yossel: April 19, 1943*." In *The Jewish Graphic Novel: Critical Approaches*, edited by Samantha Baskind and Ranen Omer-Sherman, 111–128. New Brunswick, N.J.: Rutgers University Press, 2008.

Quinn, Arthur. *Figures of Speech: 60 Ways to Turn a Phrase.* Salt Lake City, Utah: Gibbs M. Smith, 1982.

Rifas, Leonard. "War Comics." In *The Routledge Companion to Comics*, edited by Frank Bramlett, Roy T. Cook, and Aaron Meskin, 183–191. New York: Routledge, 2017.

Robbins, Trina. *Lily Renée, Escape Artist.* Minneapolis: Graphic Universe, 2011.

Romero-Jódar, Andrés. *The Trauma Graphic Novel.* New York: Routledge, 2017.

Rosenbaum, Thane. "An Act of Defiance." In *Elijah Visible: Stories*, 57–86. New York: St. Martin's Griffin, 1996.

———. "Cattle Car Complex." In *Elijah Visible: Stories*, 1–12. New York: St. Martin's Griffin, 1996.

Roth, Michael S. "Why Photography Matters to the Theory of History: *Images in Spite of All: Four Photographs from Auschwitz* by Georges Didi-Huberman and Shane B. Lillis, and *Why Photography Matters as Art as Never Before* by Michael Fried." *History and Theory* 49, no. 1 (February 2010): 90–103.

Roth, Philip. "The Conversion of the Jews." In *Goodbye, Columbus and Five Short Stories*, 137–158. New York: Modern Library, 1966.

———. *The Counterlife.* New York: Farrar, Straus and Giroux, 1988.

———. *Why Write? Collected Nonfiction 1960–2003.* New York: Library of America, 2017.

Schieber, Ava Kadishson. *Present Past.* Evanston, Ill.: Northwestern University Press, 2016.

Schivelbusch, Wolfgang. *The Railway Journey: The Industrialization of Time and Space in the Nineteenth Century.* Berkeley: University of California Press, 1986.

Schlipphacke, Heidi. "The Future of Melancholia: Freud, Fassbinder, and Anxiety after War." *Pacific Coast Philology* 52, no. 1 (2017): 6–21.

Schwartz, Delmore. *In Dreams Begin Responsibilities and Other Stories.* New York: New Directions, 1978.

Sim, David. *Judenhauss.* Kitchener, Ontario: Aardvark-Vanaheim, 2008.

Simon, Andrea. *Bashert: A Granddaughter's Holocaust Quest.* Jackson: University Press of Mississippi, 2002.

Sobel, Marc. "The Rutu Modan Interview." *Comics Journal*, May 29, 2013. http://www.tcj.com/rutu-modan/2/.

"The Songs They Sang: A Musical Narrative of the Vilna Ghetto." *St. Kilda News*, November 6, 2014. St. Kilda, Australia. Accessed July 24, 2018. http://stkildanews.com/the-songs-they-sang-a-musical-narrative-of-the-vilna-ghetto/.

Sontag, Susan. *On Photography.* New York: Farrar, Straus and Giroux, 1973.

———. *Regarding the Pain of Others.* New York: Farrar, Straus and Giroux, 2003.

Spiegelman, Art. "Ballbuster: Bernard Krigstein's Life between the Panels." *New Yorker*, July 22, 2002. Accessed June 27, 2018. https://www.newyorker.com/magazine/2002/07/22/ballbuster.

———. *Breakdowns: Portrait of the Artist as a Young %@&*!* New York: Pantheon, 2008.

———. *Maus I: A Survivor's Tale: My Father Bleeds History*. New York: Pantheon, 1986.

———. *Maus II: A Survivor's Tale: And Here My Troubles Began*. New York: Pantheon, 1991.

Stein, Arlene. *Reluctant Witnesses: Survivors, Their Children, and the Rise of Holocaust Consciousness*. New York: Oxford University Press, 2014.

Steinberg, Emily. "Berlin Story: Time, Memory, Place." *Cleaver Magazine*, December 15, 2017. https://www.cleavermagazine.com/berlin-story-time-memory-place-by-emily-steinberg.

Suleiman, Susan Rubin. "The Edge of Memory: Literary Innovation and Childhood Trauma." In *The Future of Memory*, edited by Richard Crownshaw, Jane Kilby, and Antony Rowland, 93–109. New York: Berghahn Books, 2010.

———. "The 1.5 Generation: Thinking about Child Survivors and the Holocaust." *American Imago* 59, no. 3 (2002): 277–295.

Sundquist, Eric J. "Black Milk: A Holocaust Metaphor." In *New Directions in Jewish American and Holocaust Literature: Reading and Teaching*, edited by Victoria Aarons and Holli Levitsky, 21–45. Albany: State University of New York Press, 2019.

Tabachnick, Stephen E. *The Cambridge Companion to the Graphic Novel*. Cambridge, U.K.: Cambridge University Press, 2017.

———. *Teaching the Graphic Novel*. New York: MLA, 2009.

Tanakh: A New Translation of the Holy Scriptures According to the Traditional Hebrew Text. Philadelphia: Jewish Publication Society, 1985.

Tezuka, Osamu. *Adolf: A Tale of the Twentieth Century*. Translated by Yuji Oniki. San Francisco: Cadence Books, 1995.

Torday, Daniel. *The Last Flight of Poxl West*. New York: St. Martin's, 2015.

Valent, Paul. *Child Survivors of the Holocaust*. New York: Brunner-Routledge, 2002.

Versaci, Rocco. *This Book Contains Graphic Language: Comics as Literature*. New York: Continuum, 2007.

Watts, Irene, and Marianne E. Shoemaker. *Good-Bye Marianne*. Toronto, Ontario: Tundra Books, 2008.

Whitlock, Gillian. "Autographics: The Seeing 'I' of the Comics." *Modern Fiction Studies* 52, no. 4 (2006): 965–979.

Wiesel, Elie. *Night*. Translated by Marion Wiesel. New York: Hill and Wang / Farrar, Straus and Giroux, 2006.

———. "Nobel Acceptance Speech." Nobelprize.org. Nobel Media AB (2014). June 4, 2018. http://www.nobelprize.org/nobel_prizes/peace/laureates/1986/wiesel-acceptance_en.html.

———. "An Old Acquaintance." In *Legends of Our Time*, 39–53. New York: Holt, Rinehart and Winston, 1968.

Yelin, Barbara. *Irmina*. London: SelfMadeHero, 2014.

Index

Page numbers in *italics* refer to figures.

About the Author

VICTORIA AARONS holds the position of O. R. and Eva Mitchell Distinguished Professor of Literature in the English Department at Trinity University, where she teaches courses on American Jewish and Holocaust literatures.